CADOGAN

KT-393-258

Dana Facaros & Michael Pauls

Rome Venice & Florence

Cadogan Guides
West End House, 11 Hills Place, London W1R 1AH
e-mail: guides@cadogan.demon.co.uk

The Globe Pequot Press
6 Business Park Road, PO Box 833, Old Saybrook,
Connecticut 06475–0833

Copyright © Dana Facaros and Michael Pauls 1997,1999
Illustrations © Horatio Monteverde 1994

Book and cover design by Animage
Cover photographs: outside © Ellen Rooney
                   inside © Kicca Tommasi
Maps © Cadogan Guides, drawn by Map Creation Ltd

Series Editor: Vicki Ingle

Editing: Catherine Charles
Updating: Jon Eldan, Claudia McNulty, Nicky Swallow
Proofreading: Vicky Harris
Indexing: Judith Wardman
Production: Book Production Services

**A catalogue record for this book is available
from the British Library**

ISBN: 1-86011-902-6

Printed in Great Britain by Cambridge University Press

The author and publishers have made
every effort to ensure the accuracy of the
information in the book at the time of
going to press. However, they cannot
accept any responsibility for any loss,
injury or inconvenience resulting from the
use of information contained in this guide.

About the Authors

Dana Facaros and Michael Pauls are professional travel writers. They lived in Italy for three years, and have been there about a zillion times since, and reckon they could whip 98 per cent of the world's non-Italian population in Italian trivial pursuit questions (except for the sport ones). They now live in Ireland.

Acknowledgements

A big thank you to Jon, Claudia and Nicky for their diligent updating, and to Catherine and everyone at Cadogan, as usual.

Please Help Us Keep This Guide Up to Date

We have done our best to ensure that the information in this guide is correct at the time of going to press. But places and facilities are constantly changing, and standards and prices fluctuate. We would be delighted to receive any comments concerning existing entries or omissions. Significant contributions will be acknowledged in the next edition, and authors of the best letters will receive a copy of the Cadogan Guide of their choice

Contents

Guide to the Guide

For many Italophiles with little time to spare, combining visits to two or three cities is the best option; indeed many tour operators (including those listed on p.6) offer such holidays tailor-made. If you prefer to draw up your own itinerary and choose your own accommodation, the **Travel** and **Practical** sections will help you get to Italy, travel between cities, and select a place to stay from the wide variety of grand or charming hotels and *pensioni* that Italy has to offer.

Italy in Perspective sets the context, leading you gently through its history, art, architecture and cultural heritage. The three glorious cities of **Rome**, **Venice** and **Florence** are then covered in detail, each with its own background of history and art, and all the sights you might choose to visit: museums, art galleries, cathedrals, marketplaces or simply those atmospheric streets that are a pleasure just to wander around. Each chapter ends with a practical guide to where to stay and eating out, shopping and nightlife, cafés and bars.

Finally there is a **language** section including pronunciation advice, general phrases and a detailed menu reader, as well as a list of suggestions for **further reading**, for those who want to explore any topic in greater detail.

If your visit whets your appetite and you decide next time to devote longer to one particular city, Cadogan's city guides, with their detailed walks and tours, will help you explore in more depth (*see* p.216).

Introduction

Italy dangles from the centre of western Europe like a Christmas stocking, stuffed to the brim with marvels, some as grand as a Verdi opera or Brunelleschi's dome over Florence Cathedral, some as weird and unexpected as the pagan tombs buried underneath St Peter's in Rome, or Galileo's erect middle finger, carefully, significantly preserved in a reliquary in Florence's science museum.

Even first-time visitors, with eyes and brains spinning, soon become uneasily aware that for every Italian cliché, every Mount Vesuvius, St Mark's Basilica and Leonardo's *Last Supper*, Italy has a hundred other natural wonders and artistic showpieces that any other nation would die for. Someone once tried to count up all the works of art, and concluded that there were three per inhabitant, no less. This national patrimony is echoed by even the most ephemeral arts, whether cranked out by the fashion and design workshops or simmered in the kitchen: for every Italian dish or wine you've been craving to try on its home turf, expect a hundred other delights you've never heard of before.

Even the common, everyday Italy that co-exists next to the overflow of museums, art cities, ruins and rivieras is an extravagant, daunting place to digest, and as the headlines of recent years confirm (the advent of Berlusconi's Forza Italia, the Mafia trials, the bribery scandals), it is a country that operates on rules entirely unlike those in force back home, full of contradictions and paradoxes, depths and shallows. As an Umbrian friend told us, you cry twice in Italy: when you first arrive and when you have to leave. In the meantime, pack your intellect, gird your senses and watch out, not only for pickpockets but for a country that might just pick your heart.

Not counting the islands, there are about 260,000 square kilometres of Italy, roughly the size of the island of Britain (Americans can think of it as a New York, a Pennsylvania, and most of a New Jersey). Even with some 55 million Italians, busily tending the world's fifth or sixth most opulent economy, the country never seems too crowded. Some large patches of urban sprawl exist—in the Po Valley, for example, or around the Bay of Naples—but the Italians enjoy each other's company, and generally live in tightly packed cities, hill towns and villages, with plenty of good green countryside in between. It is about 1000km, as the crow flies, from Mont Blanc to the furthest corner of Puglia, the 'heel' of the Italian boot (1400km if you're driving), and the long peninsula is in most places 150–250km across.

Rome

Lazio, ancient *Latium*, is best known as home of the Eternal City, Rome, a thoroughly modern metropolis behind which you can seek out the Romes of the Caesars and the popes. The population has exploded to about four million, to whom you need to add the swarms of tourists who sometimes seem as much part of the city as the natives themselves. Search well and you will still find the Roman *dolce vita*, the very soul of a city that can never fail to impress.

Venice

Venetia, in the northeastern corner of Italy, is the most prosperous region in the republic, the most industrial, expensive and dramatically scenic, the land of Alps and lakes. It encompasses roughly the region controlled by Venice from the 14th and 15th centuries until the conquest of Napoleon. The main attraction is, of course, Venice itself, one of the world's most extraordinary visions—a city of churches and palaces, carnivals and canals.

Florence

On the western coast of central Italy lies Tuscany, for many the archetypical image of Italy—rolling hills, faded ochre farmhouses and stone villas, cypresses and hill towns—the background to a thousand Renaissance paintings. Florence probably needs no introduction, the jewel of Tuscany's medieval and Renaissance art cities, best known for Italy's finest museums, which are filled almost entirely by art made by the Florentines themselves.

Travel

Getting There

By Air
From the UK and Ireland

Rome and Venice have an excellent choice of year-round flights; Florence has fewer direct flights, but is well connected by rail to Pisa. Scheduled services are, in the main, more expensive than charters.

major carriers

Alitalia: London, ✆ (0171) 602 7111, Dublin, ✆ (01) 844 6035.
British Airways: ✆ (0345) 222 111.
Air UK: ✆ (0345) 666 777.
Meridiana: ✆ (0171) 839 2222.
Aer Lingus, Dublin, ✆ (01) 705 3333, or Belfast, ✆ (0645) 737 747.

APEX or **SuperAPEX** fares can be excellent value; they have to be booked seven days ahead and include a Saturday night stay, and are usually unchangeable and non-refundable.

low-cost carriers

Go: ✆ (0845) 605 4321, a branch of British Airways, operates flights between Stansted and Venice (7 times a week) and Rome (14 times a week);
Ryanair: ✆ (0541) 569 569, offer flights from Stansted to Treviso near Venice.

charter flights

Many inexpensive charter flights are available to popular Italian destinations in summer. You may find cheaper fares by combing the small ads in the travel pages, or from a specialist agent (use a reputable ABTA-registered one), which offer good student and youth rates too. The main problems with cheaper flights tend to be inconvenient or unreliable flight schedules, and booking restrictions. Take good travel insurance, however cheap your ticket is.

discount agencies and youth fares

Italy Sky Shuttle, 227 Shepherd's Bush Rd, London W6 7AS, ✆ (0181) 748 1333.
Italflights, 125 High Holborn, London WC1V 6QA, ✆ (0171) 405 6771.
Italy Sky Bus, 37 Harley Street, London W1N 1DB, ✆ (0171) 631 3444.
Trailfinders, 215 Kensington High Street, London W8, ✆ (0171) 937 5400.
Budget Travel, 134 Lower Baggot Street, Dublin 2, ✆ (01) 661 1866.
Untied Travel, Stillorgan Bowl, Stillorgan, Dublin, ✆ (01) 288 4346/7.

Besides saving 25 per cent on regular flights, young people under 26 have the choice of flying on special discount charters.

Campus Travel, 52 Grosvenor Gardens, London SW1, ✆ (0171) 730 3402, with branches at most UK universities; *www.campustravel.co.uk*

STA, 74/86 Old Brompton Rd, London SW7, ✆ (0171) 937 9921, and other branches.

USIT, Aston Quay, Dublin 2, ✆ (01) 679 8833, and other branches in Ireland.

From Mainland Europe

Air travel between Italy and other parts of Europe can be expensive, especially for short hops. Some airlines (**Alitalia, Qantas, Air France**, etc.) offer excellent rates on the European stages of intercontinental flights, and Italy is an important touchdown for many long-haul services to the Middle or Far East. Amsterdam, Paris and Athens are good places to find cheap flights.

From the USA and Canada

The main Italian air gateways for direct flights from North America are Rome and Milan, though, if you're doing a grand tour, check fares to other European destinations (Paris or Amsterdam, for example) which may well be cheaper.

Alitalia: (USA) ✆ (800) 223 5730, (Canada) ✆ (800) 563 5954, sometimes run World Offers when prices drop substantially.

British Airways: ✆ (800) 247 9297.

Delta: ✆ (800) 241 414.

Air Canada: ✆ (800) 555 1212.

KLM: ✆ (800) 361 5330, from Toronto and Montreal.

It may be worth catching a cheap flight to London (New York–London fares are always very competitive) and then flying on from there. Prices are rather more from Canada, so you may prefer to fly from the States.

charters, discounts and special deals

For discounted flights, try the small ads in newspaper travel pages (e.g. *New York Times, Chicago Tribune, Toronto Globe & Mail*). Numerous travel clubs and agencies also specialize in discount fares, but may require an annual membership fee.

discount agencies and youth fares

Airhitch, 2472 Broadway, Suite 200, New York, NY 10025, ✆ (212) 864 2000.

Council Travel, 205 East 42nd Street, New York, NY 10017, ✆ (1 800) 743 1823. Major specialists in student and charter flights; branches all over the USA.

Last Minute Travel Club, 132 Brookline Avenue, Boston, MA 02215, ✆ (800) 527 8646.

Now Voyager, 74 Varick Street, Suite 307, New York, NY 10013, ✆ (212) 431 1616, for courier flights.

Board Courier Services, ✆ (514) 633 0740, for courier flights from Canada.

STA, 48 East 11th Street, New York, NY 10003, ✆ (212) 627 3111, or freephone ✆ (1 800) 777 0112.

Travel Cuts, 187 College Street, Toronto, Ontario M5T 1P7, ✆ (416) 979 2406. Canada's largest student travel specialists; branches in most provinces.

By Rail

You can still travel by train and ferry from London to Rome; it takes the best part of 24 hours and costs around £160 second-class return (plus £14 for a couchette). Or you can take a Eurostar to Paris and a high-speed train to Italy, which only takes about 12 hours, but costs around £500.

The **Orient Express** deserves a mention: it whirls you from London through Paris, Zurich, Innsbruck and Verona to Venice in a luxurious cocoon of traditional twenties and thirties glamour, with beautifully restored Pullman/wagon-lits. It's fiendishly expensive—and quite unforgettable for a once-in-a-lifetime treat. Current prices (including meals) are about £1095 per person (London–Venice one-way). Several operators offer packages including smart Venice hotels and return flights home. Contact **Venice-Simplon Orient Express**, Suite 200, Hudson's Place, Victoria Station, London SW1, ✆ (0171) 928 6000, for more information.

Interail (UK) or **Eurail** passes (USA/Canada) give unlimited travel for under-26s throughout Europe for one or two months. Various other cheap youth fares (BIJ tickets etc.) are also available; organize these before you leave home.

If you will only be travelling within Italy, inclusive rail passes may not be worthwhile. Fares on FS (*Ferrovie dello Stato*), the Italian state railway, are among the lowest (km for km) in Europe, and one of the special Italian tourist passes may be a better bet (*see* 'Getting Around'). You can pick up the Italian rail timetable (2 vols) at any station in Italy for about L4500 each.

Rail Europe Travel Centre, (UK) 179 Piccadilly, London W1, ✆ (0990) 300 003; (USA) 226–30 Westchester Ave, White Plains, NY 10604, ✆ (914) 682 2999, or ✆ (800) 438 7245.

Eurostar, EPS House, Waterloo Station, London SE1, ✆ (0345) 881 881.

International Rail Centre, London Victoria Station, adjacent to Platform 2.

Eurotrain, 52 Grosvenor Gardens, London SW1, ✆ (0171) 730 8518.

Wasteels Travel, (UK) adjacent Platform 2, London Victoria Station, ✆ (0171) 834 7066; (USA) 5728 Major Boulevard, Suite 308, Orlando, FL 32819.

CIT, (UK) Marco Polo House, 3–5 Lansdowne Rd, Croydon, Surrey, ✆ (0891) 71551 (50p a minute), ✆ (0181) 681 1712; (USA) 15 West 44th Street, 10th Floor, New York, NY 10036, ✆ (800) 248 7245, ✆ (888) FAX CIT; (Canada) 1450 City Councillors St, Suite 750, Montreal H3A 2E6, ✆ (514) 845 4310.

Accommodation Line Ltd, 11–12 Hanover Square, London W1, sell a pocket-sized Italian rail timetable (£6 plus 50p postage).

By Road

by bus and coach

Eurolines, London Victoria Coach Station, ✆ (0990) 808 080, are booked in the UK through National Express (return ticket London–Rome £130; single £90). Within Italy, you can obtain more information on long-distance bus services from any CIT office.

by car

Italy is the best part of 24 hours' drive from the UK, even if you stick to fast toll roads. Calais–Florence via Nancy, Lucerne and Lugano is about 1042km. The most scenic and hassle-free route is via the Alps but, if you take a route through Switzerland, expect to pay around £14 (30SFr) for motorway use. In winter the passes may be closed and you will have to use the expensive tunnels (one-way tolls from about L37,000 for a small car). You can avoid some of the driving by putting your car on the train. **Express Sleeper Cars** run to Milan from Paris or

Boulogne (infrequently in winter). The **Italian Auto Club** (ACI), ✆ 06 44 77, offers reasonably priced breakdown assistance.

To bring a GB-registered car into Italy, you need a **vehicle registration document, full driving licence** and **insurance papers** (these must be carried at all times when driving). Non-EU citizens should preferably have an **international driving licence** which has an Italian translation incorporated. Your vehicle should display a nationality plate indicating its country of registration. Before travelling, check everything is in perfect order; minor infringements like worn tyres or burnt-out sidelights can cost you dear. A **red triangular hazard sign** is obligatory; also recommended are a spare set of bulbs, a first-aid kit and a fire extinguisher. Spare parts for non-Italian cars can be difficult to find, especially Japanese models. Before crossing the Italian border, remember to fill up with petrol; *benzina* is still expensive in Italy.

For more information on driving in Italy contact the **AA**, ✆ (0990) 500 600, or **RAC**, ✆ (0800) 550 550 in the UK, and **AAA**, ✆ (407) 444 4000, in the USA.

Entry Formalities

Passports and Visas

EU nationals with a valid passport can enter and stay in Italy as long as they like. Citizens of the USA, Canada, Australia and New Zealand need only a valid passport to stay up to three months in Italy, unless they get a visa in advance from an Italian embassy or consulate:

UK, 38 Eaton Place, London SW1X, ✆ (0171) 235 9371; 32 Melville Street, Edinburgh EH3 7HA, ✆ (0131) 226 3631; 2111 Piccadilly, Manchester, ✆ (0161) 236 3024.

Ireland, 63–65 Northumberland Road, Dublin, ✆ (01) 660 1744; 7 Richmond Park, Stranmillis, Belfast BT9 5EF, ✆ (01232) 668 854.

USA, 690 Park Avenue, New York, NY, ✆ (212) 737 9100; 12400 Wilshire Blvd, Suite 300, Los Angeles CA, ✆ (213) 820 0622.

Canada, 136 Beverley Street, Toronto, ✆ (416) 977 1566.

Australia, Level 45, The Gateway Building, Macquarie Place, Circular Quay, Sydney 2000, NSW, ✆ (02) 2478 442.

New Zealand, 34 Grant Rd, Thorndon, Wellington, ✆ (04) 7473 5339.

France, 47 rue de Varennes, 73343 Paris, ✆ 01 45 44 38 90.

Germany, Karl Finkelnburgstrasse 49–51, 5300 Bonn 2, ✆ (0228) 82 00 60.

Netherlands, Herengracht 609, 1017 CE Amsterdam, ✆ (3120) 624 0043.

By law you should register with the police within eight days of your arrival in Italy. In practice this is done automatically for most visitors when they check in at their first hotel.

Customs

EU nationals over the age of 17 can now import a limitless amount of goods for personal use. Non-EU nationals have to pass through the Italian Customs which are usually benign. How the frontier police manage to recruit such ugly, mean-looking characters to hold the submachine guns and dogs from such a good-looking population is a mystery, but they'll let you be if you don't look suspicious and haven't brought along more than 200 cigarettes or 100 cigars, or not more than a litre of hard drink or three bottles of wine, a couple of cameras, a movie camera, 10 rolls of film for each, a tape-recorder, radio, record-player, one canoe less than 5.5m, sports equipment for personal use, and one TV (though you'll have to pay for a licence for it at Customs). You can take the same items listed above home with you without hassle—except of course your British pet. USA citizens may return with $400 worth of merchandise—keep your receipts.

Pets must always be accompanied by a bilingual Certificate of Health from your local Veterinary Inspector.

Currency

There are no limits to how much money you bring into Italy: legally you may not export more than L20,000,000 in Italian banknotes, a sum unlikely to trouble many of us, though officials rarely check.

Special-interest Holidays

A selection of specialist companies are listed below. Not all of them are necesssarily ABTA-bonded; we recommend you check before booking.

in the UK

Cresta Italy, Holiday House, Victoria Street, Altrincham, Cheshire WA14 1ET, ✆ (01345) 125 333.

Italian Escapades, 227 Shepherds Bush Rd, London W6 7AS, ✆ (0181) 748 2661.

Italiatour, 205 Holland Park Avenue, London W11 4XB, ✆ (0171) 371 1114.

Magic of Italy, 227 Shepherds Bush Road, London W6 7AS, ✆ (0181) 748 7575.

Abercrombie & Kent, Sloane Square House, Holbein Place, London SW1W 8NS, ✆ (0171) 730 9600; city breaks.

Brompton Travel, Brompton House, 64 Richmond Road, Kingston-upon-Thames, Surrey KT2 5EH, ✆ (0181) 549 3334; tailor-made trips and opera.

Citalia, Marco Polo House, 3–5 Lansdowne Road, Croydon CR9 1LL, ✆ (0181) 686 5533; opera.

Kirker, 3 New Concordia Wharf, Mill Street, London SE1 2BB, ✆ (0171) 231 3333; city breaks and tailor-made tours.

Martin Randall Travel, 10 Barley Mow Passage, Chiswick, London W4 4PH, ✆ (0181) 742 3355; cultural tours with expert guides.

in the USA/Canada

Dailey-Thorp Travel, 330 West 58th Street, New York, NY 10019, ✆ (212) 307 1555; music and opera.

Esplanade Tours, 581 Boyston Street, Boston, MA 02116, ✆ (617) 266 7465; art and architecture.

Maupintour, 1515 St Andrew's Drive, Lawrence, KS 66047, ✆ (913) 843 1211.

Olson Travelworld, 970 West 190th Street, Suite 425, Torrance, CA 90502, ✆ (310) 354 2600.

Italy has an excellent network of airports, railways, highways and byways and you'll find getting around fairly easy—until one union or another takes it into its head to go on strike (to be fair they rarely do it during the high holiday season, but learn to recognize the word in Italian: *sciopero* (SHO-per-o), and do as the Romans do—quiver with resignation). There's always a day or two's notice, and strikes usually last only a day, just long enough to throw a spanner in the works if you have to catch a plane. Keep your ears open and watch for notices posted in the stations.

By Air

Air traffic within Italy is intense, with up to ten flights a day on popular routes. Domestic flights are handled by Alitalia, ATI (its internal arm) or Avianova. Air travel makes most sense when hopping between north and south. Shorter journeys are often just as quick (and much less expensive) by train or even bus if you include check-in and airport travelling times.

Domestic flight costs are comparable to those in other European countries, and a complex system of discounts is available (some only at certain times of year). Each airport has a bus terminal in the city; ask about schedules as you purchase your ticket to avoid hefty taxi fares. Baggage allowances vary between airlines. Tickets can be bought at CIT offices and other large travel agencies.

By Rail

FS national train information: © 1478 888 088 (open 7am–9pm); *www.fs-on-line.com*

Italy's national railway, the **FS** (*Ferrovie dello Stato*), is well-run, inexpensive and often a pleasure to ride; some of the trains are sleek and high-tech, but much of the rolling stock hasn't been changed for fifty years. Possible FS unpleasantnesses you may encounter, besides a strike, are delays, crowding (especially at weekends and in the summer), and crime on overnight trains, where someone rifles your bags while you sleep. Reserve a seat in advance (*fare una prenotazione*): the fee is small and can save you hours standing in some train corridor. On the more expensive trains, and for sleepers and couchettes on overnight trains, **reservations** are mandatory. Check when you purchase your ticket in advance that the date is correct; tickets are only valid the day they're purchased unless you specify otherwise.

It is easier to buy tickets at a travel agent in one of the city centres. Fares are strictly determined by the kilometres travelled. The system is computerized and runs smoothly, at least until you try to get a reimbursement for an unused ticket (usually not worth the trouble). Be sure you ask which platform (*binario*) your train arrives at; the big permanent boards in the stations are not always correct. Always remember to stamp your ticket (*convalidare*) in the not-very-obvious yellow machines at the head of the platform before boarding the train. Failure to do so could result in a fine. If you get on a train without a ticket you can buy one from the conductor, with an added 20 per cent penalty. You can also pay a conductor to move up to first class or get a couchette, if there are places available.

There is a fairly straightforward **hierarchy of trains**. At the bottom of the pyramid is the humble, sometimes excruciatingly slow, *Locale* (euphemistically known sometimes as an

Accelerato) which often stops even where there's no station in sight. When you're checking the schedules, beware of what may look like the first train to your destination—if it's a *Locale*, it will be the last to arrive. A *Diretto* stops far less, an *Expresso* just at the main towns. *Intercity* trains whoosh between the big cities and rarely deign to stop. *Eurocity* trains link Italian cities with major European centres. Both of these services require a supplement—some 30 per cent more than a regular fare. The *ETR 500 pendolino* trains, similar to the French TGV, can travel at up to 186mph. Reservations are free, but must be made at least five hours before the trip, and on some trains there are only first-class coaches. The super-swish, super-fast *Eurostars* make very few stops, have both first- and second-class carriages, and carry a supplement which includes an obligatory seat reservation.

The FS offers several **passes**. The 'Flexi Card' (marketed as a 'Freedom Pass' in the UK) allows unlimited travel for either four days within a month (L206,000), 8 days within a month (L287,000), or 12 days within a month (L368,000) plus seat reservations and supplements on Eurostars. The *Kilometrico* allows 3000kms of travel, made on a maximum of 20 journeys, and is valid for two months (second class L206,000, first class L338,000); one advantage is that it can be used by up to five people at the same time—however, supplements are payable on *Intercity* trains. Other discounts are available for day returns, families, senior citizens and the under-26s.

Refreshments on routes of any great distance are provided by bar cars or trolleys; you can usually get sandwiches and coffee from vendors along the tracks at intermediary stops. Station bars often have a good variety of take-away travellers' fare; consider at least investing in a plastic bottle of mineral water, since there's no drinking water on the trains.

Besides trains and bars, Italy's stations offer other **facilities**. Most have a *deposito*, where you can leave your bags for hours or days for a small fee. The larger ones have porters (who charge L1000–1500 per piece) and some even have luggage trolleys; major stations have an *albergo diurno* ('day hotel', where you take a shower, get a shave and have a haircut, etc.), information offices, currency exchanges open at weekends (not at the most advantageous rates, however), hotel-finding and reservation services, kiosks with foreign papers, restaurants, etc. You can also arrange to have a rental car awaiting you at your destination—Avis, Hertz, Aurotrans and Maggiore are the firms most widespread in Italy.

Beyond that, some words need to be said about riding the rails on the most serendipitous national line in Europe. The FS may have its strikes and delays, its petty crime and bureaucratic inconveniences, but when you catch it on its better side it will treat you to a dose of the real Italy before you even reach your destination. If there's a choice, try for one of the older cars, depressingly grey outside but fitted with comfortably upholstered seats, Art Deco lamps and old pictures of the towns and villages of the country. The washrooms are invariably clean and pleasant. Best of all, the FS is relatively reliable, and even if there has been some delay you'll have an amenable station full of clocks to wait in; some of the station bars have astonishingly good food (some do not), but at any of them you may accept a well-brewed cappuccino and look blasé until the train comes in. Try to avoid travel on Friday evenings, when the major lines out of the big cities are packed. The FS is a lottery; you may find a train uncomfortably full of Italians (in which case stand by the doors, or impose on the salesmen in first class, where the conductor will be happy to change your ticket). Now and then, you may just have a beautiful 1920s compartment all to yourself for the night—even better if you're travelling with your beloved—and be serenaded on the platform.

By Coach and Bus

Inter-city coach travel is sometimes quicker than train travel, but also a bit more expensive; you will find regular coach connections only where there is no train to offer competition. Coaches almost always depart from the vicinity of the train station, and tickets usually need to be purchased before you get on. If you can't get a ticket before the coach leaves, get on anyway and pretend you can't speak a word of Italian; the worst that can happen is that someone will make you pay for a ticket.

By Car

If you're planning a tour of the cities with few excursions into the countryside around you'll be better off not driving at all: parking is impossible, traffic impossible, deciphering one-way streets, signals and signs impossible. However, if you're planning to tour the surrounding countryside a car undoubtedly gives immeasurable freedom.

Third-party **insurance** is a minimum requirement in Italy (and you should be a lot more than minimally insured, as many of the locals have none whatever!). Obtain a Green Card from your insurer, which gives automatic proof that you are fully covered. Also get hold of a **European Accident Statement** form, which may simplify things if you are unlucky enough to have an accident. Always insist on a full translation of any statement you are asked to sign. Breakdown assistance insurance is obviously a sensible investment.

Petrol (*benzina*, unleaded is *benzina senza piombo*, and diesel *gasolio*) is still very expensive in Italy (around L1500 per litre; fill up before you cross the border). Many petrol stations close for lunch in the afternoon, and few stay open late at night, though you may find a 'self-service' where you feed a machine nice smooth L10,000 notes. Motorway (*autostrada*) tolls are quite high. Rest stops and petrol stations along the motorways stay open 24 hours.

Italians are famously anarchic behind a wheel. The only way to beat the locals is to join them by adopting an assertive and constantly alert driving style. Bear in mind the ancient maxim that he/she who hesitates is lost (especially at traffic lights, where the danger is less great of crashing into someone at the front than being rammed from behind). All drivers from boy racers to elderly nuns seem to tempt providence by overtaking at the most dangerous bends, and no matter how fast you are hammering along the *autostrada* (toll motorway), plenty will whizz past at apparently supersonic rates. North Americans used to leisurely speed limits and gentler road manners will find the Italian interpretation of the highway code especially stressful. Speed limits (generally ignored) are officially 130kph on motorways (110kph for cars under 1100cc or motorcycles), 110kph on main highways, 90kph on secondary roads, and 50kph in built-up areas. Speeding fines may be as much as L500,000, or L100,000 for jumping a red light (a popular Italian sport).

If you are undeterred by these caveats, you may actually enjoy driving in Italy, at least away from the congested tourist centres. Signposting is generally good, and roads are usually excellently maintained. Some of the roads are feats of engineering that the Romans themselves would have admired—bravura projects suspended on cliffs, crossing valleys on vast stilts and winding up hairpins.

Buy a good road map (the Italian Touring Club series is excellent). The **Automobile Club of Italy** (ACI) (Viale Amendola 36, Florence, ✆ 055 24861; Viale C. Colombo 261, Rome, ✆ 06 514 971, and Via Marsala 8, Rome, ✆ 06 495 9352, is a good friend to the foreign motorist.

Besides having bushels of useful information and tips, they can be reached from anywhere by dialling 116—also use this number if you have to find the nearest service station. If you need major repairs, the ACI can make sure the prices charged are according to their guidelines.

Hiring a Car

Hiring a car (*autonoleggio*) is simple but not particularly cheap. Remember to take into account that some hire companies require a deposit amounting to the estimated cost of the hire. The minimum age limit is usually 25 (sometimes 23) and the driver must have held their licence for over a year. Most major rental companies have offices in airports or main stations, though it may be worthwhile checking prices of local firms. If you need a car for longer than three weeks, leasing may be a more economic alternative. The National Tourist Office has a list of firms in Italy that hire caravans (trailers) or camper vans. Non-residents are not allowed to buy cars in Italy.

It is probably easiest to arrange your car hire with a domestic firm before you depart and, in particular, to check-out fly-drive discounts.

Avis, (UK) ✆ (018)1 848 8733, (USA) ✆ (800) 331 1084.

Hertz, (UK) ✆ (0990) 996 699, (Dublin) ✆ (01) 660 2255, (USA) ✆ (800) 654 3001, (Canada) ✆ (800) 263 0600.

Eurodollar, (UK) ✆ (01895) 233 300.

Car Rental Direct, (UK) ✆ (0171) 625 7766.

Hitch-hiking

It is illegal to hitch on the *autostrade*, though you may pick up a lift near one of the toll booths. Don't hitch from the city centres, head for suburban exit routes. For the best chances of getting a lift, travel light, look respectable and take your shades off. Hold a sign indicating your destination if you can. Risks for women are lower in northern Italy than in the more macho south, but it is not advisable to hitch alone. Two or more men may encounter some reluctance. On major roads, heading out of town, you may sometimes see scantily clad women, usually of African origin, standing or sitting on stools on the edges of corn fields trying to attract your attention. These are not hitch-hikers, although you may still pick them up.

By Moped

Mopeds, vespas and scooters are the vehicles of choice for a great many Italians. You will see them everywhere. In the traffic-congested towns this is a ubiquity born of necessity; when driving space is limited, two wheels are always better than one. Despite the obvious dangers of this means of transport, there are clear benefits to moped-riding in Italy. For one thing it is cheaper than car hire and can prove an excellent way of covering a town's sites in a limited space of time. Furthermore, because Italy is such a scooter-friendly place, car drivers are more conditioned to their presence and so are less likely to hurtle into them when taking corners. Nonetheless, you should only consider hiring a moped if you have ridden one before (Italy's hills and alarming traffic are no place to learn) and, despite local examples, you should always wear a helmet. Also, be warned, some travel insurance policies exclude claims resulting from scooter or motorbike accidents.

Practical A–Z

Children

Even though a declining birthrate and the legalization of abortion may hint otherwise, children are still the royalty of Italy, and are pampered, often obscenely spoiled, probably more fashionably dressed than you are, and never allowed to get dirty. Surprisingly, most of them somehow manage to be well-mannered little charmers. If you're bringing your own *bambini* to Italy, they'll receive a warm welcome everywhere. Many hotels offer advantageous rates for children and have play areas, and most of the larger cities have permanent **Luna Parks**, or funfairs. Rome's version in the EUR (a residential suburb south of the city) is huge and charmingly old-fashioned (a great trade-off for a day in the Vatican Museums). Italians don't like zoos and there are only a few small ones, but there's a so-so drive-through **Safari Park** near Rome which may amuse for a while. Apart from endless quantities of pizza, spaghetti and ice cream, **Venice** could have been specifically designed for kids, and there's always the **Carnival**. If your kids know some Italian, there is a **puppet theatre** in Rome, and if a **circus** visits town, you're in for a treat: it will either be a sparkling showcase of daredevil skill or a poignant, family-run, modern version of Fellini's *La Strada*.

Climate and When to Go

'*O Sole Mio*' notwithstanding, all of Italy isn't always sunny; it rains just as much in Rome every year as in London. **Summer** comes on dry and hot in the south and humid and hot in much of the northern lowlands and inland hills; and Venice tends to swelter. You can probably get by without an umbrella, but take a light jacket for cool evenings. For average touring, August is probably the worst month to stump through Italy. Transport facilities are jammed to capacity, prices are at their highest, and the large cities are abandoned to hordes of tourists while the locals take to the beach.

Spring and **autumn** are perhaps the loveliest times to go; the weather is mild, places aren't crowded, and you won't need your umbrella too much, at least until November. **Winter** is the best time to go if you want the museums to yourself. Beware though, it can rain and rain.

Average Temperatures in °C (°F)

	January	April	July	October
Florence	5.6 (42)	13.3 (55)	25.0 (77)	15.8 (60)
Rome	7.4 (44)	14.4 (58)	25.7 (79)	17.7 (63)
Venice	3.8 (38)	12.6 (54)	23.6 (74)	15.1 (59)

Average Monthly Rainfall in Millimetres (inches)

	January	April	July	October
Florence	61 (3)	74 (3)	23 (1)	96 (4)
Rome	74 (3)	62 (3)	06 (3)	123 (5)
Venice	58 (2)	77 (3)	37 (1)	66 (3)

Crime

There is a fair amount of petty crime in Italy—purse-snatchings, pickpocketing, minor thievery of the white-collar kind (always check your change) and car break-ins and theft—but violent crime is rare. Nearly all mishaps can be avoided with adequate precautions. Scooter-borne purse-snatchers can be foiled if you stay on the inside of the pavement and keep a firm hold on your property (sling your bag-strap across your body, not dangling from one shoulder); pickpockets strike in crowded buses or trams and gatherings; don't carry too much cash, and split it so you won't lose the lot at once. In cities and popular tourist sites, beware groups of scruffy-looking women or children with placards, apparently begging for money. They use distraction techniques to perfection. The smallest and most innocent-looking child is generally the most skilful pickpocket. If you are targeted, the best technique is to grab sharply hold of any vulnerable possessions or pockets and shout furiously. (Italian passers-by or plain-clothes police will often come to your assistance if they realize what is happening.) Be extra careful in train stations, don't leave valuables in hotel rooms, and always park your car in garages, guarded lots or on well-lit streets, with portable temptations well out of sight. Purchasing small quantities of soft drugs for personal consumption is technically legal in Italy, though what constitutes a small quantity is unspecified, and if the police don't like you to begin with, it will probably be enough to get you into big trouble.

Political terrorism, once the scourge of Italy, has declined greatly in recent years, mainly thanks to special quasi-military squads of black-uniformed national police, the *Carabinieri*. Local matters are usually in the hands of the *Polizia Urbana*; the nattily dressed *Vigili Urbani* concern themselves with directing traffic and handing out parking fines. If you need to summon any of them, dial ✆ **113**.

Disabled Travellers

Italy has been relatively slow off the mark in its provision for disabled visitors. Cobblestones, uneven or non-existent pavements, the appalling traffic conditions, crowded public transport and endless flights of steps in many public places are all disincentives. Progress is gradually being made, however. A national support organization in your own country may well have specific information on facilities in Italy, or will at least be able to provide general advice. The Italian tourist office or CIT (travel agency) can also advise on hotels, museums with ramps and so on. If you book rail travel through CIT, you can request assistance if you are wheelchair-bound.

Royal Association for Disability & Rehabilitation (RADAR), 25 Mortimer St, London W1N 8AB, ✆ (0171) 637 5400, sell a guide, *Holidays & Travel Abroad: A Guide for Disabled People* (£3.50).

Society for the Advancement of Travel for the Handicapped (SATH), 347 Fifth Avenue, Suite 610, New York, NY 10016, ✆ (212) 447 7284.

Mobility International, 228 Borough High Street, London SE1, ✆ (0171) 403 5688, or PO Box 3551, Eugene, OR 97403, ✆ (503) 343 1284.

Australian Council for the Rehabilitation of the Disabled (ACROD), 55 Charles Street, Ryde, New South Wales, ✆ (02) 9809 4488.

Embassies and Consulates

UK, Lungarno Corsini 2, **Florence**, ✆ 055 284 133; Via XX Settembre 80/a, **Rome**, ✆ 06 482 5441.

Ireland, Largo Nazareno 3, **Rome**, ✆ 06 678 2541.

USA, Lungarno Vespucci 38, **Florence**, ✆ 055 239 8276; Via V. Veneto 119/a, **Rome**, ✆ 06 46741.

Canada, Via Zara 30, **Rome**, ✆ 06 440 3028.

Australia, Via Alessandria 215, **Rome**, ✆ 06 852 721.

New Zealand, Via Zara 28, **Rome**, ✆ 06 440 2928.

France, Palazzo Farnese, **Rome**, ✆ 06 686 011.

Germany, Via Po 25c, **Rome**, ✆ 06 884 741.

Netherlands, Via Cavour 81, **Florence**, ✆ 055 475 249; Via Michele Mercati 8, **Rome**, ✆ 06 322 1141.

Festivals

There are literally thousands of festivals answering to every description in Italy. Every *comune* has at least one or two honouring patron saints, at which the presiding Madonna is paraded through the streets decked in fairy lights and gaudy flowers. Shrovetide and Holy Week are great focuses of activity. *Carnival*, having been suppressed and ignored for decades, has been revived in many places, displaying the gorgeous music and pageantry of the *Commedia dell'Arte* with Harlequin and his motley crew. In Venice the handmade carnival masks now constitute a new art form and make delightful, if expensive, souvenirs. In Rome the Supreme Pontiff himself officiates at the Easter ceremonies.

Other festivals are more earthily pagan, celebrating the land and the harvest in giant phallic towers. Some are secular affairs sponsored by political parties (especially the Communists and Socialists), where everyone goes to meet friends. There are great costume pageants dating back to the Middle Ages or Renaissance, an endless round of carnivals, music festivals, opera seasons and antique fairs. Whatever the occasion, eating is a primary pastime at all Italian jamborees, and all kinds of regional specialities are prepared. Check at the local tourist office for precise dates, which alter from year to year, and often slide into the nearest weekend.

March/April	Holy Week and Easter: Scoppio del Carro (Explosion of the Cart), **Florence**; Good Friday Procession led by the Pope, **Rome.**
May	Vogolonga, **Venice** (the 'long row' from San Marco to Burano).
May/June	Maggio Musicale Fiorentino, **Florence.**
June	Historical Regatta of the Four Ancient Maritime Republics (boat race between the rival sea-towns of Pisa, **Venice**, Amalfi and Genoa—location alternates).
June 21	Infiorata, Genzano (**Rome**); Gioco del Calcio, **Florence** (football in medieval costume).
July	Feast of the Redeemer, **Venice** (fireworks, gondola procession).

July and August	Outdoor opera, Terme di Caracalla, **Rome**.
August	International Film Festival, **Venice**.
September	Historic Regatta, **Venice**.
October	**Venice** marathon.
November	Festa della Salute, **Venice**.
December	Opera and ballet at La Fenice (when it reopens) and Teatro Goldoni, **Venice**. Feast of St Lucy, **Venice** (torchlight procession, bonfire and balloon launch). Advent and Christmas celebrations.

Food and Drink

There are those who eat to live and those who live to eat, and then there are the Italians, for whom food has an almost religious significance, unfathomably linked with love, La Mamma, and tradition. In this singular country, where millions of otherwise sane people spend much of their waking hours worrying about their digestion, standards both at home and in restaurants are understandably high. Few Italians are gluttons, but all are experts on what is what in the kitchen; to serve a meal that is not properly prepared and more than a little complex is tantamount to an insult.

For the visitor this national culinary obsession comes as an extra bonus to the senses—along with Italy's remarkable sights, music and the warm sun on your back, you can enjoy some of the best tastes and smells the world can offer, prepared daily in Italy's kitchens and fermented in its countless wine cellars. Eating *all'Italiana* is not only delicious and wholesome, but now undeniably trendy. Foreigners flock here to learn the secrets of Italian cuisine and the even more elusive secret of how the Italians can live surrounded by such delights and still fit into their sleek Armani trousers.

Breakfast (*colazione*) in Italy is no lingering affair, but an early-morning wake-up shot to the brain: a *cappuccino* (incidentally, first thing in the morning is the only time of day at which any self-respecting Italian will touch the stuff), a *caffè latte* (white coffee) or a *caffè lungo* (a generous portion of espresso), accompanied by a croissant-type roll, called a *cornetto* or *briosce*, or a fancy pastry. This repast can be consumed in any bar and repeated during the morning as often as necessary. Breakfast in most Italian hotels seldom represents great value.

Lunch (*pranzo*), generally served around 1pm, is the most important meal of the day for the Italians, with a minimum of a first course (*primo piatto*—any kind of pasta dish, broth or soup, or rice dish or pizza), a second course (*secondo piatto*—a meat dish, accompanied by a *contorno* or side dish—a vegetable, salad or potatoes), followed by fruit or dessert and coffee. You can, however, begin with a platter of *antipasti*—the appetizers Italians do so brilliantly—ranging from warm seafood delicacies to raw ham (*prosciutto crudo*), salami in a hundred varieties, lovely vegetables, savoury toasts, olives, pâté and many many more. There are restaurants that specialize in *antipasti*, and they usually don't take it amiss if you decide to forget the pasta and meat and just nibble on these scrumptious hors-d'œuvres (though in the end it will probably cost more than a full meal). Most Italians accompany their meal with wine and mineral water—*acqua minerale*, with or without bubbles (*con* or *senza gas*), which supposedly aids digestion—concluding their meals with a *digestivo* liqueur.

Cena, the **evening meal**, is usually eaten around 8pm. This is much the same as *pranzo* although lighter, without the pasta; a pizza and beer, eggs or a fish dish. In restaurants, however, they offer all the courses, so if you have only a sandwich for lunch you can have a full meal in the evening.

In Italy the various terms for types of **restaurants**—*ristorante*, *trattoria* or *osteria*—have been confused. A *trattoria* or *osteria* can be just as elaborate as a restaurant, though rarely is a *ristorante* as informal as a traditional *trattoria*. Unfortunately the old habit of posting menus and prices in the windows has fallen from fashion, so it's often difficult to judge variety or prices. Invariably the least expensive eating place is the *vino e cucina*, a simple establishment serving simple cuisine at simple everyday prices. It is essential to remember that the fancier the fittings, the fancier the **bill**, though neither of these points has anything at all to do with the quality of the food. If you're uncertain, do as you would at home—look for lots of locals. When you eat out, mentally add to the bill (*conto*) the bread and cover charge (*pane e coperto*, between L2000 and L4000), and a 15 per cent service charge. This is often included in the bill (*servizio compreso*); if not, it will say *servizio non compreso*, and you'll have to do your own arithmetic. Additional tipping is at your own discretion, but never do it in family-owned and -run places.

People who haven't visited Italy for years and have fond memories of eating full meals for under £1 will be amazed at how much **prices** have risen; though in some respects eating out is still a bargain, especially when you figure out how much all that wine would have cost you at home. You'll often find restaurants offering a *menu turistico*—full, set meals of usually meagre inspiration for L20,000–30,000. More imaginative chefs often offer a *menu degustazione*—a set-price gourmet meal that allows you to taste their daily specialities and seasonal dishes. Both of these are cheaper than if you had ordered the same food *à la carte*.

We have divided restaurants into the following price categories:

very expensive	over L80,000
expensive	L50,000–80,000
moderate	L30,000–50,000
cheap	below L30,000

When you leave a restaurant you will be given a receipt (*scontrino* or *ricevuto fiscale*) which according to Italian law you must take with you out of the door and carry for at least 60 metres. If you aren't given one, it means the restaurant is probably fudging on its taxes and thus offering you lower prices. There is a slim chance the tax police (*Guardia di Fianza*) may have their eye on you and the restaurant, and if you don't have a receipt they could slap you with a heavy fine.

There are several alternatives to sit-down meals. The 'hot table' (*tavola calda*) is a stand-up buffet where you can choose a simple prepared dish or a whole meal, depending on your appetite. The food in these can be truly impressive; many offer only a few hot dishes, pizza and sandwiches, though in every fair-sized town there will be at least one *tavola calda* with seats where you can contrive a complete dinner outside the usual hours. Little shops that sell pizza by the slice are common in city centres. At any grocer's (*alimentari*) or market (*mercato*) you can buy the materials for countryside or hotel-room picnics; some places in the smaller towns will make the sandwiches for you. For really elegant picnics, have a *tavola calda* pack up something nice for you. And if everywhere else is closed, there's always the railway station—bars will at least have sandwiches and drinks, and perhaps some surprisingly good snacks you've never heard of before. Some of the station bars also prepare *cestini di viaggio*, full-course meals in a basket to help you through long train trips. Common snacks you'll encounter include *panini* of prosciutto, cheese and tomatoes, or other meats; *tramezzini*, little sandwiches on plain, square white bread (much better than they look); and pizza, of course.

The pace of modern urban life militates against traditional lengthy homecooked repasts with the family, followed by a siesta. Many office workers in northern cities behave much as their counterparts elsewhere in Europe and consume a rapid slimline snack at lunchtime, returning home after a busy day to throw together some pasta and salad. But those with more leisure can still eat extremely well, and (if you avoid obvious expense-account places) inexpensively. Many Italian dishes need no introduction—pizza, spaghetti, lasagne and minestrone are now familiar well beyond national boundaries. What is perhaps less well known is the tremendous regional diversity at the table. Each corner of Italy prides itself on its own specialities, the shape of its pasta, its soups and sauces, its wines and desserts; expect to be overwhelmed, especially since many Italian chefs have wholeheartedly embraced the concept of *nouvelle cuisine*, or rather *nuova cucina*, and are constantly inventing dishes with new names.

Central Italy is the land of beans and chickpeas, game, tripe, salt cod (*baccalà*), *porchetta* (whole roast pork with rosemary), Florentine steaks, *saltimbocca alla romana* (veal escalopes with ham and sage) and freshwater fish in interesting guises. Tuscan and Umbrian cooking uses fresh, simple, high-quality ingredients flavoured with herbs and olive oil, and the local *porcini* mushrooms or truffles. The further south you go, the spicier and oilier things get, and the richer the puddings and cakes. Modern Romans are as adventurous at the table as their classical ancestors, and include some stomach-churning offal in their diets. But the capital is an excellent place to delve into any style of regional cooking, with dozens of restaurants from all over Italy. If you are bored poring over a menu in Italy, you've been nipped in the tastebuds.

Wine and Spirits

Italy is a country where everyday wine is cheaper than Coca-Cola or milk, and where nearly every family owns some vineyards or has some relatives who supply most of their daily needs—which are not great. Even though they live in one of the world's largest wine-growing countries, Italians imbibe relatively little, and only at meals.

If Italy has an infinite variety of regional dishes, there is an equally bewildering array of **regional wines**, many of which are rarely exported because they are best drunk young. Even wines that are well known and often derided clichés abroad, like Chianti or Lambrusco, can be wonderful new experiences when tasted on their home turf. Unless you're dining at a restaurant with an exceptional cellar, do as the Italians do and order a carafe of the local wine (*vino locale* or *vino della casa*). You won't often be wrong. Most Italian wines are named after the grape and the district they come from. If the label says DOC (*Denominazione di Origine Controllata*) it means that the wine comes from a specially defined area and was produced according to a certain traditional method. DOCG (*Denominazione d'Origine Controllata e Garantia*) is allegedly a more rigorous classification, indicating that the wines not only conform to DOC standards, but are tested by government-appointed inspectors (who are now more in evidence since a hideous methanol scandal claimed 20 lives in 1986). At present few wines have been granted this status, but the number is planned to increase steadily. *Classico* means that a wine comes from the oldest part of the zone of production, though is not necessarily better than a non-Classico. *Riserva, superiore* or *speciale* denotes a wine that has been aged longer and is more alcoholic; *Recioto* is a wine made from the outer clusters of grapes, with a higher sugar and therefore alcohol content. Other Italian wine words are *spumante* (sparkling), *frizzante* (pétillant), *amabile* (semi-sweet), *abbocato* (medium dry), *passito* (strong sweet wine made from raisins). *Rosso* is red, *bianco* white; between the two extremes lie *rubiato* (ruby), *rosato, chiaretto* or *cerasuolo* (rosé). *Secco* is dry, *dolce* sweet, *liquoroso* fortified and sweet. *Vendemmia* means vintage, a *cantina* is a cellar, and an *enoteca* is a wine shop or museum where you can taste and buy wines.

The regions of Piedmont, Tuscany and Veneto produce Italy's most prestigious red wines, while Friuli-Venezia Giulia and Trentino-Alto Adige are the greatest regions for white wines. King of the Tuscans is the mighty Brunello di Montalcino (DOCG), an expensive blockbuster. Pinot Grigio and the unusual Tocai make some of the best whites.

Italy turns its grape harvest to other uses too, producing Sicilian **Marsala**, a famous fortified wine fermented in wooden casks, ranging from very dry to flavoured and sweet and **vin santo**, a sweet Tuscan speciality often served with almond biscuits. **Vermouth** is an idea from Turin made of wine flavoured with Alpine herbs and spices. Italians are fond of post-prandial brandies (to aid digestion)—**Stock** or **Vecchia Romagna** appear on the best-known Italian brandy bottles. **Grappa** is a rough, Schnapps-like spirit drunk in black coffee after a meal (a *caffè corretto*). Other drinks you'll see in any Italian bar include **Campari**, a red bitter drunk on its own or in cocktails; **Fernet Branca**, **Cynar** and **Averno** (popular aperitif/digestifs); and a host of liqueurs like **Strega**, the witch potion from Benevento, apricot-flavoured **Amaretto**, cherry **Maraschino**, aniseed **Sambuca** or the herby **Millefiori**.

Health and Emergencies

You can insure yourself for almost any possible mishap—cancelled flights, stolen or lost baggage and health. While national health coverage in the UK takes care of its citizens while travelling, in the USA it doesn't. Check any current policies you hold to see if they cover you while abroad, and under what circumstances, and judge whether you need a special **traveller's insurance** policy. Travel agencies sell them, as well as insurance companies.

Citizens of EU countries are entitled to **reciprocal health care** in Italy's National Health Service and a 90 per cent discount on prescriptions (bring **Form E111** with you). The E111 does not cover all medical expenses (no repatriation costs, for example, and no private treatment), and it is advisable to take out separate travel insurance for full cover. Citizens of non-EU countries should check carefully that they have adequate insurance for any medical expenses, and the cost of returning home. Australia has a reciprocal health care scheme with Italy, but New Zealand, Canada and the USA do not. If you already have health insurance, a student card, or a credit card, you may be entitled to some medical cover abroad.

In an **emergency**, dial ✆ 115 for fire and ✆ 113 for an ambulance (*ambulanza*) or to find the nearest hospital (*ospedale*). Less serious problems can be treated at a *Pronto Soccorso* (casualty/first aid department) at any hospital clinic (*ambulatorio*), or at a local health unit (*Unita Sanitarial Locale*—USL). Airports and main railway stations also have **first-aid posts**.

If you have to pay for any health treatment, make sure you get a receipt, so that you can make any claims for reimbursement later.

Dispensing **chemists** (*farmacia*) are generally open from 8.30am to 1pm and from 4 to 8pm. Pharmacists are trained to give advice for minor ills. Any large town will have a *farmacia* that stays open 24 hours; others take turns to stay open (the rota is posted in the window).

No specific **vaccinations** are required or advised for citizens of most countries before visiting Italy; the main health risks are the usual travellers' woes of upset stomachs or the effects of too much sun. Take a supply of **medicaments** with you (insect repellent, anti-diarrhœal medicine, sun lotion and antiseptic cream), and any drugs you need regularly.

Most Italian doctors speak at least rudimentary English, but if you can't find one, contact your embassy or consulate for a list of English-speaking doctors. Standards of health care in the north are generally higher than in the deep south.

Public Hospitals and Medical Services

Rome, Policlinico Umberto I, Viale del Policlinico 255 (near Staz. Termini), ✆ 06 492 341.

Florence, Tourist Medical Service, Via Lorenzo il Magnifico 59, ✆ 055 475 411 (English-speaking doctors, 24-hr service).

Venice, Ospedale Civilis Riuniti di Venezia, Campo SS Giovanni e Paolo, ✆ 041 520 5622, or Ospedale del Mare, 1 Lungomare d'Annunzio, Lido, ✆ 041 526 5900.

Maps and Publications

The maps in this guide are for orientation only and to explore in any detail it is worth investing in a good, up-to-date regional map before you arrive from any of the following bookshops:

Stanford's, 12–14 Long Acre, London WC2 9LP, ✆ (0171) 836 1321.
The Travel Bookshop, 13 Blenheim Crescent, London W11, ✆ (0171) 229 5260.
The Complete Traveller, 199 Madison Ave, New York, 10016, ✆ (212) 685 9007.

Excellent maps are produced by **Touring Club Italiano**, **Michelin** and **Istituto Geografico de Agostini**. They are available at all major bookshops in Italy or sometimes on news-stands. Italian tourist offices are helpful and can often supply good area maps and town plans.

Books are more expensive in Italy than in the UK, but some excellent shops stock English-language books. A few useful ones are listed below.

The Paperback Exchange, Via Fiesolana 31r, Florence.
Feltrinelli, Via Cavour 12–20r, Florence.
Anglo-American Book Co., Via della Vite 57, Rome.
Lion Bookshop, Via del Babuino 181, Rome.
Corner Bookshop, Via del Moro 48, Rome.
Open Door Bookshop, Via della Lungaretta 25, Rome.
Economy Book Center, Via Torino 136, Rome.
Sangiorgio, Calle Larga XXII Marzo 2087, San Marco, Venice.
Serenissima, Merceria dell'Orologio 739, San Marco, Venice.

Money

It's a good idea to order a wad of lire from your home bank to have on hand when you arrive in Italy, the land of strikes, unforeseen delays and quirky banking hours (*see* below). Take great care how you carry it, however (don't keep it all in one place). Obtaining money is often a frustrating business involving much queueing and form-filling. The major banks and exchange bureaux licensed by the Bank of Italy give the best exchange rates for currency or traveller's cheques. Hotels, private exchanges in resorts and FS-run exchanges at railway stations usually have less advantageous rates, but are open outside normal banking hours.

Weekend exchange offices

Florence: Thomas Cook, Lungarno Acciaioli 6r; American Express, Via de'Guicciardini 49r.

Rome: Banco Nazionale delle Comunicazione, Stazione Termini; Thomas Cook, Piazza Barberini 21D.

Venice: American Express, S. Moise 1471; CIT, Piazza S. Marco.

In addition there are exchange offices at most airports. Remember that Italians indicate decimals with commas and thousands with full points.

Most British banks have an arrangement with the Italian banking authorities whereby you can (for a significant commission) use your bank card to take money out of Italian cash machines, but check with your bank first. Besides traveller's cheques, most banks will give also you cash on a recognized credit card or Eurocheque with a Eurocheque card (taking little or no commission), and in big cities you can find automatic tellers (ATMs) to spout cash on a Visa, American Express or Eurocheque card. You need a PIN number to use these. Make sure you read the instructions carefully, or your card may be retained by the machine. MasterCard (Access) is much less widely acceptable in Italy. Large hotels, resort-area restaurants, shops and car-hire firms will accept plastic as well; many smaller places will not. From sad experience, Italians are wary of plastic—you can't even always use it at motorway petrol stops.

You can have money transferred to you through an Italian bank but this process may take over a week, even if it's sent urgent—*espressissimo*. You will need your passport as identification when you collect it. Sending cheques by post is inadvisable.

National Holidays

Most museums, as well as banks and shops, are closed on the following national holidays.

1 January (New Year's Day)

6 January (Epiphany)

Easter Monday

25 April (Liberation Day)

1 May (Labour Day)

15 August (Assumption, also known as *Ferragosto*, the official start of the Italian holiday season)

1 November (All Saints' Day)
8 December (Immaculate Conception)
25 December (Christmas Day)
26 December (*Santo Stefano*, St Stephen's Day)

Opening Hours and Museums

Although it varies from region to region, most of Italy closes down at 1pm until 3 or 4pm to eat and properly digest the main meal of the day. Afternoon hours are from 4 to 7, often from 5 to 8 in the hot summer months. Bars are often the only places open during the early afternoon. In any case, don't be surprised if you find anywhere in Italy unexpectedly closed (or open for that matter), whatever its official stated hours.

offices

banks: *open Mon–Fri 8.30–1 and 3–4, closed weekends and on local and national holidays (see below).*

shops: *open Mon–Sat 8–1 and 3.30–7.30.* Some supermarkets and department stores stay open throughout the day.

Government-run dispensers of red tape (e.g. visa departments) often stay open for quite limited periods, usually during the mornings (*Mon–Fri*). It pays to get there as soon as they open (or before) to spare your nerves in an interminable queue. Anyway, take something to read, or write your memoirs.

museums and galleries

Many of Italy's museums are magnificent, many are run with shameful neglect, and many have been closed for years for 'restoration' with slim prospects of reopening in the foreseeable future. With two works of art per inhabitant, Italy has a hard time financing the preservation of its national heritage; it would be as well to enquire at the tourist office to find out exactly what is open and what is 'temporarily' closed before setting off on a wild-goose chase.

churches

Italy's churches have always been a prime target for art thieves and as a consequence are usually locked when there isn't a sacristan or caretaker to keep an eye on things. All churches, except for the really important cathedrals and basilicas, close in the afternoon at the same hours as the shops, and the little ones tend to stay closed. Always have a pocketful of coins for the light machines in churches, or whatever work of art you came to inspect will remain clouded in ecclesiastical gloom. Don't do your visiting during services, and don't come to see paintings and statutes in churches the week preceding Easter—you will probably find them covered with mourning shrouds.

In general, Sunday afternoons and Mondays are dead periods for the sightseer—you may want to make them your travelling days. Places without specified opening hours can usually be visited on request—but it is best to go before 1pm. We have listed the hours of important sights and museums, and specified which ones charge admission. Entrance charges vary widely; major sights are fairly steep (L10,000 plus), but others may be completely free. EU citizens under 18 and over 65 get free admission to state museums, at least in theory.

Packing

You simply cannot overdress in Italy; whatever grand strides Italian designers have made on the international fashion merry-go-round, most of their clothes are purchased domestically, prices be damned. Whether or not you want to try to keep up with the natives is your own affair. It's not that the Italians are very formal; they simply like to dress up with a gorgeousness that adorns their cities just as much as those old Renaissance churches and palaces. The few places with dress codes are the major churches and basilicas (no shorts, sleeveless shirts or strappy sundresses—women should carry a scarf to throw over the shoulders), casinos and a few posh restaurants.

Your electric appliances will work if you adapt them to run on 220 AC with two round prongs on the plug.

Post Offices

post offices: *in cities usually open Mon–Sat 8–6 or 7.*

Dealing with *la posta italiana* has always been a risky, frustrating, time-consuming affair. It is one of the most expensive and slowest postal services in Europe. Even buying the right stamps requires dedicated research and saintly patience. One of the scandals that mesmerized Italy in recent years involved the Minister of the Post Office, who disposed of literally tons of backlog mail by tossing it in the Tiber. When the news broke, he was replaced—the new minister, having learned his lesson, burned all the mail the Post Office was incapable of delivering. Not surprisingly, fed-up Italians view the invention of the fax machine as a gift from the Madonna. From these harsh judgements, however, we must exempt the Vatican City, whose special postal service (on angelic wings?) knocks spots off the rest of the country for speed and efficiency. If you're anywhere in Rome, be sure to post your mail in the Holy See. You need to buy special Vatican stamps, which provide a tidy profit for the papal coffers.

To have your mail sent *poste restante* (general delivery), have it addressed to the central post office (*Fermo Posta*) and allow three to four weeks for it to arrive. Make sure your surname is very clearly written in block capitals. To pick up your mail you must present your passport and pay a nominal charge. Stamps (*francobolli*) may be purchased in post offices or at tobacconists (*tabacchi*, identified by their blue signs with a white T). Prices fluctuate. The rates for letters and postcards (depending how many words you write!) vary according to the whim of the tobacconist or postal clerk.

You can also have money telegraphed to you through the post office; if all goes well, this can happen in a mere three days, but expect a fair proportion of it to go into commission.

Shopping

'Made in Italy' has become a byword for style and quality, especially in fashion and leather, but also in home design, ceramics, kitchenware, jewellery, lace and linens, glassware and crystal, chocolates, bells, Christmas decorations, hats, straw work, art books, engravings, handmade stationery, gold and silverware, bicycles, sports cars, woodworking, a hundred kinds of liqueurs, aperitifs, coffee machines, gastronomic specialities and antiques (both reproductions and the real thing).

If you are looking for antiques, be sure to demand a certificate of authenticity—reproductions can be very, very good. To get your antique or modern art purchases home, you will have to apply to the Export Department of the Italian Ministry of Education—a possible hassle. You will have to pay an export tax as well; your seller should know the details. Be sure to save receipts for Customs on the way home. Italians don't much like department stores, but there are a few chains—the classiest is the oldest, Rinascente, while COIN stores often have good buys in almost the latest fashions. Standa and UPIM are more like Woolworth's; they have good clothes selections, housewares, etc., and often contain basement supermarkets. The main attraction of Italian shopping, however, is to buy classy luxury items; for less expensive clothes and household items you can nearly always do better at home. Prices for clothes are generally very high.

Telephones

Public telephones for international calls may be found in the offices of **Telecom Italia**, Italy's telephone company. They are the only places where you can make reverse-charge calls (*a erre*, collect calls) but be prepared for a wait, as all these calls go through the operator in Rome. Rates for long-distance calls are among the highest in Europe. Calls within Italy are cheapest after 10pm; international calls after 11pm. Most phone booths now take either coins (L100, 200, 500 or 1000), *gettoni* (L200 tokens often given to you in place of change) or phone cards (*schede telefoniche*) available in L5000, L10,000 and sometimes L15,000 amounts at tobacconists and news-stands—you will have to snap off the small perforated corner in order to use them. Try to avoid telephoning from hotels, which often add 25% to the bill.

As with most countries, Italy has a constant need for new telephone numbers and, as with other countries, this has forced the Italian telephone authorites to change numbers, usually by adding a digit to the area code, in order to cope with demand. Also, as elsewhere, it is usually realized after a couple of years that this renumbering has been based on a severe underestimation of the potential demand and that the numbers will have to change again. In an attempt to stay one step ahead of the game, however, Telecom Italia has unveiled new plans which require people to dial the entire phone number including the area code when they make a call, even if they are calling from within that area code. We have included all former area codes with phone numbers in the guide.

Direct calls may be made by dialling the international prefix (for the UK 0044, Ireland 00353, USA and Canada 001, Australia 0061, New Zealand 0064). If you're calling Italy from abroad, dial 39 first. Many places have public fax machines, but the speed of transmission may make costs very high.

Time

Italy is on Central European Time, one hour ahead of Greenwich Mean Time and six hours ahead of Eastern Standard Time. From the last weekend of March to the end of September, Italian Summer Time (daylight-saving time) is in effect.

Toilets

Frequent travellers have noted a steady improvement over the years in the cleanliness of Italy's public conveniences, although as ever you will only find them in places like train and bus stations and bars. Ask for the *bagno*, *toilette* or *gabinetto*; in stations and the smarter bars and cafés there are washroom attendants who expect a few hundred lire for keeping the place decent. You'll probably have to ask them for paper (*carta*). Don't confuse the Italian plurals: *signori* (gents), *signore* (ladies).

Tourist Offices

Tourist information offices: *open 8–12.30 or 1 and 3–7, possibly longer in summer. Few open on Saturday afternoons or Sundays.*

Known as EPT, APT or AAST, information booths provide hotel lists, town plans and terse information on local sights and transport. Queues can be maddeningly long. English is spoken in the main centres. If you're stuck, you may get more sense out of a friendly travel agency than an official tourist office.

UK, 1 Princes Street, London W1R 8AY, ✆ (0171) 408 1254; **Italian Travel Centre**, Thomas Cook, 45 Berkeley Street, London W1A 1EB, ✆ (0171) 499 4000.

USA, 630 Fifth Ave, Suite 1565, New York, NY 10111, ✆ (212) 245 4822; 12400 Wilshire Blvd, Suite 550, Los Angeles, CA 90025, ✆ (310) 820 0098; 500 N. Michigan Ave, Suite 1046, Chicago, IL 60611, ✆ (312) 644 0990.

Australia, c/o Italian Embassy, 61–69 Macquarie St, Sydney 2000, NSW, ✆ (02) 9247 8442.

Canada, 1 Place Ville Marie, Suite 1914, Montréal, Quebec H3B 3M9, ✆ (514) 866 7667.

Japan, 2–7–14 Minimi, Aoyama, Minato-Ku, Tokyo 107, ✆ (813) 347 82 051.

France, 23 rue de la Paix, 75002 Paris, ✆ 01 42 66 66 68; 14 Avenue de Verdun, 06048 Nice, ✆ 04 93 87 75 81.

Germany, Berliner Allee 26, 4 Düsseldorf, ✆ (211) 13 22 32; Kaiserstrasse 65, 6000 Frankfurt/Main 1, ✆ (069) 2374; Goethestrasse 20, 80336 München, ✆ (089) 53 03 69.

Netherlands, Stadhouderskade 6, 1054 ES Amsterdam, ✆ (020) 616 8244.

New Zealand, c/o Italian Embassy, 36 Grant Road, Thorndon, Wellington, ✆ (04) 736 065.

Weights and Measures

1 kilogram (1000g)—2.2 lb	1 lb—0.45 kg
1 etto (100g)—0.25 lb (approx)	1 pint—0.568 litres
1 litre—1.76 pints	1 quart—1.136 litres
1 metre—39.37 inches	1 Imperial gallon—4.546 litres
1 kilometre—0.621 miles	1 US gallon—3.785 litres
1 foot—0.35 metres	1 mile—1.16 kilometres

Clothes sizes are tailored for slim Italian builds. Shoes, in particular, tend to be narrower than in most other Western countries.

clothing sizes

Women's Shirts/Dresses

UK	10	12	14	16	18
USA	8	10	12	14	16
Italy	40	42	44	46	48

Sweaters

UK	10	12	14	16
USA	8	10	12	14
Italy	46	48	50	52

Women's Shoes

UK	3	4	5	6	7	8
USA	4	5	6	7	8	9
Italy	36	37	38	39	40	41

Men's Shirts

UK/USA	14	14.5	15	15.5	16	16.5	17	17.5
Italy	36	37	38	39	40	41	42	43

Men's Suits

UK/USA	36	38	40	42	44	46
Italy	46	48	50	52	54	56

Men's Shoes

UK	5	6	7	8	9	10	11	12
USA	7.5	8	9	10	10.5	11	12	13
Italy	38	39	40	41	42	43	44	45

Where to Stay

All accommodation in Italy is classified by the Provincial Tourist Boards. Price control, however, has been deregulated since 1992. Hotels now set their own tariffs, which means that in some places prices have rocketed. After a period of rapid and erratic price fluctuation, tariffs are at last settling down again to more predictable levels under the influence of market forces. Good-value, interesting accommodation in cities can be very difficult to find.

The quality of furnishings and facilities has generally improved in all categories in recent years. Many hotels have installed smart bathrooms and electronic gadgetry. At the top end of the market, Italy has a number of exceptionally sybaritic hotels, furnished and decorated with real panache. But you can still find plenty of older-style hotels and *pensioni*, whose eccentricities of character and architecture (in some cases undeniably charming) may frequently be at odds with modern standards of comfort or even safety.

Category	Double with bath
luxury (*****)	L450–800,000
very expensive (****)	L300–450,000
expensive (***)	L200–300,000
moderate (**)	L120–200,000
cheap (*)	up to L120,000

Hotels and Guesthouses

Italian *alberghi* come in all shapes and sizes. They are rated from one to five stars, depending what facilities they offer (not their character, style or charm). The star ratings are some indication of price levels, but for tax reasons not all hotels choose to advertise themselves at the rating to which they are entitled, so you may find a modestly rated hotel just as comfortable (or more so) than a higher-rated one. Conversely, you may find a hotel offers few stars in hopes of attracting budget-conscious travellers, but charges just as much as a higher-rated neighbour. *Pensioni* are generally more modest establishments, though nowadays the distinction between these and ordinary hotels is becoming blurred. *Locande* are traditionally an even more basic form of hostelry, but these days the term may denote somewhere fairly chic. Other inexpensive accommodation is sometimes known as *alloggi* or *affittacamere*. There are usually plenty of cheap dives around railway stations; for somewhere more salubrious, head for the historic quarters. Whatever the shortcomings of the décor, furnishings and fittings, you can usually rely at least on having clean sheets.

Price lists, by law, must be posted on the door of every room, along with meal prices and any extra charges (such as air-conditioning, or even a shower in cheap places). Many hotels display two or three different rates, depending on the season. Low-season rates may be about a third lower than peak-season tariffs. During high season you should always book ahead to be sure of a room (a fax reservation may be less frustrating to organize than one by post). If you have paid a deposit, your booking is valid under Italian law, but don't expect it to be refunded if you have to cancel. Tourist offices publish annual regional lists of hotels and *pensioni* with current rates, but do not generally make reservations for visitors. Major city business hotels may offer significant discounts at weekends.

Main railway stations generally have accommodation booking desks; inevitably, a fee is charged. Chain hotels or motels are generally the easiest hotels to book, though not always the most interesting to stay in. Top of the list is CIGA (*Compagnia Grandi Alberghi*) with some of the most luxurious establishments in Italy, many of them grand, turn-of-the-century places that have been exquisitely restored. Venice's legendary Cipriani is one of its flagships. The French consortium *Relais et Châteaux* specializes in tastefully indulgent accommodation, often in historic buildings. At a more affordable level, one of the biggest chains in Italy is *Jolly Hotels*, always reliable if not all up to the same standard. Many motels are operated by the ACI (Italian Automobile Club) or by AGIP (the oil company) and usually located along major exit routes.

If you arrive without a reservation begin looking or phoning round for accommodation early in the day. If possible, inspect the room (and bathroom facilities) before you book, and check the tariff carefully. Italian hoteliers may legally alter their rates twice during the year, so printed tariffs or tourist board lists (and prices quoted in this book!) may be out of date. Hoteliers who wilfully overcharge should be reported to the local tourist office. You will be asked for your passport for registration purposes.

Prices listed in this guide are for double rooms; you can expect to pay about two-thirds the rate for single occupancy, though in high season you may be charged the full double rate. Extra beds are usually charged at about a third more of the room rate. Rooms without private bathrooms generally charge 20–30% less, and most offer discounts for children sharing parents' rooms, or children's meals. A *camera singola* (single room) may cost anything from about L25,000 upwards. Double rooms (*camera doppia*) go from about L60,000 to L250,000 or more. If you want a double bed, specify a *camera matrimoniale*.

Breakfast is usually optional in hotels, though obligatory in *pensioni*. It is usually better value to eat breakfast in a bar or café if you have any choice. In high season you may be expected to take half-board if the hotel has a restaurant, and one-night stays may be refused.

Hostels and Budget Accommodation

There aren't many youth hostels (known as *alberghi* or *ostelli per la gioventù*), but they are generally pleasant and sometimes located in historic buildings. The **Associazione Italiana Alberghi per la Gioventù** (Italian Youth Hostel Association, or AIG) is affiliated to the International Youth Hostel Federation. For a full list of hostels, contact AIG, Via Cavour 44, 00184 Roma, ✆ 06 487 1152, 🖷 06 488 0492. An international membership card will enable you to stay in any of them. You can obtain these in advance from the following organizations.

UK, Youth Hostels Association of England and Wales, 14 Southampton Street, London WC2, ✆ (0171) 836 1036.

USA, American Youth Hostels Inc., Box 37613, Washington DC 20013-7613, ✆ (202) 783 6161.

Australia, Australian Youth Hostel Association, 60 Mary Street, Surry Hills, Sydney, NSW 2010, ✆ (02) 9621 1111.

Canada, Canadian Hostelling Association, 1600 James Naismith Drive, Suite 608, Gloucester, Ontario K1B 5N4, ✆ (613) 237 7884.

(Cards can usually be purchased on the spot in many hostels if you don't already have one.)

Religious institutions also run hostels; some are single-sex, others will accept Catholics only. Rates are usually somewhere between L15,000 and L20,000, including breakfast. Discounts are available for senior citizens, and some family rooms are available. You generally have to check in after 5pm, and pay for your room before 9am. Hostels usually close for most of the daytime, and many operate a curfew. During the spring, noisy school parties cram hostels for field trips. In the summer, it's advisable to book ahead. Contact the hostels directly.

Women Travellers

Italian men, with the heritage of Casanova, Don Giovanni and Rudolph Valentino as their birthright, are very confident in their role as Great Latin Lovers, but the old horror stories of gangs following the innocent tourist maiden and pinching her bottom are way behind the times. Italian men these days are often exquisitely polite and flirt on a much more sophisticated level, especially in the more 'Europeanized' north.

Still, women travelling alone may frequently receive hisses, wolf-whistles and unsolicited comments (complimentary or lewd, depending on your attitude) or 'assistance' from local swains—usually of the balding, middle-age-crisis variety. A confident, indifferent poise is usually the best policy. Failing that, a polite 'I am waiting for my *marito*' (avoiding damaged male egos which can turn nasty), followed by a firm '*No!*' or '*Vai via!*' (Scram!) will generally solve the problem. Flashers and wandering hands on crowded buses may be an unpleasant surprise, but rarely present a serious threat (unless they're after your purse).

Risks can be greatly reduced if you use common sense and avoid lonely streets or parks and train stations after dark. Choose hotels and restaurants within easy and safe walking distance of public transport. Travelling with a companion of either sex will buffer you considerably from such nuisances (a guardian male, of course, instantly converts you into an inviolable chattel in Italian eyes). Avoid hitch-hiking alone in Italy.

Italy in Perspective

The First Italians

Some 50,000 years ago, when the Alps were covered by an ice cap and the low level of the Mediterranean made Italy a much wider peninsula than it is now, Neanderthal man graced the Ligurian Riviera with his low-browed presence. Even that, however, is not the beginning of the story. Recently, scientists have become excited over the discovery of a new type, *Homo Aeserniensis*, the first known inhabitant of Europe, living in caves around Isernia a million years ago. Italy makes a convenient bridge from Africa to Europe, and it seems that there was a lot of traffic throughout prehistory. Nevertheless, none of the earliest inhabitants of Italy left much in terms of art or culture, and the peninsula remained a backwater until about the 8th century BC. At that time, most of the population were lumped together as 'Italics', a number of powerful, distinct tribes with related languages. Among them were the **Samnites**, who dominated much of Campania and the south, the dolmen-building **Messapians** in Puglia, the **Picentes** and **Umbrii** along the northern Adriatic coast, and a boiling kettle of contentious peoples in the centre: **Sabines, Aequi, Volscii** and **Latins**. The mighty walls of their cities, called *cyclopean walls*, can still be seen today around southern Lazio. Two of Italy's most culturally sophisticated peoples lived on the islands: the **Siculi** of Sicily and the castle-building, bronze-working **Sards** of the Nuraghe culture. Both kept to themselves and interfered little with affairs on the mainland. Much of the north, the classical Cisalpine Gaul, was the stomping ground of Celtic Ligurians; at the time this area north of the Po was not really thought of as part of Italy.

750–509 BC: Greeks and Etruscans

The most interesting nations of the time, however, were two relative newcomers who contributed much towards bringing Italy out of its primitive state, the **Etruscans** and **Greeks**. With their shadowy past and as yet largely undeciphered language, the Etruscans are one of the puzzles of ancient history. According to their own traditions they arrived from somewhere in western Anatolia about 900 BC—Etruscan inscriptions have been found on the Greek island of Lemnos—probably as a sort of warrior aristocracy that imposed itself on the existing populations of Tuscany and north Lazio. By the 8th century BC they were the strongest people in Italy, grouped in a loose confederation of 12 city-states called the *Dodecapolis*. At the same time, the Greeks, whose trading routes had long covered Italy's southern coasts, began to look upon that 'underdeveloped' country as a New World for exploration and colonization. Cumae, on the Campanian coast, became the first Greek foundation in 750 BC, a convenient base for trading with the Etruscans and their newly discovered iron mines. A score of others soon followed in Sicily and along the Ionian Sea and soon they were rivalling the cities of Greece itself in wealth and culture. A third new factor in the Italian equation also appeared at this time, without much fanfare. 753 BC, according to the legends, saw the foundation of **Rome**.

Italy was ripe for civilization. In the centuries that followed, the Etruscans spread their rule and their culture over most of the north while the Italic tribes learned from Etruscans and Greeks alike. Some of them, especially the Latins and the Samnites, developed into urbanized, cultured nations in their own right. For the Greek cities, it was a golden age, as Taras (Tàranto), Metapontum, Sybaris, Croton, and especially the Sicilian cities like Syracuse and

Akragas, grew into marble metropolises that dominated central Mediterranean trade and turned much of inland Italy into tribute-paying allies. In the 6th century BC, they had more wealth than was probably good for them; stories are told of the merchants of Sybaris sending across the Mediterranean, offering fortunes for a cook who could produce the perfect sauce for seafood, and of the sentries of Akragas' army going on strike for softer pillows. From the first, also, these cities dissipated their energies by engaging in constant wars with each other. Some, like Sybaris, were completely destroyed, and by c. 400 BC, the failure of the rest to work together sent them into a slow but irreversible economic decline.

The Etruscan story is much the same. By about 600 BC the 12 cities and their allies ruled almost all northern Italy (excluding Cisalpine Gaul), and wealth from their Tuscan mines made them a political force on a Mediterranean scale. Their decline was to be as rapid as that of Magna Graecia. Repeated defeats at the hands of the wild Gauls weakened their confederation, but the economic decline that led to Etruria's virtual evaporation in the 4th century BC is harder to account for. Rome, a border city between the Etruscans and Latins, threw out its Etruscan king and established a **Republic** in 509 BC (*see* **Rome**, 'History', p.65). Somehow, probably by the absorption of conquered populations, this relatively new city managed to grow to perhaps 100,000 people, ranking it with Taras and Capua, an Etruscan colony in the growing region of Campania, as the largest on the peninsula. With an economy insufficient to support so many Romans, the city could only live by a career of permanent conquest.

509–268 BC: The Rise of Rome

After the expulsion of the Etruscans, Rome spent a hundred years at war with the various cities of Etruria, while gradually subjugating the rest of the Latins and neighbouring tribes. The little republic with the military-camp ethic was successful on all fronts, and a sacking by marauding Gauls in 390 BC proved only a brief interruption in Rome's march to conquest. Southern Etruria and Latium were swallowed up by 358 BC, and Rome next turned its attention to the only power in Italy capable of competing with her on an equal basis: the Samnites. These rugged highlanders of the southern Apennines, with their capital at Benevento, had begun to seize parts of coastal Campania. The Romans drove them out in 343–1 BC, but in the **Second Samnite War** the Samnites dealt them a severe defeat (Battle of Caudine Forks, 321 BC). In the third war, feeling themselves surrounded by Roman allies, the Samnites formed an alliance with the Northern Etruscans and Celts, leading to a general Italian commotion in which the Romans beat everybody, annexing almost all of Italy by 283 BC.

A strange interlude, delaying Rome's complete domination of Italy, came with the arrival of **Pyrrhus of Epirus**, a Greek adventurer with a large army who was invited in by the cities of Magna Graecia as a protector. From him we get the term 'Pyrrhic victories', for he outmatched the Romans in one battle after another, but never was able to follow up his advantage. After finally losing one in 275 BC, at Benevento, he quit and returned to Epirus, while the Romans leisurely took the deserted Greek cities one by one. Now the conquest was complete. All along the Romans had been diabolically clever in managing their new demesne, maintaining most of the tribes and cities as nominally independent states, while planting Latin colonies everywhere (refounded cities like Paestum, Ascoli Piceno, and Benevento were such colonies, together with new ones in the north like Florence). The great network of roads centred on Rome was extended with great speed, and a truly united Italy seemed close to becoming a reality.

268–91 BC: Empire Abroad, Disarray at Home

After all this, Rome deserved a shot at the Mediterranean heavyweight title. The current champ, the powerful merchant thalassocracy of Carthage, was alarmed enough at the successes of its precocious neighbour, and proved happy to oblige. Rome won the first bout, beating Carthage and her ally Syracuse in the **First Punic War** (264–41 BC), and gained Sicily, Sardinia, and Corsica. For the rematch, the **Second Punic War** (219–202 BC), Carthage sent **Hannibal** and his elephants from Spain into Italy over the Alps to bring the war into the Romans' backyard. Undeterred by the brilliant African general's victory at Cannae in 216 BC, where four legions were destroyed, the Romans hung on tenaciously even when Hannibal appeared at the gates of Rome. In Hannibal's absence, they took Spain and much of Africa, and after Scipio Africanus' victory at Zama in 202 BC, Carthage surrendered. The **Third Punic War** was a sorry affair. Rome only waited long enough for Carthage to miss a step in its treaty obligations before razing the city to the ground. The west conquered, Rome looked east. Already by 200 BC she had been interfering in Greek affairs. The disunited Greeks and successor states of Alexander's empire proved easy targets, and by 64 BC the legions were camped on the Cataracts of the Nile, in Jerusalem, and half across Asia Minor.

Nothing corrupts a state like easy conquests, and all this time things in Italy were going very wrong. Taxation ceased for Roman citizens, as booty provided the state with all the revenues it needed, and tens of thousands of slaves were imported. Thus Italy became a parasite nation. Vast amounts of cheap grain brought from Africa and Egypt ruined the Italian farmer, who had the choice of selling his freehold and becoming a sharecropper, joining the army, or moving to Rome as part of the burgeoning lumpenproletariat. The men who profited the most from the wars bought up tremendous amounts of land, turning Italy into a country of huge estates (*latifundia*), and becoming a new aristocracy powerful enough to stifle any attempts at reform. Only Rome, of course, and a few other cities prospered.

Not that degeneracy and social disintegration had proceeded far enough for Italy to fail to resist. Rome, and indeed all Italy, divided into extremist factions.

91–31 BC: Sixty Years of Civil War

Italy had had enough; the year 91 saw a coordinated revolt among the southern peoples called the **Social War**, which was defeated by the campaigns of Marius and **Sulla** (the Senate's darling in the army), and by an offer to extend Roman citizenship to all Italians. A military coup by Sulla followed, with the backing of the Senate. An effective dictatorship was created, and all opponents either murdered or exiled. Italy careened into anarchy, with many rural districts reverting to bandit-ridden wastelands, a setting for the remarkable revolt in 73 BC of **Spartacus**, an escaped gladiator who led a motley army of dispossessed farmers and runaway slaves—some 70,000 of them— back and forth across the south until the legions finally defeated him in 71 BC.

All this had exhausted both sides, and finally discredited senatorial rule. After Sulla's death, no one minded when the consulship and real power passed to **Pompey**, another successful general but one who cared little for politics. Like Sulla before him, Pompey soon set out for the east, where the most glory and booty were to be gained, and his departure left the stage in Rome open to 33-year-old **Julius Caesar**, a tremendously clever soldier-politician, but a good man anyhow. With his two surpassing talents, one for rhetoric and the other for attracting money, he took up the popular cause in better style than anyone had done it before. A taint of connection to the **Catiline conspiracy** of 68 BC (a revolt of adventurers, disaffected nobles, and other loose ends) proved a temporary setback, just as it advanced the fortunes of **Marcus Tullius Cicero**, the great orator, writer, and statesman who still dreamed of founding a real republic with a real constitution, opposing both extreme parties and pinning his hopes on the still-surviving Italian middle class. Few people in Rome cared for such principles, however, and after Pompey returned from bashing the Pontic Kingdom and the Cilician pirates, he, Caesar, and a wealthy building contractor named Licinius Crassus sliced up the republic between them, forming the **First Triumvirate** in 59 BC.

What Caesar really wanted, of course, was a military command. Following the accepted practice, he managed to buy himself one in the north, and undertook the conquest of most of Gaul, with well-known results. In his four years as ruler of Rome, Caesar surprised everyone, even his enemies; everything received a good dose of reform, even the calendar, and a beginning was made towards sorting out the economic mess and getting Italy back on its feet. His assassination by a clique of Republican bitter-enders in 44 BC plunged Italy into civil war again, and left historians to ponder the grand question of whether Caesar had really intended to make himself a king and finally put the now senile Republic to sleep. A **Second Triumvirate** was formed, of Caesar's adopted son Octavian, a senatorial figurehead named Lepidus, and Caesar's old friend and right-hand man, a talented, dissipated fellow named Marcus Antonius (Mark Antony), who according to one historian spent the equivalent of $3 billion (of other people's money) in his brief lifetime. While he dallied in the east with Cleopatra, Octavian was consolidating his power in Italy. The inevitable battle came in 31 BC, at Actium in Greece, and it was a complete victory for Octavian.

31 BC–AD 251: The Empire

With unchallenged authority through all the Roman lands, Octavian (soon to rename himself **Augustus**) was free to complete the reforms initiated by Caesar. For his career, and those of his successors, you may read the gossipy, shocking, and wonderfully unreliable *Lives of the Caesars* of Suetonius. All Rome tittered at the scandals of the later Julian Emperors, but reality was usually much more prosaic. **Tiberius** (AD 14–37) may have been a monster to his girlfriends and boyfriends, but he proved an intelligent and just ruler otherwise; his criminally insane successor **Caligula**, or 'Bootkin', lasted only four years (37–41) while the bureaucracy kept things going. **Claudius** (41–54) governed well and conquered southern Britain, while his stepson **Nero** (54–68) generally made a nuisance of himself in Rome but did little to disturb the system. Nevertheless, a commmander in Spain (Galba) declared him unfit to be emperor and marched on Rome to take his place; Nero just managed to commit suicide before they caught him. Now the genie was out of the bottle again, as the soldiers once more realized that the real power lay with them. Another general, Otho, commander of the Emperor's Praetorian Guard, toppled Galba, and soon lost out in turn to Vitellius, commander on the Rhine. The fourth emperor of the fateful years AD 68–69 was **Vespasian**, leader of the eastern armies. He had the strongest legions and so got to keep the job; his reign (69–79) and those of his sons **Titus** (79–81) and **Domitian** (81–96), the three Flavian Emperors, were remembered as a period of prosperity. Vespasian began the Colosseum; whether intentionally or not, this incomparable new charnel house made a perfect symbol for the renewed decadence and militarization of the state.

For the moment, however, things looked rosy. After the assassination of Domitian, another bad boy but not an especially calamitous ruler, Rome had the good fortune to be ruled by a series of high-minded and intelligent military men, who carefully chose their successors in advance to avoid civil war. The so-called **Antonine Emperors** presided over the greatest age of prosperity the Mediterranean world ever knew; in Italy they ran a surprisingly modern state (though one still based on slave labour) that would seem familiar to us today: public libraries, water boards to maintain the aqueducts, rent control, agricultural price supports, low-cost loans for starting new businesses and many other such innovations. The first of the Antonines was **Nerva** (96–98), followed by **Trajan** (98–117) and **Hadrian** (117–138), both great soldiers and builders on a monumental scale, especially in Rome; after them came **Antoninus Pius** (138–61), little known only because his reign was so peaceful, and **Marcus Aurelius** (161–80), soldier, statesman, and Stoic philosopher. His choice for successor was his useless son **Commodus** (180–93) and the string of good emperors was broken.

The 2nd-century prosperity was not without its darker side. The arts were in serious decline, as if the imagination of the Greco-Roman Mediterranean was somehow failing. Education was in poor shape, and every sort of fatuous mysticism imported from the East permeated the minds of the people. Economically, this period saw the emergence of the well-known north–south split in Italy.

251–475: Decline and Fall

For all it cost to maintain them, the legions were no longer the formidable military machine of Augustus' day. They were bureaucratic and a little tired, and their tactics and equipment were also falling behind those of the Persians and even some of the more clever German barbarians. The Goths were the first to demonstrate this, in 251, when they overran the Balkans, Greece, and Asia Minor. Five years later Franks and Alemanni invaded Gaul, and in 268 much of the east detached itself from the empire under the leadership of Odenathus of Palmyra. Somehow the empire recovered and prevailed, under dour soldier-emperors like **Aurelian** (270–5), who built Rome's walls, and **Diocletian** (284–305), who completely revamped the structure of the state and economy. His fiscal reforms, such as the fixing of prices and a decree that every son had to follow the trade of his father, ossified the economy and made the creeping decline of Italy and all western Europe harder to arrest.

More than ever, the Empire had become an outright military dictatorship, in a society whose waning energies were entirely devoted to supporting a bloated, all-devouring army and bureaucracy. The confused politics of the 4th century are dominated by **Constantine** (306–37), who ruled both halves of the Empire, defeated various other contenders (Battle of the Milvian Bridge, outside Rome, in 312), and founded the new eastern capital of Constantinople. He adroitly moved to increase his and the Empire's political support by favouring Christianity. Though still a small minority in most of the Empire, the Christians' strong organization and determination made them a good bet for the future.

The military disasters began in 406, with Visigoths, Franks, Vandals, Alans, and Suevi over-running Gaul and Spain. Italy's turn came in 408, when Western Emperor Honorius, ruling from the new capital of Ravenna, had his brilliant general Stilicho (who himself happened to be a Vandal) murdered. A Visigothic invasion followed, leading to Alaric's sack of Rome in 410. St Augustine, probably echoing the thoughts of most Romans, wrote that it seemed the end of the world must be near. Rome should have been so lucky; judgement was postponed long enough for **Attila the Hun** to pass through Italy in 451. Then Gaiseric the Vandal, who had set up a pirate kingdom in Africa, raided Italy and sacked Rome again in 455. So completely had things changed, it was scarcely possible to tell the Romans from the barbarians. By the 470s, the real ruler in Italy was a Gothic general named **Odoacer**, who led a half-Romanized Germanic army and probably thought of himself as the genuine heir of the Caesars. In 476, he decided to dispense with the lingering charade of the Western Empire. The last emperor, young, silly Romulus Augustulus, was packed off to premature retirement in Naples, and Odoacer had himself crowned King of Italy at Pavia.

475–1000: The Dark Ages

At the beginning, the new Gothic-Latin state showed some promise. Certainly the average man was no worse off than he had been under the last emperors; trade and cities even revived a bit. In 493, Odoacer was replaced (and murdered) by a rival Ostrogoth, **Theodoric**, nominally working on behalf of the Eastern Emperor at Byzantium.

A disaster as serious as those of the 5th century began in 536, with the invasion of Italy by the Eastern Empire, part of the relentlessly expansionist policy of the great **Justinian**. The historical irony was profound; in the ancient homeland of the Roman Empire, Roman troops now came not as liberators, but foreign, largely Greek-speaking conquerors. Justinian's brilliant generals, Belisarius and Narses, ultimately prevailed over the Goths in a series of terrible wars that lasted until 563, but the damage to an already stricken society and economy was incalculable. Italy's total exhaustion was exposed only five years later, when the **Lombards**, a Germanic tribe who worked hard to earn the title of barbarian, overran northern Italy and parts of the south, establishing a kingdom at Pavia and separate duchies in Benevento and Spoleto. A new pattern of power appeared, with semi-independent Byzantine dukes defending many coastal areas, the Byzantine Exarchs of Ravenna controlling considerable territory on the Adriatic and in Calabria, and Lombard chiefs ruling most of the interior. The popes in Rome, occasionally allied with the Lombards against Byzantium, became a force during this period, especially after the papacy of the clever, determined **Gregory the Great** (590–604). Scion of the richest family in Italy, Gregory took political control in Rome during desperate times, and laid the foundations for the papacy's claims to temporal power.

With trade and culture at their lowest ebb, the 7th century marks the rock bottom of Italian history. The 8th showed some improvement; while most of the peninsula lay in feudal darkness, **Venice** was beginning its remarkable career as a trading city, and independent Amalfi and Naples emulated its success on the Tyrrhenian coast. The popes, along with other bishops who had taken advantage of the confused times to become temporal powers, intrigued everywhere to increase their influence; they finally cashed in with a Frankish alliance in the 750s. At the time the Lombard kings were doing well, finally conquering Ravenna (751) and considerable territories formerly under the dominion of the popes, who invited in **Charlemagne** to protect them.

When Charlemagne's empire disintegrated following his death in 814, Italy reverted to a finely balanced anarchy. Altogether the 9th century was a bad time, with Italy caught between the Arab raiders and the endless wars of petty nobles and battling bishops in the north. The 10th century proved somewhat better—perhaps much better than the scanty chronicles of the time attest. Even in the worst times, Italy's cities never entirely disappeared.

A big break for them, and for Italy, came in 961 with the invasion of the German **Otto the Great**, heir to the imperial pretensions of the Carolingians. He deposed the last feeble King of Italy, Berengar II of Ivrea, and was crowned Holy Roman Emperor in Rome the following year. Not that any of the Italians were happy to see him, but the strong government of Otto and his successors beat down the great nobles and allowed the growing cities to expand their power and influence. A new pattern was established; Germanic emperors would be meddling in Italian affairs for centuries, not powerful enough to establish total control, but at least usually able to keep out important rivals.

1000–1154: The Rise of the *Comuni*

On the eve of the new millennium, most Christians were convinced that the turn of the calendar would bring with it the end of the world. On the other hand, if there had been economists and social scientists around, they would have had ample evidence to reassure everyone that things were looking up. Especially in the towns, business was very good, and the political prospects even brighter. The first mention of a truly independent *comune* (plural: *comuni*; a term used throughout this book, meaning a free city state; the best translation might be 'commonwealth') was in Milan, where in 1024 a popular assembly is recorded, deciding which side the city would take in the Imperial Wars.

Throughout this period the papacy had declined greatly in power and prestige, a political football kicked between the emperors and the piratical Roman nobles. Beginning in the 1050s, a remarkable Tuscan monk named Hildebrand controlled papal policy, working behind the scenes to reassert the influence of the Church. When he became Pope himself, in 1073, **Gregory VII** immediately set himself in conflict with the emperors over the issue of investiture—whether the Church or secular powers could name Church officials. The various Italian (and European) powers took sides on the issue, and 50 years of intermittent war followed.

Southern Italy knew a different fate. The first **Normans** arrived about 1020, on pilgrimages to Monte Sant'Angelo in the Gargano. They liked the opportunities they saw for conquest, and soon younger sons of Norman feudal families were moving into the south, first as mercenaries but gradually gaining large tracts of land for themselves in exchange for their services. Usually allied to the popes, they soon controlled most of Puglia and Calabria.

1154–1300: Guelphs and Ghibellines

While all this was happening, of course, the First Crusade (1097–1130) occupied the headlines. It was, in part, a result of the new militancy of the papacy begun by Gregory VII. For Italy, especially Pisa and Venice, the two states with plenty of boats to help ship Crusaders, the affair meant nothing but pure profit. Trade was booming everywhere, and the accumulation of money helped the Italians to create modern Europe's first banking system. It also financed the continued independence of the *comuni*, which flourished everywhere, with a big enough surplus for building-projects like Pisa's cathedral complex. Culture and science were flourishing, too, with a big boost from contact with the Byzantines and the Muslims of Spain and Africa. By the 12th century, far in advance of most of Europe, Italy had attained a prosperity unknown since Roman times. Even Italian names were changing, an interesting sign of the beginnings of national consciousness; quite suddenly the public records (such as they were) show a marked shift from Germanic to classical and Biblical surnames: fewer Ugos, Othos, and Astolfos, more Giuseppes, Giovannis, Giulios, and Flavios.

Emperors and popes were still embroiled in the north. **Frederick I Barbarossa** of the Hohenstaufen—or Swabian—dynasty was strong enough in Germany, and he made it the cornerstone of his policy to reassert imperial power in Italy. Beginning in 1154, he crossed the Alps five times, molesting free cities that asked nothing more than the right to continually fight one another. He spread terror, utterly destroying Milan in 1161, but a united front of cities called the Lombard League defeated him in 1176. Frederick's greatest triumph in Italy came by arranging a marriage with the Normans, leaving his grandson **Frederick II** not only Emperor but King of Sicily, giving him a strong power base in Italy itself.

The second Frederick's career dominated Italian politics for 30 years (1220–50). With his brilliant court, in which Italian was used for the first time (alongside Arabic and Latin), his half-Muslim army, his incredible processions of dancing girls, eunuchs, and elephants, he provided Europe with a spectacle the like of which it had never seen. Frederick founded universities (as at Naples), gave Sicily a written constitution (perhaps the world's first), and built geometrically arcane castles and towers all over the south. The popes excommunicated him at least twice.

The battle of pope and emperor had become serious. All Italy divided into factions: the **Guelphs**, under the leadership of the popes, supported religious orthodoxy, the liberty of the *comuni*, and the interests of their emerging merchant class. The **Ghibellines** stood for the Emperor, statist economic control, the interests of the rural nobles, and religious and intellectual tolerance. Frederick's campaigns and diplomacy in the north met with very limited success, and his death in 1250 left the outcome very much in doubt.

His son **Manfred**, not Emperor but merely King of Sicily, took up the battle with better luck; Siena's defeat of Florence in 1260 gained that city and most of Tuscany for the Ghibellines. The next year, however, Pope Urban IV began an ultimately disastrous precedent by inviting in **Charles of Anjou**, a powerful, ambitious leader and brother of the King of France. As protector of the Guelphs, Charles defeated Manfred (1266) and murdered the last of the Hohenstaufens, Conradin (1268). He held unchallenged sway over Italy until 1282, when the famous revolt of the Sicilian Vespers started the party wars up again. By now, however, the terms *Guelph* and *Ghibelline* had ceased to have much meaning; men and cities changed sides as they found expedient.

Some real changes did occur out of all this sound and fury. In 1204 Venice hit its all-time biggest jackpot when it diverted the Fourth Crusade to the sack of Constantinople, winning for itself a small empire of islands in the Adriatic and Levant. Genoa emerged as its greatest rival in 1284, when its fleet put an end to Pisa's prominence at the Battle of Meloria. And elsewhere around the peninsula, some cities were falling under the rule of military *signori* whose descendants would be styling themselves counts and dukes—the Visconti of Milan, the della Scala of Verona, the Malatesta of Rimini. Everywhere the freedom of the *comuni* was in jeopardy; after so much useless strife the temptation to submit to a strong leader often proved overwhelming. During Charles of Anjou's reign the popes extracted the price for their invitation. The Papal State, including much of central Italy, was established in 1278. But most importantly, the Italian economy never seemed to mind the trouble. Trade and money flowed as never before; cities built new cathedrals and created themselves incredible skyscraper skylines, with the tall tower-fortresses of the now urbanized nobles. And it was, in spite of everything, a great age for culture—the era of Guelphs and Ghibellines was also the time of Dante (b. 1265) and Giotto (b. 1266).

1300–1494: Renaissance Italy

This paradoxical Italy continued into the 14th century, with a golden age of culture and an opulent economy side by side with almost continuous war and turmoil. With no serious threats from the emperors or any other foreign power, the myriad Italian states were able to menace each other joyfully without outside interference. One of the secrets to this state of affairs was that war had become a sort of game, conducted on behalf of cities by bands of paid mercenaries led by *condottieri*, who were never allowed to enter the cities themselves. The arrangement suited everyone well.

By far the biggest event of the 14th century was the **Black Death** of 1347–8, in which it is estimated Italy lost one-third of its population. The shock brought a rude halt to what had been 400 years of almost continuous growth and prosperity, though its effects did not prove a permanent setback for the economy. In fact, the plague's grim joke was that it actually made life better for most of the Italians who survived; working people in the cities, no longer over-crowded, found their rents lower and their labour worth more, while in the country farmers were able to increase their profits by tilling only the best land.

It is impossible to speak of 'Italian history' in this period, with the peninsula split up into long-established, cohesive states pursuing different ends and warring against one another. Italian statesmen understood the idea of a balance of power long before political theorists invented the term, and, despite all the clatter and noise, most probably believed Italy was enjoying the best of all possible worlds. Four major states, each a European power in its own right, dom-inated the region's politics: first **Venice**, the oldest and most glorious, with its oligarchic but singularly effective constitution, and its exotic career of trade with the East. The Venetians waged a series of wars against arch-rival Genoa, finally exhausting her after the War of Chioggia in 1379. After that, they felt strong enough to make a major change in policy. Once serenely aloof from Italian politics, Venice now carved out a small land empire for itself, by 1428 including Verona, Padua, Vicenza, Brescia and Bergamo.

Florence, the richest city-state thanks to its banking and wool trade, also enjoyed good fortune, extending its control over most of Tuscany, and gaining a seaport with its conquest of now decadent Pisa in 1406. In 1434, **Cosimo de' Medici**, head of the largest banking house, succeeded in establishing a de facto dictatorship. Even though the forms of the old republic were maintained, Florence was well on its way to becoming a signorial state like its greatest rival, **Milan**. Under the Visconti, Milan had become rich and powerful, basing its success on the manufactures of the city (arms and textiles) and the bountiful, progressively managed agri-culture of southern Lombardy. Its greatest glory came during the reign of **Gian Galeazzo Visconti** (1385–1402), who bought himself a ducal title from the Emperor and nearly conquered all north Italy, before his untimely death caused his plans to unravel.

In the south, the huge **Kingdom of Naples** suffered from the heritage of the Normans, who had made it the only part of Italy where north-European-style feudalism had taken root. When times changed, the backward rural barons who dominated the south retarded its commerce and its culture. Despite such promising periods as the reign of the King of Aragon, **Alfonso the Magnanimous** (1442–58), a prototypical Renaissance prince and patron of the arts who seized Naples and added it to his domains, the south was falling far behind the rest of Italy.

And what of the Renaissance? No word has ever caused more mischief for the understanding of history and culture—as if Italy had been Sleeping Beauty, waiting for some Prince

Charming of classical culture to come and awaken it from a thousand-year nap. On the contrary, Italy even in the 1200s was richer, more technologically advanced, and far more artistically creative than it had ever been in the days of the Caesars. The new art and scholarship that began in Florence in the 1400s and spread across the nation grew from a solid foundation of medieval accomplishment. The gilded, opulent Italy of the 15th century felt complacently secure in its long-established cultural and economic pre-eminence. A long spell of freedom from outside interference lulled the nation into believing that its political disunity could continue safely forever; except perhaps for the sanguinely realistic Florentine Niccolò Machiavelli, no one realized that Italy in fact was a plum waiting to be picked.

1494–1529: The Wars of Italy

The Italians brought the trouble down on themselves, when Duke Ludovico of Milan invited the French King Charles VIII to cross the Alps and assert his claim to the throne of Milan's enemy, Naples. Charles did just that, and the failure of the combined Italian states to stop him (at the inconclusive Battle of Fornovo, 1494) showed just how helpless Italy was at the hands of emerging monarchies like France or Spain. When the Spaniards saw how easy it was, they too marched in, and restored Naples to its Spanish king the following year (an Aragonese dynasty, cousins to Ferdinand and Isabella, had ruled Naples since 1442). Before long the German Emperor and even the Swiss entered this new market for Italian real estate. The popes did as much as anyone to keep the pot boiling. Alexander VI and his son Cesare Borgia carried the war across central Italy in an attempt to found a new state for the Borgia family, and Julius II's madcap policy led him to egg on the Swiss, French and Spaniards in turn, before finally crying, 'Out with the barbarians!' when it was already too late.

By 1516, with the French ruling Milan and the Spanish in control of the south, it seemed as if a settlement would be possible. The worst possible luck for Italy, however, came with the accession of the insatiable megalomaniac **Charles V** to the throne of Spain in that year; in 1519 he bought himself the crown of the Holy Roman Empire, making him the most powerful ruler in Europe since Charlemagne. Charles felt he needed Milan as a base for communications between his Spanish, German and Flemish possessions, and as soon as he had emptied Spain's treasury, driven her to revolt, and plunged Germany into civil war, he turned his attentions to Italy. The wars began anew, bloodier than anything Italy had seen for centuries, climaxing with the defeat of the French at Pavia in 1525, and the sack of Rome by an out-of-control imperial army in 1527. The French invaded once more, in 1529, and were defeated this time at Naples by the treachery of their Genoese allies. All Italy, save only Venice, was now at the mercy of Charles and the Spaniards.

1529–1600: Italy in Chains

The final treaties left Spanish viceroys in Milan and Naples, and dukes and counts toeing the Spanish line almost everywhere else. Besides Venice and the very careful Republic of Lucca, the last bastions of Italian liberty were Siena and Florence, where the Medici had been thrown out and the republic re-established. Charles' army besieged and took the city in 1530, giving it back to the Medici, who gained the title of Grand Dukes of Tuscany. They collaborated with Spain in extinguishing Siena's independence, despite a desperate seven-year resistance (1552–9), and the new Medici state assumed roughly the borders of Tuscany today.

The broader context of these events, of course, was the bitter struggles of the Reformation and Counter-Reformation. In Italy, the new religious angle made the Spaniards and the popes natural allies. With the majority of the peninsula still nominally controlled by local rulers, and an economy that continued to be sound, both the Spanish and the popes realized that the only real threat would come not from men, but from ideas. Under the banner of combating Protestantism, they commenced a reign of terror across Italy. In the 1550s, the revived Inquisition began its manhunt for free-thinkers of every variety. A long line of Italian intellectuals trudged to the stake, while many more buried their convictions or left for exile in Germany or England.

Despite the oppression, the average Italian at first had little to complain about. Spanish domination brought peace and order to a country that had long been a madhouse of conflicting ambitions. Renaissance artists attained a virtuosity never seen before, just in time to embellish the scores of new churches, palaces, and villas of the mid 16th-century building boom. The combined Christian forces had turned back the Turkish threat at Malta (1566) and Lepanto (1571), and some Italians were benefiting greatly from Spanish imperialism in the New World—especially the Genoese, who rented ships, floated loans, and snatched up a surprising amount of the gold and silver arriving from America.

1600–1796: The Age of Baroque

Nevertheless, the first signs of decay were already apparent. Palladio's country villas for the Venetian magnates, and Michelozzo's outside Florence, are landmarks in architecture but also one of the earliest symptoms. In both cities, the old mercantile economies were failing, and the wealthy began to invest their money unproductively in land instead of risking it in business or finance. Venice, between its wars with the Turks and its loss of the spice trade when the Portuguese discovered the route to the Indies, suffered the most. By 1650 she no longer had an important role to play in European affairs, though the Venetians kept their heads and made their inevitable descent into decadence a serene and enjoyable one.

The troubles were not limited to these two cities. After 1600 nearly everything started to go wrong for the Italians. The textiles and banking of the north, long the engines of the economy, both withered in the face of foreign competition, and the old port towns (with the exceptions of Genoa and the new city of Livorno) began to look half empty as the English and Dutch muscled them out of the declining Mediterranean trade. Worst off of all was the south, under direct Spanish or papal rule. Combining incompetence and brutality with outrageously high taxes (the Spaniards' to finance foreign wars, the popes' to build up Rome), they rapidly turned the already poor south into a nightmare of anarchic depravity, haunted by legions of bandits and beggars, and controlled more tightly than ever by its violent feudal barons. To everyone's surprise, the south rose up and staged an epic rebellion. Beginning in Naples (Masaniello's Revolt, 1647), the disturbances soon spread all over the south and Sicily. For over a year peasant militias ruled some areas, and makeshift revolutionary councils defended the cities. When the Spanish finally defeated them, however, they massacred some 18,000, and tightened the screws more than ever.

Bullied, humiliated and increasingly impoverished, 17th-century Italy at least tried hard to keep up its ancient prominence in the arts and sciences. Galileo looked through telescopes, Monteverdi wrote the first operas, and hundreds of talented though uninspired artists cranked out pretty pictures to meet the continuing high demand. Bernini and Borromini turned Rome into the capital of Baroque—the florid, expensive coloratura style that serves as a perfect symbol for the age itself, an age of political repression and thought control where art itself became a political tool. Baroque's heavenly grandeur and symmetry helped to impress everyone with the majesty of Church and state. At the same time, Baroque scholars wrote books that went on for hundreds of pages without saying anything, but avoided offending the government and the Inquisition.

By the 18th century, there were very few painters, or scholars, or scientists. There were no more heroic revolts either. Italy in this period hardly has any history at all; with Spain's increasing decadence, the great powers decided the futures of Italy's major states, and used the minor ones as a kind of overflow tank to hold surplus princes and those dispossessed by wars elsewhere (Napoleon on Elba was the last and most famous of these). In 1713, after the War of the Spanish Succession, the Habsburgs of **Austria** came into control of Milan and Lombardy, Mantua and the Kingdom of Naples. The House of Lorraine, related to the Austrians, won Tuscany upon the extinction of the Medici in 1737. These new rulers improved conditions somewhat.

1796–1830: Napoleon, Restoration, and Reaction

Napoleon, that greatest of Italian generals, arrived in the country in 1796 on behalf of the French revolutionary Directorate, sweeping away the Piedmontese and Austrians and setting up republics in Lombardy (the 'Cisalpine Republic'), Liguria, and Naples (the 'Parthenopean Republic'). Italy woke with a start from its Baroque slumbers, and local patriots gaily joined the French cause. In 1799, however, while Napoleon was off in Egypt, the advance through Italy by an Austro-Russian army, aided by Nelson's fleet, restored the status quo. This was often accompanied by bloody reprisals, as peasant mobs led by clerics like the 'Army of the Holy Faith' marched across the south massacring liberals and French sympathizers.

In 1800 Napoleon returned in a campaign that saw the great victory at Marengo, giving him the opportunity once more to reorganize Italian affairs. Napoleon crowned himself King of Italy; Joseph Bonaparte and later Joachim Murat ruled at Naples. Elisa Bonaparte and her husband got Tuscany. Rome was annexed to France, and the Pope was carted off to Fontainebleau. Napoleonic rule lasted only until 1814, but in that time important public works were begun and laws, education and everything else reformed after the French model; immense Church properties were expropriated, and medieval relics everywhere put to rest—including the Venetian Republic, which Napoleon for some reason took a special delight in liquidating. The French, however, soon wore out their welcome. Besides hauling much of Italy's artistic heritage off to the Louvre, implementing high war taxes and conscription (some 25,000 Italians died in the invasion of Russia), and brutally repressing a number of local revolts, they systematically exploited Italy for the benefit of the Napoleonic élite and the crowds of speculators who came flocking over the Alps. When the Austrians and English came to chase all the little Napoleons out, no one was sad to see them go.

Almost immediately, revolutionary agitators and secret societies like the famous *Carbonari* emerged that would keep Italy convulsed in plots and intrigues. A large-scale revolt in Naples forced the reactionary King Ferdinand to grant a constitution (1821), but when Austrian troops came down to crush the rebels he revoked it. The French July Revolution of 1830 also spread to Italy, encouraged by the liberal King **Carlo Alberto** in Piedmont-Savoy, but once more the by now universally hated Austrians intervened.

1848–1915: The Risorgimento and United Italy

Conspirators of every colour and shape, including the legendary **Giuseppe Mazzini**, had to wait another 18 years for their next chance. Mazzini, a sincere patriot and democrat, agitated frenetically all through the years 1830–70, beginning by founding the *Young Italy* movement, all with little practical effect.

The big change came in the revolutionary year of 1848, when risings in Palermo and Naples (in January) anticipated even those in Paris itself. Soon all Italy was in the streets. Piedmont and Tuscany won constitutions from their rulers, and the people of Milan chased out the Austrians after a month of extremely bloody fighting; at the same time the Venetian Republic was restored. Carlo Alberto, the hope of most Italians for a war of liberation, marched against the Austrians, but his two badly bungled campaigns allowed the enemy to re-establish control over the peninsula. By June 1849, only Venice, under Austrian blockade, and the recently declared Roman Republic were left. Rome, led by Mazzini, and with a small army under **Giuseppe Garibaldi**, a former sailor who had fought in the wars of independence in Latin America, beat off several attacks from foreign troops invited in by the Pope. The republic finally succumbed to a large force sent by, of all people, the republic of President Louis Napoleon (soon to declare himself Napoleon III) in France. Garibaldi's dramatic escape to safety in San Marino (he was trying to reach Venice, itself soon to surrender) gave the Risorgimento one of its great heroic myths.

Despite failure on a grand scale, at least the Italians knew they would get another chance. Unification was inevitable, but there were two irreconcilable contenders for the honour of accomplishing it. On one side, the democrats and radicals dreamed of a truly reborn, revolutionary Italy, and looked to the popular hero Garibaldi to deliver it; on the other, moderates wanted the Piedmontese to do the job, ensuring a stable future by making **Vittorio Emanuele II** King of Italy. Vittorio Emanuele's Minister, the polished, clever **Count Camillo Cavour**, spent the 1850s getting Piedmont in shape for the struggle, building its economy and army, participating in the Crimean War to earn diplomatic support, and plotting with the French for an alliance against Austria.

War came in 1859, and French armies did most of the work in conquering Lombardy. Tuscany and Emilia revolted, and Piedmont was able to annex all three. In May 1860, Garibaldi and his red-shirted 'Thousand' sailed from Genoa—Cavour almost stopped them at the last minute—and landed in Sicily, electrifying Europe by repeatedly beating the Bourbon forces in a quick march across the island. The Thousand had become 20,000, and when they crossed the straits bound for Naples it was clear that the affair was reaching its climax. On 7 September, Garibaldi entered Naples, and though he proclaimed himself temporary dictator on Vittorio Emanuele's behalf, the Piedmontese were alarmed enough to occupy Umbria and the Marches. The King met Garibaldi on 27 October, near Teano, and after finding out what little regard the Piedmontese had for him, the greatest and least self-interested leader modern Italy has known went off to retirement on the island of Caprara.

Just as the French made all this possible, some more unexpected help from outside allowed the new Italy to add two missing pieces and complete its unification. When the Prussians defeated Austria in the war of 1866, Italy was able to seize the Veneto. Only Rome was left, defended by a French garrison, and when the Prussians beat France at Sedan in 1870, the Italian army marched into Rome almost without opposition.

The first decades of the Italian Kingdom were just as unimpressive as its wars of independence. A liberal constitutional monarchy was established, but the parliament almost immediately decomposed into cliques and political cartels representing various interests. Finances started in disorder and stayed that way, and corruption became widespread. Peasant revolts occurred in the south, as people felt cheated by inaction after the promises of the Risorgimento, and organized brigandage became a problem, partially instigated by the Vatican as part of an all-out attempt to discredit the new regime. The outlines of foreign policy often seemed to change monthly, though like the other European powers Italy felt it necessary to snatch up some colonies. The attempt revealed the new state's limited capabilities, with embarrassing military disasters at the hands of the Ethiopians at Dogali in 1887, and again at Adowa in 1896.

After 1900, with the rise of a strong socialist movement, strikes, riots, and police repression often occupied centre stage in Italian politics. Even so, important signs of progress, such as the big new industries in Turin and Milan, showed that at least the northern half of Italy was becoming a fully integral part of the European economy. The 15 years before the war, prosperous and contented ones for many, came to be known by the slightly derogatory term *Italietta*, the 'little Italy' of modest bourgeois happiness, an age of sweet Puccini operas, the first motorcars, blooming 'Liberty'-style architecture, and Sunday afternoons at the beach.

1915–1945: War, Fascism, and War

Italy could have stayed out of the First World War, but let the chance to do so go by for the usual reasons—a hope of gaining some new territory, especially Trieste. Also, a certain segment of the intelligentsia found the *Italietta* boring and disgraceful: irredentists of all stripes, some of the artistic futurists, and the perverse, idolized poet **Gabriele D'Annunzio**. The groups helped Italy leap blindly into the conflict in 1915, with a big promise of boundary adjustments dangled by the beleaguered Allies. Italian armies fought with their accustomed flair, masterminding an utter catastrophe at Caporetto (October 1917) that any other nation but Austria would have parleyed into a total victory. No thanks to their incompetent generals, the poorly armed and equipped Italians somehow held firm for another year, until the total exhaustion of Austria allowed them to prevail (at the Battle of Vittorio Veneto you see so many streets named after), capturing some 600,000 prisoners in November 1918.

In return for 650,000 dead, a million casualties, severe privation on the home front, and a war debt higher than anyone could count, Italy received Trieste, Gorizia, the South Tyrol, and a few other scraps. Italians felt they had been cheated, and nationalist sentiment increased, especially when D'Annunzio led a band of freebooters to seize the half-Italian city of Fiume in September 1919, after the peace conferences had promised it to Yugoslavia. The Italian economy was in a shambles, and, at least in the north, revolution was in the air; workers in Turin raised the Red Flag over the Fiat plants and organized themselves into soviets. The troubles had encouraged extremists of both right and left, and many Italians became convinced that the liberal state was finished.

Enter **Benito Mussolini**, a professional intriguer in the Mazzini tradition with bad manners and no fixed principles. Before the War he had found his real talent as editor of the Socialist Party paper *Avanti*—the best it ever had, tripling the circulation in a year. When he decided that what Italy really needed was war, he left to found a new paper, and contributed mightily to the jingoist agitation of 1915. In the post-War confusion, he found his opportunity. A little bit at a time, he developed the idea of **Fascism**, at first less a philosophy than an astute use of mass propaganda and a sense for design. (The *fasces*, from which the name comes, were bundles of rods carried before ancient Roman officials, a symbol of authority. *Fascii* also referred to organized bands of rebellious peasants in 19th-century Sicily.) With a little discreet money supplied by frightened industrialists, Mussolini had no trouble in finding recruits for his black-shirted gangs, who found their first success beating up Slavs in Trieste and working as a sort of private police for landowners in stoutly socialist Emilia-Romagna.

Mussolini's accession to power came on an improbable gamble. In the particularly anarchic month of October 1922, he announced that his followers would march on Rome. King Vittorio Emanuele III refused to sign a decree of martial law to disperse them, and there was nothing to do but offer Mussolini the post of prime minister. At first, he governed Italy with undeniable competence. Order was restored, and the economy and foreign policy handled intelligently by non-Fascist professionals. In the 1924 elections, despite the flagrant rigging and intimidation, the Fascists only won a slight majority.

One politician who was not intimidated was Giacomo Matteotti, and when some of Mussolini's close associates took him for a ride and murdered him, a major scandal erupted. Mussolini survived it, and during 1925 and 1926 the Fascists used parliamentary methods to convert Italy into a permanent Fascist dictatorship.

Compared to the governments that preceded him, Mussolini looked quite impressive. Industry advanced, great public works were undertaken, with special care towards the backward south, and the Mafia took some heavy blows at the hands of a determined Sicilian prefect named Mori. In the words of one of Mussolini's favourite slogans, painted on walls all over Italy, 'Whoever stops is lost'.

Mussolini couldn't stop, and the only possibility for new diversions lay with the chance of conquest and empire. His invasion of Ethiopia and his meddling in the Spanish Civil War, both in 1936, compromised Italy into a close alliance with Nazi Germany. Mussolini's confidence and rhetoric never faltered as he led an entirely unprepared nation into the biggest war ever. Once more, Italian ineptitude at warfare produced embarrassing defeats on all fronts, and only German intervention in Greece and North Africa saved Italy from being knocked out of the War as early as 1941. The Allies invaded Sicily in July 1943, and the Italians began to look for a clever way out. They seized Mussolini during a meeting of the Grand Council, packed him into an ambulance and sent him off first to Ponza, then to a little ski hotel up in the Apennines. The new government under Marshal Badoglio didn't know what to do, and confusion reigned supreme.

While British and American forces slogged northwards, in this ghetto of the European theatre, with the help of the Free French, Brazilians, Costa Ricans, Poles, Czechs, New Zealanders and Norwegians, the Germans poured in divisions to defend the peninsula. They rescued Mussolini, and set him up in a puppet state called the Italian Social Republic in the north. In September 1943, the Badoglio government signed an armistice with the Allies, too late to keep the War from dragging on another year and a half, as the Germans made good use of Italy's difficult terrain to slow the Allied advance. Meanwhile Italy finally gave itself something to be proud of, a determined, resourceful Resistance that established free zones in many areas, and harassed the Germans with sabotage and strikes. The *partigiani* caught Mussolini in April 1945, while he was trying to escape to Switzerland; after shooting him and his mistress, they hung him by his feet from the roof of a petrol station in Milan.

1945–the Present

Post-war Italian *cinema verità*—Rossellini's *Rome, Open City*, or de Sica's *Bicycle Thieves*—captures the atmosphere better than words ever could. In a period of serious hardships that older Italians still remember, the nation slowly picked itself up and returned things to normal. A referendum in June 1946 made Italy a republic, but only by a narrow margin. The first governments fell to the new Christian Democrat Party under Alcide de Gasperi, which has run the show ever since in coalitions with a preposterous band of smaller parties. The main opposition has been provided by the Communists, surely one of the most remarkable parties of modern European history. With the heritage of the only important socialist philosopher since Marx, Antonio Gramsci, and the democratic and broad-minded leader Enrico Berlinguer, Italian communism is something unique in the world, with its stronghold and showcase in the well-run, prosperous cities of the Emilia-Romagna.

The fifties was Rome's decade, when Italian style and Italian cinema caught the imagination of the world. Gradually, slowly, a little economic miracle was happening; *Signor Rossi*, the average Italian, started buzzing around in his first classic Fiat *cinquecento*, northern industries boomed, and life cruised slowly back to normal. The south continued to lag behind, despite the sincere efforts of the government and its special planning fund, the *Cassa per il Mezzogiorno*. Though the extreme poverty and despair of the post-War years gradually disappeared, even today there is little evidence that the region is catching up with the rest of the country. Nationally, the *Democristiani*-controlled government soon evolved a Byzantine style of politics that only an Italian could understand. Through the constant parade of collapsing and reforming cabinets, nothing changed; all deals were made in the back rooms and everyone, from the Pope to the Communists, had a share in the decision-making. One wouldn't call it democracy with a straight face, but for four decades it worked well enough to keep Italy on its wheels. The dark side of the arrangement was the all-pervasive corruption that the system fostered. It is fascinating to read the work of journalists only a few years ago, seeing how almost without exception they would politely sidestep the facts; Italy was run by an unprincipled political machine, whose members were raking in as much for themselves as they could grab, and everyone knew it, only it couldn't be said openly, for lack of proof. Even more sinister was the extent to which the machine would go to keep on top.

The seventies—Italy's 'years of lead'—witnessed the worst of the political sleaze, along with a grim reign of terrorism, culminating in the kidnapping and murder in 1978 of an honourable Christian Democrat prime minister, Aldo Moro. All along, the attacks were attributed to 'leftist groups', though even at the time many suspected that some of the highest circles in the government and army were controlling or manipulating them, with the possible collusion of the CIA. They were indeed, and only recently has some of the truth begun to seep out. On another front, Italians woke up one morning in 1992 to find that the government had magically vacuumed 7 per cent of the money out of all their savings accounts, an 'emergency measure' to meet the nation's colossal budget deficit—a deficit caused largely by the thievery of the political class and its allies in organized crime.

Italians are a patient lot but, as everyone knows, the lid has blown off, and at the time of writing Italy is well into a very Italian sort of revolution. The business started in the judiciary, the one independent and relatively uncorrupt part of the government. In the early nineties, heroic prosecutors Giovanni Falcone and Paolo Borsellino went after the Sicilian Mafia with some success, and were spectacularly assassinated for it, causing national outrage. Meanwhile, in Milan, a small group of prosecutors and judges found a minor political kickback scandal that has led them, through years of quiet and painstaking work, to the golden string that is currently unravelling the whole rotten tangle of Italian political depravity—what Italians call the *tangentopoli*, or 'bribe city'. For over a year, the televised hearings of Judge Antonio di Pietro and his Operation *Mani Pulite* ('clean hands') team from Milan were the nation's favourite and most fascinating serial.

The future of the Italian 'revolution' looks more uncertain than ever. Expect bigger and stranger surprises in the years to come.

Art and Architecture

You'd have to spend your holiday in a baggage compartment to miss Italy's vast piles of architecture and art. The Italians estimate there is one work of art per capita in their country, which is more than anyone could see in a lifetime—especially since so much of it is locked away in museums that are in semi-permanent 'restoration'. Although you may occasionally chafe at not being able to see certain frescoes, or at finding a famous palace completely wrapped up in the ubiquitous green netting of the restorers, the Italians on the whole bear the burden of keeping their awesome patrimony dusted off and open for visitors very well. Some Italians find it insupportable living with the stuff all around them; the futurists, for instance, were worried that St Mark's might be blown up by foreign enemies in the First World War— but only because they wanted to do it themselves, as was their right as Italian citizens.

Pre-Etruscan

To give a chronological account of the first Italian artists is an uncomfortable task. The peninsula's mountainous terrain saw many isolated developments and many survivals of ancient cultures even during the days of the sophisticated Etruscans and Romans. Most ancient of all, however, is the palaeolithic troglodyte culture on the Riviera, credited with creating some of the first artworks in Europe—chubby images of fertility goddesses. The most remarkable works from the Neolithic period up until the Iron Age are the thousands of graffiti rock incisions in several isolated Alpine valleys north of Lake Iseo.

After 1000 BC Italic peoples all over the peninsula were making geometrically painted pots, weapons, tools and bronze statuettes. The most impressive culture, however, was the tower-building, bronze-working Nuraghe civilization on **Sardinia**, of which echoes are seen in many cultures on the mainland. Among the most intriguing and beautiful artefacts to have survived are those of the Villanova culture; the statues and inscriptions of the little-known Middle Adriatic culture, and the statue-steles of an unknown people north of Viareggio.

Etruscans and Greeks (8th–2nd centuries BC)

With the refined, art-loving Etruscans we begin to have architecture as well as art. Not much has survived, thanks to the Etruscans' habit of building in wood and decorating with terracotta, but we do have plenty of distinctive rock-cut tombs, many of which contain exceptional frescoes that reflect Aegean Greek styles. The best of their lovely sculptures, jewellery, vases, and much more are in the Villa Giulia in **Rome**—where you can also see a reconstructed temple façade. There are also fine Etruscan holdings in the archaeology museum in **Florence**.

The Etruscans imported and copied many of their vases from their ancient Greek contemporaries, from Greece proper and the colonies of Magna Graecia in southern Italy; there are many other excavated Greek cities, but usually only foundations remain. The Archaeological Museum in the **Vatican** contains an impressive collection of ancient Greek vases, statues and other types of art.

Roman (3rd century BC–5th century AD)

Italian art during the Roman hegemony is mostly derivative of the Etruscan and Greek, with a special talent for mosaics, wall paintings, glasswork and portraiture; architecturally, the Romans were brilliant engineers, the inventors of concrete and grand exponents of the arch. Even today their constructions, such as aqueducts, amphitheatres, bridges, baths, and of course the Pantheon, are most impressive.

Of course **Rome** itself has no end of ancient monuments; also in the vicinity there is **Ostia Antica**, Rome's ancient port, and **Tivoli**, site of Hadrian's great villa. Rome also has a stellar set of museums filled with Roman antiquities—the National Museum in Diocletian's Baths, the Vatican Museum, the Capitoline Museums, and the Museum of Roman Civilization at EUR.

Early Middle Ages (5th–10th century)

After the fall of the Roman Empire, civilization's lamp flickered most brightly in Ravenna, where Byzantine mosaicists adorned the glittering churches of the Eastern Exarchate. Theirs was to be the prominent style in pictorial art and architecture until the 13th century. Apart from Ravenna, there are fine mosaics and paintings of the period in **Rome**, in a score of churches such as Sant'Agnese, San Clemente and Santa Prassede; in Rome the Italian preference for basilican churches and octagonal baptistries began in Constantine's day, and the development of Christian art and architecture through the Dark Ages can be traced there better than anywhere else. There are also many paintings in the catacombs. Other good Ravenna-style mosaics may be seen in Torcello Cathedral in **Venice**, where the fashion lingered long enough to create St Mark's.

'Lombard' art, really the work of the native population under Lombard rule, revealed an original talent in the 7th–9th centuries, as well as a new style, presaging the Romanesque.

Romanesque (11th–12th centuries)

At this point, when an expansive society made new advances in art possible, north and south Italy went their separate ways, each contributing distinctive styles in sculpture and architecture. We also begin to learn the identities of some of their makers. The great Lombard cathedrals are masterworks of brick art and adorned with blind arcading, bas-reliefs and lofty campaniles. **Florence** developed its own particularist black and white style, exemplified in truly amazing buildings like the Baptistry and San Miniato.

The outstanding architectural advance of this period is the Puglian Romanesque, a style closely related to contemporary Norman and Pisan work—it is impossible to say which came first. This period also saw the erection of urban skyscrapers by the nobility—family fortress-towers built when the *comuni* forced local barons to move into the towns. Larger cities once had literally hundreds of them, before the townspeople succeeded in getting them demolished. In many cases extremely tall towers were built simply for decoration and prestige.

Late Medieval–Early Renaissance (13th–14th centuries)

In many ways this was the most exciting and vigorous phase in Italian art history, an age of discovery when the power of the artist was almost like that of a magician. Great imaginative leaps occurred in architecture, painting, and sculpture, especially in Tuscany. From Milan to Assisi, a group of masons and sculptors known as the *Campionese Masters* built magnificent brick cathedrals and basilicas. Some of their buildings reflect the Gothic style of the north while in others you can see the transition from that same Gothic to Renaissance. In **Venice**, an ornate, half-oriental style called Venetian-Gothic still sets the city's palaces and public buildings apart, and influenced the exotic Basilica di Sant'Antonio in **Padua**. This was also an era of transition in sculpture, from stiff Romanesque stylization to the more realistic, classically inspired works of the great Nicola Pisano and his son Giovanni, and his pupil Arnolfo di Cambio (in **Florence**).

Painters, especially in Rome and Siena, learned from the new spatial and expressive sculpture. Most celebrated of the masters in the dawn of the Italian Renaissance is, of course, the solemn Giotto. Sienese artists Duccio di Buoninsegna, Simone Martini and Pietro and Ambrogio Lorenzetti gave Italy its most brilliant exponents of the International Gothic style—though they were also important precursors of the Renaissance. Their brightly coloured scenes, embellished with a thousand details, helped make Siena into the medieval dream-city it is today. In Florence, the works of Orcagna, Gentile da Fabriano and Lorenzo Monaco continued that city's unique approach, laying a foundation for Florence's launching of the Renaissance.

Rome, for one of the few times in its history, achieved artistic prominence with home-grown talent. The city's architecture from this period (as seen in the campaniles of Santa Maria in Cosmedin and Santa Maria Maggiore) has largely been lost under Baroque remodellings, but the paintings and mosaics of Pietro Cavallini and his school, and the intricate, inlaid stone pavements and architectural trim of the Cosmati family and their followers (derived from the Amalfi coast style) can be seen all over the city; both had an influence that extended far beyond Rome itself.

The Renaissance (15th–16th centuries)

The origins of this high noon of art are very much the accomplishment of quattrocento **Florence**, where sculpture and painting embarked on a totally new way of educating the eye (*see* **Florence**, p.164). The idea of a supposed 'rediscovery of antiquity' has confused the understanding of the time. In general, artists broke new ground when they expanded from the traditions of medieval art; when they sought merely to copy the forms of ancient Greece and Rome the imagination often faltered.

Florentine art soon became recognized as the standard of the age. By 1450 Florentine artists were spreading the new style to the north, where Leonardo da Vinci and Bramante spent several years. Michelangelo and Bramante, among others, carried the Renaissance to **Rome**, where it thrived under the patronage of enlightened popes. The most significant art in the north came out of **Venice**, which had its own distinct school led by Mantegna and Giovanni Bellini (*see* 'Venetian Art', p.115).

Despite the brilliant triumphs in painting and sculpture, the story of Renaissance architecture is partially one of confusion and retreat. **Florence**, with Brunelleschi, Alberti and Michelozzo, achieved its own special mode of expression, a dignified austerity that proved difficult to transplant elsewhere. In most of Italy the rediscovery of the works of Vitruvius, representing the authority of antiquity, killed off Italians' appreciation of their own architectural heritage; with surprising speed the dazzling imaginative freedom of medieval architecture was lost forever. Some work still appeared, however, notably Codussi's palaces and churches in **Venice**.

High Renaissance and Mannerism (16th century)

At the beginning of the cinquecento an Olympian triumvirate of Michelangelo, Raphael and Leonardo da Vinci held court at the summit of European art. But in this time when Italy was losing her self-confidence, and was soon to lose her essential liberty, artistic currents tended towards the dark and subversive. More than anyone, it was Michelangelo who tipped the balance from the cool, classical Renaissance into the turgid, stormy, emotionally fraught movement the critics have labelled Mannerism. Among the few painters left in exhausted Florence, he had the brilliant, deranged Jacopo Pontormo and Rosso Fiorentino to help. Other painters lumped in with the Mannerists, such as Giuliano Romano in Mantua and Il Sodoma around Siena, broke new ground while maintaining the discipline and intellectual rigour of the early Renaissance. Elsewhere, and especially among the fashionable Florentine painters and sculptors, art was decaying into mere interior decoration.

For **Venice**, however, it was a golden age, with the careers of Titian, Veronese, Tintoretto, Sansovino and Palladio.

In architecture, attempts to recreate ancient styles and the classical orders won the day. In Milan, and later in **Rome**, Bramante was one of the few architects able to do anything interesting with it, while Michelangelo's great dome of St Peter's put a cap on the accomplishments of the Renaissance. Other talented architects found most of their patronage in Rome, which after the 1520s became Italy's centre of artistic activity: Ligorio, Peruzzi, Vignola and the Sangallo family among them.

Baroque (17th–18th centuries)

Rome continued its artistic dominance to become the capital of Baroque, where the socially irresponsible genius of artists like Bernini and Borromini was approved by the Jesuits and indulged by the tainted ducats of the popes. As an art designed to induce temporal obedience and psychical oblivion, its effects are difficult to describe, but you can see for yourself in the three great churches along Corso Vittorio Emanuele in Rome and a host of other works (Bernini's Piazza Navona fountains and St Peter's colonnades).

More honest cities, such as Florence and Venice, chose to sit out the Baroque era, though **Florence** at first enthusiastically approved the works of 16th-century proto-Baroque sculptors like Ammannati, Giambologna and Cellini. Not all artists fitted the Baroque mould; genius could survive in a dangerous, picaresque age, most notably in the person of Caravaggio.

Neoclassicism and Romanticism (late 18th–19th centuries)

Baroque proved to be a hard act to follow, and in these centuries Italian art and architecture almost ceased to exist. Two centuries of stifling oppression had taken their toll on the national imagination, and for the first time Italy not only ceased to be a leader in art, but failed even to make significant contributions.

The one bright spot in 18th-century Italian painting was **Venice**, where Giambattista Tiepolo and son adorned the churches and palaces of the last days of the Serenissima. Other Venetians, such as Antonio Canaletto and Francesco Guardi, painted their famous canal scenes for Grand Tourists. In the 19th century, the Italian Impressionist movement, the *Macchiaioli*, led by Giovanni Fattori, was centred in the city of **Florence**. In sculpture, the neoclassical master Antonio Canova stands almost alone, a favourite in the days of Napoleon. Some of his best works may be seen in **Rome**'s Villa Borghese. In architecture, it was the age of grand opera houses and the late 19th-century Gallerias in Milan and Naples.

20th Century

The turn-of-the-century Liberty Style (Italian Art Nouveau) failed to spread as widely as its counterparts in France and central Europe. The age saw the construction of new Grand Hotels, casinos and villas in nearly every resort, for example in **Venice**.

In the 20th century two Italian art movements attracted international attention: futurism, a response to Cubism, concerned with the relevancy to the present ('the art that achieves speed, achieves success'), a movement led by Boccioni, Gino Severini and Giacomo Balla (well-represented in the National Gallery of Modern Art, **Rome**); and the mysterious, introspective metaphysical world of Giorgio De Chirico, whose brethren—Modigliani, Giorgio Morandi and Carlo Carrà—were masters of silences. Their works, and others by modern Italian and foreign artists, are displayed in the museums of **Rome** and **Venice**.

Architecture in this century reached its (admittedly low) summit in the Fascist period (the EUR suburb in **Rome**, and public buildings everywhere in the south). Mussolinian architecture often makes us smile but, as the only Italian school in the last 200 years to have achieved a consistent sense of design, it presents a challenge to all modern Italian architects—one they have so far been unable to meet. In **Rome** you can see the works of the most acclaimed Italian architect of this century, Pier Luigi Nervi; good post-War buildings are very difficult to find, and the other arts have never yet risen above the level of dreary, saleable postmodernism. Much of the Italians' artistic urge has been sublimated into the shibboleth of Italian design— clothes, sports cars, suitcases, kitchen utensils, etc. At present, though business is good, Italy is generating little excitement in these fields. Europe expects more from its most artistically talented nation; after the bad centuries of shame and slumber a free and prosperous Italy may well find its own voice and its own style to help interpret the events of the day. If Italy ever does begin to speak with a single voice, whatever it has to say will be worth hearing.

Literature

Non è questo 'l terren, ch' i' toccai pria?
Non è questo il mio nido,
Ove nudrito fui sí dolcemente?
Non è questa la patria in ch' io mi fido,
Madre benigna e pia,
Che copre l'un e l'altro mio parente?
Per Dio, questo la mente
Talor vi mova; e con pietà guardate
Le lagrime del popol doloroso,
Che sol da voi riposo,
Dopo Dio, spera: e, pur che voi mostriate
Segno, alcun di pietate,
Vertú contra furore
Prenderà l'arme; e fia 'l combatter corto;
Ché l'antiquo valore
Ne l' italici cor non è ancor morto.

Petrarch (1304–74)

Is not this precious earth my native land?
And is not this the nest
From which my tender wings were taught to fly?
And is not this soil upon whose breast,
Loving and soft, faithful and true and fond,
My father and my gentle mother lie?
'For love of God,' I cry,
Some time take thought of your humanity
And spare your people all their tears and grief!
From you they seek relief
Next after God. If in your eyes they see
Some marks of sympathy,
Against this mad disgrace
They will arise, the combat will be short
For the stern valour of our ancient race
Is not yet dead in the Italian heart.

trans. William Dudley Foulke LL D (1915)

Few countries have as grand a literary tradition—even Shakespeare made extensive use of Italian stories for his plots. Besides all the great Latin authors and poets of ancient Rome, the peninsula has produced a small shelf of world classics in the Italian language; try to read a few before you come to Italy, or bring them along to read on the train. (All the books listed below are available in English translations, and may often be found in the English sections of Italian bookstores.) Once you've visited some of the settings of Dante's *Divine Comedy*, and come to know at least historically some of the inhabitants of the Inferno, Purgatorio and Paradiso, the old classic becomes even more fascinating.

Dante (1265–1321) was one of the first poets in Europe to write in the vernacular, and in doing so incorporated a good deal of topographical material from his 13th-century world. His literary successor, Petrarch (1304–74), has been called by many 'the first modern man'; in his poetry the first buds of humanism were born, deeply felt, complex, subtle, and fascinating today as ever (his *Canzoniere* is widely available in English). The third literary deity in Italy's late-medieval/early-Renaissance trinity is Boccaccio (1313–75), whose imagination, humour and realism is most apparent in his 'Human Comedy' the *Decameron*, a hundred stories 'told' by a group of young aristocrats who fled into the countryside from Florence to escape the plague of 1348. Boccaccio's detached point of view had the effect of disenchanting Dante's ordered medieval cosmos, clearing the way for the renaissance of the secular novel.

Dante, Petrarch and Boccaccio exerted a tremendous influence over literary Europe, and in the 15th and 16th centuries a new crop of Italian writers continued in the vanguard—Machiavelli in political thought (*The Prince*), though he also wrote two of the finest plays of the Renaissance (*Mandragola* and *Clizia*); Ariosto in the genre of knightly romance (*Orlando Furioso*, the antecedent of Spenser's *Faerie Queene*, among many others); Benvenuto Cellini in autobiography; Vasari in art criticism and history (*The Lives of the Artists*); Castiglione in etiquette, gentlemanly arts and behaviour (*The Courtier*); Alberti in architecture and art theory (*Della Pintura*); Leonardo da Vinci in a hundred different subjects (the *Notebook*, etc.); even Michelangelo had time to write a book's worth of sonnets, now translated into English.

Other works from the period include the writings and intriguing play (*The Candlemaker*) of the great philosopher and heretic Giordano Bruno (perhaps the only person to be excommunicated from three different churches); the risqué, scathing writings of Aretino, the 'Scourge of Princes'; the poetry and songs of Lorenzo de' Medici; and the *Commentaries* by Pope Pius II (Enea Silvio), a rare view into the life, opinions, and times of one of the most accomplished Renaissance men, not to mention the only autobiography ever written by a pope.

Baroque Italy was a quieter place, dampened by the censorship of the Inquisition. The Venetians kept the flame alight: Casanova's picaresque *Life*, the tales of Carlo Gozzi and the plays of Goldoni. Modern Italian literature, unlike many, has an official birthdate—the publication in 1827 of Alessandro Manzoni's *I Promessi Sposi* ('The Betrothed'), which not only spoke with sweeping humanity to the concerns of pre-Risorgimento Italy, but also spoke in its own language—a new everyday Italian that nearly everyone was able to understand, no matter what their regional dialect; the novel went on to become a symbol of the aspiration of national unity.

The next writer with the power to capture the turbulent emotions of his time was Gabriele D'Annunzio, whose life of daredevil, personally tailored patriotism and superman cult strongly contrast with the lyricism of his poetry and some of his novels—still widely read in Italy.

Meanwhile, and much more influentially, Pirandello, the philosophical Sicilian playwright and novelist obsessed with absurdity, changed the international vocabulary of drama before the Second World War.

The post-War era saw the appearance of neorealism in fiction as well as cinema, and the classics, though available in English, are among the easiest books to read in Italian—Cesare Pavese's *La luna e i falò* (The Moon and the Bonfires), Carlo Levi's tragic *Cristo si è fermato a Eboli* (Christ Stopped at Eboli) or Vittorini's *Conversazione in Sicilia*. Other acclaimed works of the post-War era include *The Garden of the Finzi-Contini* (about a Jewish family in Fascist Italy) by Giorgio Bassani, and another book set during the Fascist era, *That Awful Mess on Via Merulana* by Carlo Emilio Gadda; then there's the Sicilian classic that became famous around the world—*The Leopard* by Giuseppe di Lampedusa.

The late Italo Calvino, perhaps more than any other Italian writer in the past two decades, enjoyed a large international following—his *Italian Folktales*, *Marcovaldo*, *The Baron in the Trees*, and *If on a Winter's Night a Traveller* (which includes the first chapters of about 10 novels) were all immediately translated into English; perhaps the best of them is *Invisible Cities*, an imaginary dialogue between Marco Polo and Kublai Khan. Much maligned Sicily continued to produce some of Italy's best literature, from the pens of Leonardo Sciascia and Gesualdo Bufalino. The current celebrity of Italian literature is of course Umberto Eco, Professor of Semiotics at Bologna University, whose *The Name of the Rose* kept readers all over the world at the edge of their seats over the murders of a handful of 14th-century monks in a remote Italian monastery, while magically evoking, better than many historians, all the political and ecclesiastical turmoil of the period.

Italy has also inspired countless of her visitors, appearing as a setting in more novels, poems and plays than tongue can tell. There is also a long list of non-fiction classics, some of which make fascinating reading and are readily available in most bookshops: Goethe's *Italian Journey*, Ruskin's *The Stones of Venice*, D. H. Lawrence's *Etruscan Places* and *Twilight in Italy*, Hilaire Belloc's *The Path to Rome*, Norman Douglas's *Old Calabria*, Jan Morris's *Venice*, Mary McCarthy's *The Stones of Florence* and *Venice Observed*, and many others, including the famously over-the-top travellers' accounts of Edward Hutton and the ever-entertaining H. V. Morton. For the Italian point of view from the outside looking in, read the classic *The Italians* by the late Luigi Barzini, former correspondent for the *Corriere della Sera* in London.

Music and Opera

Italy has contributed as much to Western music as any country—and perhaps a little more. It was an Italian monk, Guido d'Arezzo, who devised the musical scale; it was a Venetian printer, Ottaviano Petrucci, who invented a method of printing music with movable type in 1501—an industry Italian printers monopolized for years (which is why we play *allegro* and not *schnell*). Italy also gave us the *pianoforte*, because unlike the harpsichord you could play both soft and loud, and the accordion, invented in the Marches, and the violins of the Guarneri and Stradivarius of Cremona, setting a standard for the instrument that has never been equalled. But Italy is most famous as the mother of opera, the most Italian of arts.

Italian composers first came into their own in the 14th century, led by the half-legendary, blind Florentine Landini, whose *Ecco la Primavera* is one of the first Italian compositions to come down to us. Although following international trends introduced by musicians from

France and the Low Countries, musicologists note from the start a special love of melody, even in earlier Italian works, as well as a preference for vocal music over the purely instrumental.

Landini was followed by the age of the *frottolas* (secular verses accompanied by lutes), especially prominent in the court of Mantua. The *frottolas* were forerunners of the *madrigal*, the greatest Italian musical invention during the Renaissance. Although sung in three or six parts, the text of the madrigals was given serious consideration, and was sung to be understood; at the same time church music had become so polyphonically rich and sumptuous (most notoriously at St Mark's in Venice) that it drowned out the words of the Mass. Many melodies used were from secular and often bawdy songs, and the bishops at the Council of Trent (1545–63) seriously considered banning music from the liturgy. The day was saved by the Roman composers, led by Palestrina, whose solemn, simple, but beautiful melodies set a standard for all subsequent composers.

Two contrasting strains near the end of the 16th century led to the birth of opera: the Baroque love of spectacle and the urge to make everything, at least on the surface, more beautiful, more elaborate, more showy. Musically there were the lavish Florentine *intermedii*, performed on special occasions between the acts of plays; the *intermedii* used elaborate sets and costumes, songs, choruses and dances to set a mythological scene.

At the same time, in Florence, a group of humanist intellectuals who called themselves the *Camerata* came to the conclusion from their classical studies that ancient Greek drama was not spoken, but sung, and took it upon themselves to try to recreate this pure and classical form. One of their chief theorists was Galileo's father Vincenzo, who studied Greek, Turkish and Moorish music and advocated the clear enunciation of the words, as opposed to the Venetian tendency to merge words and music as a single rich unit of sound.

One of the first results of the Camerata's debates was court musician Jacopo Peri's *L'Euridice*, performed in Florence in 1600. Peri used a kind of singing speech (recitative) to tell the story, interspersed with a few melodic songs. No one, it seems, asked for an encore; opera had to wait a few years, until the Duchess of Mantua asked her court composer, Claudio Monteverdi (1567–1643), to compose something like the work she had heard in Florence. Monteverdi went far beyond Peri, bringing in a large orchestra, designing elegant sets, adding dances and many more melodic songs (*arias*). His classic *L'Orfeo* (1607), still heard today, and *L'Arianna* (unfortunately lost but for fragments) were the first operatic 'hits'. Monteverdi moved on to bigger audiences in Venice, which soon had 11 opera houses. After he died, though, Naples took over top opera honours, gaining special renown for its clear-toned *castrati*.

Other advances were developing in the more pious atmosphere of Rome, where Corelli was perfecting the concerto and composing his famous *Christmas Concerto*. In Venice, Vivaldi greatly expanded the genre by composing some four hundred concerti for whatever instruments happened to be played in the orchestra of orphaned girls where he was concert-master.

The 18th century saw the sonata form perfected by harpsichord master Domenico Scarlatti. Opera was rid of some of its Baroque excesses and a division was set between serious works and the comic *opera buffa*; Pergolesi (1710–36—his *Il Flaminio* was the basis for Stravinsky's *Pulcinella*) and Cimarosa (1749–1801) were the most sought-after composers, while the now infamous Salieri, antagonist of Mozart, charmed the court of Vienna. Italian composers held sway throughout Europe; they contributed more than is generally acknowledged today towards the founding of modern music.

Italy innovated less in the 19th century; at this time most of its musical energies were devoted to opera, becoming the reviving nation's clearest and most widely appreciated medium of self-expression. All of the most popular Italian operas were written in the 19th and early 20th centuries, most of them by the 'Big Five'— Bellini, Donizetti, Rossini, Verdi and Puccini. For Italians, Verdi (1813–1901) is supreme, the national idol even in his lifetime, whose rousing operas were practically the battle hymns of the Risorgimento. Verdi, more than anyone else, re-established Italy on the musical map; his works provided Italy's melodic answer to the ponderous turbulence of Richard Wagner. After Verdi, Puccini held the operatic stage, though not entirely singlehandedly; the later 19th century gave us a number of composers best remembered for only one opera: Leoncavallo's *Pagliacci,* Mascagni's *Cavalleria Rusticana,* Cilea's *Adriana Lecouvreur,* and many others down to obscure composers like Giordano, whose *Fedora,* famous for being the only opera with bicycles on stage, is revived frequently in his hometown of Foggia.

Of more recent Italian, and Italian-American, composers there's *The Pines of Rome* of Respighi (whose works were among the few 20th-century productions that the great Toscanini deigned to direct) and Gian Carlo Menotti, surely the best loved, not only for his operas but for founding the Spoleto Festival. Lately there are the innovative post-War composers Luigi Nono and Luciano Berio, two respected names in contemporary academic music.

Next to all of this big-league culture, however, there survive remnants of Italy's traditional music—the pungent tunes of Italian bagpipes (*zampogna*), the ancient instrument of the Apennine shepherds, often heard in the big cities (especially in the south) at Christmas time; the lively *tarantellas* of Puglia; country accordion music, the fare of many a rural *festa*; and the great song tradition of the country's music capital, Naples, the cradle of everyone's favourite cornball classics, but also of many haunting, passionate melodies of tragedy and romance that are rarely heard abroad—or, to be honest, in Italy itself these days.

Opera season in Italy runs roughly from November to May. The Teatro dell'Opera in Rome and the Teatro Comunale in Florence can both put on excellent and innovative productions; and hopefully La Fenice in Venice will reopen before too long. Summer festivals are an excellent place to hear music; check through the list of festivals on pp.14–15.

Cinema

After the Second World War, when Italy was at its lowest ebb, when it was financially and culturally bankrupt, when its traditional creativity in painting, architecture and music seemed to have dried up, along came a handful of Italian directors who invented a whole new language of cinema. Neorealism was a response to the fictions propagated by years of Fascism; it was also a response to the lack of movie-making equipment after the Romans—their eyes suddenly opened after a decade of deception and mindless 'White Telephone' comedies— pillaged and sacked Cinecittà in 1943. Stark, unsentimental, often shot in bleak locations with unprofessional actors, the genre took shape with directors like Roberto Rossellini (*Roma, Open City,* 1945), Vittorio de Sica (*Bicycle Thieves,* 1948) and Luchino Visconti (*The Earth Trembles,* 1948).

Although neorealism continued to influence Italian cinema (Rossellini's films with Ingrid Bergman, like *Europa 51* and *Stromboli,* Fellini's classic *La Strada* with Giulietta Masina and Anthony Quinn, Antonioni's *The Scream*), Italian directors began to go off in their own directions. The post-War period was the golden age of Italian cinema, when Italy's Hollywood, Cinecittà, produced scores of films every year. Like the artists of the Age of Mannerism, a new generation of individualistic (or egoistic) directors created works that needed no signature, ranging from Sergio Leone's ultra-popular kitsch westerns to the often jarring films of the Marxist poet Pasolini (*Accattone*, *The Decameron*). This was the period of Visconti's *The Damned*, Antonioni's *Blow Up*, Lina Wertmuller's *Seven Beauties*, De Sica's *Neapolitan Gold*, Bertolucci's *The Conformist*, and the classics of the indefatigable maestro Federico Fellini—*I Vitelloni*, *La Dolce Vita*, *Juliet of the Spirits*, *The Clowns*, *Satyricon*.

In the seventies the cost of making films soared and the industry went into recession. Increasingly, directors went abroad or sought out actors with international appeal in order to reach a larger audience, to help finance their films (Bertolucci's *Last Tango in Paris* with Marlon Brando and *1900* with Donald Sutherland, the overripe Franco Zeffirelli's *Taming of the Shrew* with Taylor and Burton, Visconti's *Death in Venice*). Fellini was one of the few who managed to stay home (*Roma, Amarcord*, and later *Casanova* (although admittedly with Donald Sutherland in the lead role), *City of Women*, *The Ship Sails On*, *Orchestra Rehearsal* and *Intervista*, a film about Cinecittà itself).

Although funding became even scarcer in the eighties, new directors appeared to recharge Italian cinema, often with a fresh lyrical realism and sensitivity. Bright stars of the decade included Ermanno Olmi (the beautiful *Tree of the Wooden Clogs* and *Cammina, Cammina*), Giuseppe Tornatore's sentimental and nostalgic *Cinema Paradiso* (1988), Paolo and Vittorio Taviani (*Padre Padrone*, *Night of the Shooting Stars*, *Kaos* and *Good Morning Babilonia*), Francesco Rosi (*Christ Stopped at Eboli*, *Three Brothers*, *Carmen* and *Cronaca d'una morte annunciata*), and Nanni Moretti (*La Messa é finita*), unfortunately rarely seen outside of festivals and film clubs abroad, while Zeffirelli (*La Traviata*) and Bertolucci (*1900, The Last Emperor*) continued to represent Italy in the world's movie-houses. Comedy found new life in Mario Monticelli's hilarious *Speriamo che sia femina* and in Bruno Bozzetto, whose animation features (especially *Allegro Non Troppo*, a satire of Disney's *Fantasia*) are a scream.

So far the 1990s have served up fairly thin gruel, a recession of inspiration to go with the economy. Worthy exceptions have been *Il Ladro dei bambini* (1992) by Gianni Amelio, *Mediterraneo* (1991) by Gabriele Salvatores, about Italian soldiers marooned on a Greek island, and Nanni Moretti's travelogue to the Ionian islands, *Caro Diario* (1994). This was also the decade that Fellini spun his final reel. Although critics at home and abroad sometimes complained that he repeated himself in his last films (*Ginger and Fred* and *La Voce della Luna*, 1990), his loyal fans eagerly awaited each new instalment of his personal fantasy, his alternative hyper-Italy that exists on the other side of the looking glass in the gossamer warp of the silver screen. The last director regularly to use Cinecittà ('Cinecittà is not my home; I just live there,' he once said), his demise may well bring about the end of Rome's pretensions as Hollywood on the Mediterranean.

Italian films are windows of the nation's soul, but if you don't understand Italian you may want to see them at home, where you have the advantage of subtitles. English-language films in Italy rarely receive the same courtesy, however—Italians like their movies dubbed. Check listings for films labelled '*versione originale*'—you're bound to find a few in Rome (*see* p.105), and often in other big cities as well. There are also Italy's film festivals (where films tend to be subtitled); the most important one is in Venice (last week of August to first week of September); Florence hosts a documentary festival in December.

Bella Figura

The longer you stay in Italy, the more inscrutable it becomes. Nothing is ever quite as it seems, and you'll find yourself changing your ideas about things with disconcerting frequency. Part of the reason is the obsession to *fare una bella figura*, 'to make a good impression or appearance', one of the most singular traits of the Italian people. You notice it almost immediately upon arrival. Not only is every Italian an immaculately smart fashion victim, but they always seem to be modelling their spiffy threads—posing, gesturing, playing to an audience when they have one, which is nearly always, because Italians rarely move about except in small herds. Their cities are their stage. Long-time observers of the phenomenon have even noted that each city's women tend to dress themselves in colours that complement the local brick or stone.

The Italians' natural grace and elegance may be partly instinctive; even back in the 14th century, foreigners invariably noted their charming manners and taste for exquisite clothes. Many a painting of the Madonna served not only piety's sake, but also advertised the latest Milanese silks or Venetian brocades. Appearance supplanted reality in a thousand ways in the Renaissance, especially after the discovery of artificial perspective, which made artistic representations seem much more clever and interesting than the real thing. Fake, painted marble supplanted real marble, even if the fake cost more; Palladio built marble palaces out of stucco; *trompe l'œil* frescoes embellished a hundred churches; glorious façades on cathedrals and palaces disguise the fact that the rest is shabby, unfinished brick. The gentleman's bible of the day, Castiglione's *The Courtier*, advises that it is no use doing a brave and noble deed unless someone is watching.

Bella figura pleases the eye but irritates just about everything else. Fashionable conformity has a way of spreading from mere clothing and gestures to opinions, especially in the provinces; the Italians remain the masters of empty flattery and compliments, and will say anything to please: 'Yes, straight ahead!' they'll often reply when you need directions, hoping it will make you happy even if they've never heard of your destination.

Nor does fashion slavery show any sign of abating; now that more Italians have more money than ever before, they are using it for fur coats, rarely necessary in most of the country's winters, and for designer clothes for the whole family. Even little children go to bed with visions of fashion dancing in their heads.

Brick Italy, Marble Italy

'Italy', begins the 1948 Constitution, 'is a republic based on labour'—an unusual turn of phrase, perhaps, but one entirely in keeping with a time when a thoroughly humbled Italy was beginning to get back on its feet after the War. The sorrows of the common man occupied the plots of post-War *cinema verità*, and artists and writers began to celebrate themes of Faith, Bread and Work as if they were in the employ of the Church's *Famiglia Cristiana* magazine. To outsiders it must have seemed that Italy was undergoing a serious change, but careful observers would have noted only another oscillation in the grandest, oldest dichotomy in Italian history. Brick Italy was once more in the driver's seat.

Brick Italy is a nation of hard work, humility and piety that knows it must be diligent and clever to wrest a comfortable living from the thin soil of this rocky, resource-poor peninsula. Marble Italy knows its citizens are perfectly capable of doing just that, just as they always have, and seeks to celebrate that diligence and cleverness by turning it into opulence, excess and foreign conquest. The two have been contending for Italy's soul ever since Roman quarrymen discovered the great veins of Carrara marble during the Republican era. Brick Italy's capital in former times was brilliant, republican Siena; right now it is virtuous, hard-working socialist Bologna, a city with more bricks that Woolworth's has nickels. Its triumphs came with the Age of the Comunes, with the modest genius of the Early Renaissance, and with the hard-won successes of the last 40 years. Marble Italy reached its height in the days of Imperial Rome; its capital is Rome, always and forever. After the medieval interlude, marble made its great comeback with the High Renaissance, Spaniardism and Michelangelo, the high priest of marble. The Age of Baroque belonged to it completely, as did the brief era of Mussolini. Some confirmed Marble cities are Naples, Genoa, Turin, Pisa, Parma, Trieste, Perugia and Verona. Brick partisans include Pavia, Livorno, Lucca, Arezzo, Cremona and Mantua. Florence and Venice, the two medieval city-republics that eventually became important states on their own, are the two cities that most successfully straddle the fence. Look carefully at their old churches and palaces: you will often find marble veneer outside and solid brick underneath.

Keep all this in mind when you ponder the infinite subtleties of Italian history. It isn't always a perfect fit; medieval Guelphs and Ghibellines each had a little brick and a little marble in them, and the contemporary papacy changes from one to the other with every shift of the wind. Mussolini would have paved Italy over in marble if he had been able—but look at the monuments he could afford, and you'll see more inexpensive travertine and brick than anything else. For a while in the eighties, with Italy's economic successes and the glitz of Milanese fashion and design, it looked as if Marble Italy was about to make another comeback. But today, with Italy in the midst of its long and torturous revolution, the situation is unclear. If and when a new regime emerges, will its monument to itself be a beautiful symbol of republican aspirations, like Siena's brick Palazzo del Pubblico, or a florid marble pile like Rome's Altar of the Nation, the monument to Italian unification (and one of the biggest hunks of kitsch on this planet)?

Commedia dell'Arte

The first recorded mention of Arlecchino, or Harlequin, came when the part was played by a celebrated actor named Tristano Martinelli in 1601—the year that also saw the début of *Hamlet*. Theatre as we know it was blooming all over Europe in those times: Shakespeare and Marlowe, Calderón and Lope de Vega in Spain, the predecessors of Molière in France. All of these had learned their craft from late-Renaissance Italy, where the *commedia dell'arte* had created a fashion that spread across the continent. The great companies, such as the Gelosi, the Confidenti and the Accesi, toured the capitals, while others shared out the provinces. Groups of ten or twelve actors, run as co-operatives, they could do comedies, tragedies or pastorals, to their own texts, and provide music, dance, magic and juggling between acts.

The audiences liked the comedies best of all, with a set of masked stock characters, playing off scenes between the *magnificos*, the great lords, and the *zanni*, or servants, who provide the slapstick, half-improvised comic relief. These represented every corner of Italy: Arlecchino is a Bergamese; Balanzone, the wise doctor who 'cures with Latin', is from Bologna; white-clad, warbling Pulcinello a true Neapolitan; Meneghino, the piratical warrior, a Milanese; the drunkard Rugantino is a Roman; and the nervous rich merchant Pantalone is a Venetian; while the maid Colombina apparently belongs to all. To spring the plot there would be a pair of *inamorati*, or lovers—unmasked, to remind us that only those who are in love are really alive.

It had nothing to do with 'art'. *Arte* means a guild, to emphasize that these companies were made up of professional players. The term was invented in 1745 by Goldoni (who wrote one of the last plays of the genre, *Arlecchino, servitore di due padrone*); in the 1500s the companies were often referred to as the *commedia mercenaria*—they would hit town, set up a stage on trestles, and start their show within the hour.

Cultured Italians of the day often deplored the way the 'mercenary' shows were driving out serious drama, traditionally written by scholarly amateurs in the princely courts. In the repressive climate of the day, caught between the Inquisition and the Spanish bosses, a culture of ideas survived only in free Venice. Theatre retreated into humorous popular entertainment, but the Italians still found a way to say what was on their minds. A new character appeared, the menacing but slow-witted Capitano, who always spoke with a Spanish accent, and Italians learned from the French how to use Arlecchino to satirize the hated Emperor Charles V himself—playing on the French pronunciation of the names *harlequin* and *Charles Quint*.

Arlecchino may have been born in Oneta, a village north of Bergamo, but he carries a proud lineage that goes back to the ancient Greeks and Romans. From his character and appearance, historians of the theatre trace him back to the antique planipedes, comic mimes with shaved heads (everyone knew Arlecchino wore his silly nightcap to cover his baldness). Other scholars note his relationship to the 'tricksters' of German and Scandinavian mythology, and it has even been claimed that his costume of patches is that of a Sufi dervish. No doubt he had a brilliant career all through the Middle Ages, though it was probably only in the 1500s that he took the form of the Arlecchino we know. At that time, young rustics from the Bergamese valleys would go to Venice, Milan and other cities to get work as *facchini*, porters. They all seemed to be named Johnny—*Zanni* in dialect—which became the common term for any of the clownish roles in the plays; it's the origin of our word 'zany'.

The name 'Arlecchino' seems actually to have been a French contribution. At the court of Henri III, a certain Italian actor who played the role became a protégé of a Monsieur de Harlay, and people started calling him 'little Harlay', or Harlequin. The character developed into a stock role, the most beloved of all the *commedia dell'arte* clown masks: simple-minded and easily frightened, yet an incorrigible prankster, a fellow as unstable as his motley dress. His foil was usually another servant, the Neapolitan Puricinella, or Punchinella—Punch—more serious and sometimes boastful, but still just as much of a buffoon. Try to imagine them together on stage, and you'll get something that looks very much like Stan Laurel and Oliver Hardy. No doubt these two have always gone through the world together, and we can hope they always will.

Pasta

Croton and Sybaris, among other Greek cities of the Ionian Sea, take the credit for introducing the Italians to their future hearts' delight. A small, cylindrical form of pasta called *makaria*—perhaps the original *macaroni*—was a ritual food eaten at funeral banquets; by 600 BC, the Sybarites, always on the hunt for new culinary experiences, had invented the rolling pin and were turning out *tagliatelle* and maybe even *lasagne*. Not yet having tomatoes, they were unable to perfect the concept, but, in a nation that often has trouble baking a decent loaf of bread, this delicious, aesthetically stimulating and eminently practical new staple found a warm welcome everywhere. Pasta's triumphal march northwards finally slowed to a halt in the rice paddies and treacherous *polenta* morasses of Lombardy, but everywhere else it remains in firm control.

Pasta does have its cultural ramifications. The artists of the Futurist movement wanted to declare war on spaghetti, and many of today's Italian *nouveaux riches* wouldn't be caught dead ordering any form of pasta in a restaurant (this, ironically, at a time when their counterparts in northern Europe and America wax ever more enthusiastic about it). Do you think that pasta is all the same? Well, so do millions of Italians, though an equal number revel in the incredible variety of pasta forms and fashions; in your travels you'll find the same flour and water turned into broad *pappardelle* and narrow *linguini* ('tiny tongues'), stuffed delights like *ravioli* and *tortellini*, regional specialities like Puglian *orecchietti* ('little ears') and Sardinia's *malorreddus*, that resemble miniature trilobites. Other inviting forms, among the 400 or so known shapes, include *vermicelli* ('little worms'), *lumacconi* ('slugs'), *bavette* ('dribbles') and *strangolopreti* ('priest chokers'). But even these fail to satisfy the nation's culinary whims, and every so often one of the big pasta companies commissions a big-name fashion designer to come up with a new form.

The Pinocchio Complex

The Italians, as much as they adore their *bambini*, have produced but one recognized classic of children's literature, the story of a naughty wooden puppet who must pass through trials and tribulations before he can become a real boy—a stable, responsible child, a blessing to his father in his old age.

Since the Risorgimento, the Italian government has been a bit of a Pinocchio to the old country that painfully carved it out of wood, admittedly half petrified and half rotted from the start. Each ring of the thick trunk told a dire tale of defeat and tyranny, corruption, papal misgovernment, foreign rule and betrayal. From this piece of flotsam the Italians created a new creature, a national state that sits in the class of real governments like a mischievous, exasperating puppet. This Pinocchio is the bad boy of the EU, with more violations of its trade rules than any other nation. Every day its parliament is in session, its nose grows a little bit longer. With its creaky wooden bureaucracy, unpredictable and not blessed with the soundest of judgements, it is constantly led astray by scheming foxes and cats—like the Mafia, power-hungry cabals of 'freemasons', southern landowners, Mussolinis, popes, Jesuits and whale-sized special interests that threaten to gobble it down whole. The parties that make up its *commedia dell'arte* coalitions, like flimsy wooden limbs and joints, are liable to trip up or fly off at any moment, making the poor marionette collapse (something that since 1946 has occurred an average of once every 11 months).

Just as Pinocchio, by some unexplained power, is able to walk without strings, so Italy, without a real government, functions with remarkable smoothness, and even prospers. Understandably, as Europe grows ever closer together, having a wooden-headed political system becomes more and more embarrassing. Constitutional reform, with the 1993 referendum that changed the electoral system, may prove a threat to this puppet's career. And, with the revelations of the last few years, Italians are beginning to interest themselves in the all-important question of who, all this time, has been pulling the strings.

Rome

On a Saturday night variety show, the television host discusses the founding of Rome with two comedians dressed up as Romulus and Remus; turning to Remus, the sillier-looking of the pair, he asks: 'What did you ever do?' Remus gets a big laugh by proudly claiming, 'Well, I founded Lazio.'

Despite being the location of the capital city, Lazio does not get much respect from the average Italian, who thinks of it as a sort of vacuum that needs to be crossed to get to Rome. Northerners often lump it in with Campania and Calabria as part of the backward south. To an extent it is, though great changes have come in the last 60 years with land reclamation and new industry. Lazio's problem is a simple one: Rome, that most parasitic of all cities. Before there was a Rome this was probably the wealthiest and most densely populated part of non-Greek Italy, the homeland of the Etruscans as well as the rapidly civilizing nations of Sabines, Aequi, Hernici, Volscii and the Latins themselves, from whom Lazio (*Latium*) takes its name.

After the Roman triumph the Etruscan and Italic cities shrivelled and died; those Romans who proved such good governors elsewhere caused utter ruin to their own backyard. A revival came in the Middle Ages when Rome was only one of a score of squabbling feudal towns, but once again, when the popes restored Rome, Lazio's fortunes declined. To finance their grandiose building projects, Renaissance popes literally taxed Lazio into extinction; whole villages and large stretches of countryside were abandoned, and land drained in medieval times reverted to malarial swamps. Modern Rome, at least since Mussolini's day, has begun to mend its ways; the government still considers Lazio a development area, and pumps a lot of money into it.

Rome

To know what Rome is, you might pay a visit to the little church of San Clemente, unobtrusively hidden away on the back streets behind the Colosseum. The Baroque façade conceals a 12th-century basilica with a beautiful marble choir screen 600 years older. In 1857 a cardinal from Boston discovered the original church of 313 underneath the church, one of the first great Christian basilicas. And beneath that have been discovered the remains of two ancient buildings and a Temple of Mithras from the time of Augustus; from it you can walk out into a Roman alley that looks exactly as it did 2000 years ago, now some 30ft below ground level. There are commemorative plaques in San Clemente, placed there by a Medici duke, a bishop of New York, and the last chairman of the Bulgarian Communist Party.

You are not going to get to the bottom of this city, or even begin to understand it, whether your stay is for three days or a month. With its legions of headless statues, acres of paintings, 913 churches and megatons of artistic sediment, this metropolis of aching feet will wear down even the most resolute of travellers (and travel writers). The name Rome passed out of the plane of reality into legend some 2200 years ago, when princes as far away as China first began to hear of the faraway city and its invincible armies building an empire in the West. At the same time the Romans were cooking up a personified goddess, the Divine Rome, and beginning the strange myth of their city's destiny to conquer and pacify the world, a myth that would still haunt Europe a thousand years later.

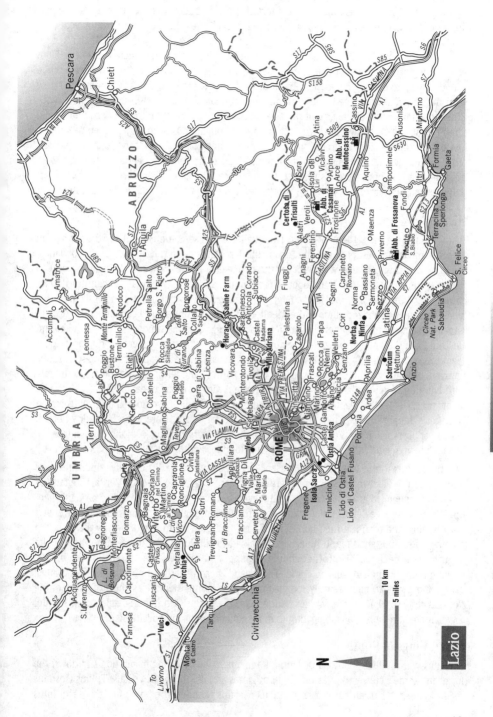

Lazio

63

You may find it requires a considerable effort of the imagination to break through to the past Romes of the Caesars and popes. You will need to peel away the increasingly thick veneer of the 'Third Rome', the thoroughly up-to-date creation of post-Reunification Italy. Ancient Rome at the height of its glory had perhaps a million and a half people; today there are four million, and at any given time at least half of them will be pushing their way into the Metro train while you are trying to get off. The popes, for all their experience in spectacle and ceremony, rarely steal the show, sharing the stage with an overabundance of preposterous politicians, with Cinecittà and the rest of Italy's cultural apparatus, and of course with the tourists, who sometimes put on the best show in town. The old-guard Romani, now a minority, often bewail the loss of old Rome's slow and easy pace, its vintage brand of *dolce vita* that once impressed other Italians, let alone foreigners. Lots of money, lots of traffic and an endless caravan of tour buses have a way of compromising even the most beautiful cities. Don't worry; the present is only one snapshot from a 2600-year history, and no one has ever left Rome disappointed.

History

Historians believe the settlement of the Tiber Valley began some time about 1000 BC, when an outbreak of volcanic eruptions in the Alban Hills forced the Latin tribes down to the lowlands. But remembering that every ancient legend conceals a kernel of truth, it would be best to follow the accounts of Virgil, the poet of the empire, and Livy, the great 1st-century Roman chronicler. When Virgil wrote, in the reign of Augustus, Greek culture was an irresistible force in all the recently civilized lands of the Mediterranean. For Rome, Virgil concocted the story of Aeneas, fleeing from Troy after the Homeric sack and finding his way over the sea to Latium. Descent from the Trojans, however specious, connected Rome to the Greek world and made it seem less of an upstart in its Imperial age. As Virgil tells it, Aeneas' son Ascanius founded Alba Longa, a city that by the 800s was leader of the Latin Confederation. Livy takes up the tale with Numitor, a descendant of Ascanius and rightful King of Alba Longa, tossed off the throne by his usurping brother Amulius. In order that Numitor should have no heirs, Amulius forced Numitor's daughter Rhea Silvia into service as a Vestal Virgin. Here Rome's destiny begins, with an appearance in the Vestals' chambers of the god Mars, staying just long enough to leave Rhea Silvia pregnant with the precocious twins Romulus and Remus.

When Amulius found out he of course packed them away in a little boat, which the gods directed up the Tiber to a spot somewhere near today's Piazza Bocca della Verità. The famous she-wolf then looked after the babies, until they were found by a shepherd, who brought them up. When Mars revealed to the grown twins their origin, they returned to Alba Longa to sort out Amulius, and then returned home (in 753 BC, traditionally) to found the city the gods had ordained. Romulus soon found himself constrained to kill Remus, who would not believe the auguries that declared his brother should be king, and this sets the pattern for the bloody millennium of Rome's history to come. The legends portray early Rome as a glorified pirates' camp, and the historians are only too glad to agree. Finding themselves short of women, the Romans stole some from the Sabines. Not especially interested in farming or learning a trade, they adopted the hobby of subjugating their neighbours and soon polished it to an art.

Seven Kings of Rome

Romulus was the first, followed by Numa Pompilius, who by divine inspiration laid down the forms for Rome's cults and priesthoods, its auguries and its College of Vestals. Tullius Hostilius made Rome ruler of all Latium, and Ancus Martius founded the port of Ostia. Tarquinius

Priscus was an Etruscan, and probably gained his throne thanks to a conquest by one of the great Etruscan city-states. Tarquin made a city of Rome, building the first real temples, the Cloaca Maxima and the first Circus Maximus. Servius Tullius restored Latin rule, inaugurated the division of the citizens between patricians and plebeians, and built a great wall to keep the Etruscans out. It apparently did not work, for as next king we find the Etruscan Tarquinius Superbus (about 534 BC), another great builder. His misfortune was to have a hot-headed son like Tarquinius Sextus, who imposed himself on a noble and virtuous Roman maiden named Lucretia (cf. Shakespeare's *Rape of Lucrece*). She committed public suicide in the morning; the enraged Roman patricians, under the leadership of Lucius Junius Brutus, then chased out proud Tarquin and the Etruscan dynasty forever. The Republic was established before the day was out, with Brutus as First Consul, or Chief Magistrate.

The Invincible Republic

Taking an oath never to allow another king in Rome, the patricians designed a novel form of government, a republic (*res publica*—public thing) governed by the two consuls elected by the Senate (the patricians' assembly); later innovations in the constitution would include a tribune, an official with inviolable powers elected by the plebeians to protect their interests. The two classes fought like cats and dogs at home but combined with impressive resolve in their foreign wars. Etruscans, Aequi, Hernici, Volscii, Samnites and Sabines were all defeated by Rome's citizen armies. By 270 BC Rome had eliminated all its rivals to become master of Italy. It had taken about 200 years, and in the next 200 Roman rule would be established from Spain to Egypt. In the three Punic Wars against Carthage (264–146 BC) Rome gained most of the western Mediterranean; Greece, North Africa and Asia Minor were absorbed in small bites over the next 100 years. Rome's history was now the history of the Western world.

Imperial Rome

When the Romans took Greece they first met Culture, and it had the effect on them that puberty has on little boys. After some bizarre behaviour, evidenced in the continuous civil wars, the Romans began tarting up their city in the worst way, vacuuming all the gold, paintings, statues, cooks, poets and architects out of the civilized East. Beginning perhaps with Pompey, every contender for control of the now constitutionally deranged Republic added some great work to the city centre: Pompey's theatre, the Julian Basilica, and something from almost every emperor up to Constantine. Julius Caesar and Augustus were perhaps Rome's greatest benefactors, initiating every sort of progressive legislation, turning dirt lanes into paved streets and erecting new forums, temples and the vast network of aqueducts. In their time Rome's population probably reached the million mark, surpassing Antioch and Alexandria as the largest city in the Western world.

It was Augustus who effectively ended the Republic in 27 BC, by establishing his personal rule and reducing the old constitution to a series of formalities. During the Imperial era that followed, Rome's position as administrative and judicial centre of the Empire created a new cosmopolitan population as people from every province—from Britain to Mesopotamia—crowded in. The city also became the capital of banking and the financial markets—and also of religion; Rome's policy was always to induct everyone's local god as an honorary Roman, and every important cult image and relic was abducted to the Capitoline Temple. The Emperor himself was *Pontifex Maximus*, head priest of Rome, whose title derives from the early Roman veneration of bridges (*pontifex* means 'keeper of bridges'). St Peter, of course, arrived, and was duly martyred in AD 67. His successor, Linus, became the first pope—or *pontiff.*

For all its glitter, Rome was still the complete economic predator, producing nothing and consuming everything. At times almost half the population of Roman citizens (as opposed to slaves) was on the public dole. Uncertain times made Aurelian give Rome a real defensive wall in 275. By 330 the necessity of staying near the armies at the front led the Western Emperors to spend most of their time at army headquarters in Milan. Rome became a bloated backwater and, after three sacks of the city, there was no reason to stay. The sources disagree: perhaps 100,000 inhabitants were left by the year 500, perhaps as few as 10,000.

Rome in the Shadows

Rome never quite went down the drain in the Dark Ages. Its lowest point in prestige undoubtedly came in the 14th century, when the popes were at Avignon, but the number of important churches built, and mosaics created (equal in number if not quality to those of Ravenna), testify to the city's continuing importance. There was certainly enough to attract a few more sacks. Rome at this time must have been a fascinating place, much too big for its population though still thinking of itself as the centre of the Western world. The Forum was mostly abandoned, as were the gigantic baths, rendered useless as the aqueducts decayed and no one had the means to repair them. Almost all of the temples and basilicas survived, converted to Christian churches. Hadrian's massive tomb on the banks of the Tiber was converted into a fortress, the Castel Sant'Angelo, an impregnable haven of safety for the popes in times of trouble.The popes deserve credit for keeping Rome alive, but the tithe money trickling in from across Europe confirmed the city in its parasitical behaviour. Charlemagne visited the city in 800; during a prayer vigil in St Peter's on Christmas Eve, Pope Leo III sneaked up behind him and set an imperial crown on his head. The surprise coronation established the precedent of Holy Roman Emperors having to cross over the Alps to receive their crown from the pope; for centuries to come Rome was able to keep its hand in the political struggles of all Europe.

Arnold of Brescia and Rienzo

Not that Rome ever spoke with one voice; over the next 500 years it was only the idea of Rome, as the spiritual centre of the universal Christian community, that kept the actual city of Rome from disappearing altogether. Down to some 20–30,000 people, Rome evolved a sort of stable anarchy, in which the major contenders for power were the popes and various noble families. Very often outsiders would get into the game. A remarkable woman named Theodora seized the Castel Sant'Angelo in the 880s; with the title of Senatrix she and her daughter Marozia ruled Rome for decades. Various German emperors seized the city, but were never able to hold it. In the 10th century, things got even more complicated as the Roman people began to assert themselves, and nine of the 24 popes managed to get themselves murdered. In the 1140s a Jewish family, the Pierleoni, held power, and a Jewish antipope sat enthroned in St Peter's. Mighty Rome occupied itself with a series of wars against its neighbouring village of Tivoli, and usually lost. A sincere monkish reformer appeared, the Christian and democrat Arnold of Brescia; he recreated the Senate and almost succeeded in establishing Rome as a free *comune*, but somehow in 1155 he fell into the hands of the German Emperor Frederick Barbarossa, who sold him to the English pope (Adrian IV) for hanging.

Too many centuries of this made Rome uncomfortable for the popes, who frequently removed themselves to Viterbo during the 13th century. The final indignity came when, under French pressure, the papacy decamped entirely to Avignon in 1309. Pulling strings from a distance, the papacy only made life more complicated for the Romans left behind. Cola di Rienzo stepped into the vacuum they created. The son of an innkeeper, he had a good enough education to read Latin inscriptions and the works of Livy, Cicero and Tacitus. Obsessed by the idea of re-establishing Roman glory, he talked at the bewildered inhabitants until they caught the fever too. With Rienzo as Tribune of the People, the Republic was reborn in May 1347. Corrupted by power, however, an increasingly fat and ridiculous Rienzo was hustled out of Rome by the united nobles before the year was out. His return to power, in 1354, ended with his murder by a mob after only two months. Rome was now at its lowest ebb, with only some 15,000 people, and prosperity and influence were not to be restored until after 1447.

The New Rome

In the more settled conditions of the 15th century, a new papacy emerged, richer and more sophisticated. Political power was always its goal, and a series of talented Renaissance popes saw their best hopes for achieving this by rebuilding Rome. Under Julius II (1503-13) the papal domains for the first time were run like a modern state; Julius also laid plans for the rebuilding of St Peter's, beginning, with his architect, Bramante, the great building programme that was to transform the city. New streets were laid out, especially the Via Giulia and the grand avenues radiating from the Piazza del Popolo.

Over the next two centuries hundreds of churches were either built or rebuilt, and cardinals and nobles lined the streets with imposing new palaces. A new departure in urban design was developed in the 1580s, under Sixtus V, and piazzas were cleared in front of the major religious sites, each with its Egyptian obelisk, linked by a network of straight boulevards. The New Rome, symbol of the Counter-Reformation and the majesty of the popes, was, however, bought at a terrible price. Besides Bramante's destruction of medieval Rome, buildings that had survived substantially intact for 1500 years were cannibalized for their marble and, to pay for their programme, the popes taxed the economy of the Papal States out of existence. Worst of all, the new papacy in the 16th century instituted terror as an instrument of public policy. The popes tried to extend their power by playing a game of high-stakes diplomacy between Emperor Charles V of Spain and King Francis I of France, but reaped a bitter harvest in the 1527 sack of Rome. An out-of-control, destructive imperial army occupied the city for almost a year, while Pope Clement VII looked on helplessly from the Castel Sant'Angelo. The popes subsequently became part of the Imperial-Spanish system and political repression was fiercer than anywhere else in Italy; the Inquisition was refounded in 1542, and book-burnings, the torture of freethinkers and executions became even more common than in Spain itself.

The End of Papal Rule

By about 1610 workmen were adding the last stones to the cupola of St Peter's. It was the end of an era, but the building continued. A thick accretion of Baroque, like coral, collected over Rome. Bernini did his Piazza Navona fountain in 1650, and the Colonnade for St Peter's 15 years later. The political importance of the popes, however, disappeared with surprising finality as they drifted into irrelevance during the Thirty Years War and after.

Rome was left to enjoy a decadent but rather pleasant twilight. A brief interruption came when revolutionaries in 1798 once again proclaimed the Roman Republic, and a French army sent the pope packing. Rome later became part of Napoleon's empire, but papal rule was restored in 1815. Another republic appeared in 1848, but this time a French army besieged the city and had the Pope propped back on his throne by July 1849. For twenty years Napoleon III maintained a garrison in Rome to look after the Pope, and consequently Rome became the last part of Italy to join the new Italian kingdom. After the French defeat in the war of 1870, Italian troops blew a hole in the old Aurelian wall near the Porta Pia and marched in. Pius IX locked himself in the Vatican and pouted; the popes were to be 'prisoners' until Mussolini's Concordat of 1929, by which they recognized the Italian state. As capital of the new state, Rome underwent another building boom; new streets made circulation a little easier; villas and gardens disappeared under endless blocks of speculative building; long-needed projects like the Tiber embankments were built; and, at the same time, the kingdom strove to impress the world with gigantic, absurd public buildings and monuments, such as the Altar of the Nation and the Finance Ministry on Via XX Settembre. Growth has been steady; from some 200,000 people in 1879, Rome has since increased twentyfold.

The Twentieth Century

In 1922 the city was the objective of Mussolini's 'March on Rome', when he used his black-shirts to demand and win complete power in the Italian government. Mussolini wanted to revive the greatness of ancient Rome and to create a 'New Roman Empire' for Italy, and it was under Fascism that many of the relics of ancient Rome were first opened up as public monuments in order to remind Italians of their great heritage. His greatest legacy, however, was the EUR suburb to the south—the projected site of a world exhibition for 1942, and a huge showcase of his preferred Fascist-classical architecture. Since the War Rome has continued to grow fat as the capital of the often ramshackle, notoriously corrupt, never-changing political system thrown up by the Italian Republic, and the headquarters of the smug *classe politica* that ran it. Nevertheless, Romans have joined in Italy's 'Moral Revolution', abusing the old-style political bosses like the rest of the country, despite the fact that a great many in this city of civil servants themselves benefited from the system. The city has been led by a mayor from the Green Party since 1993, and is currently in the throes of preparation for the Holy Year 2000. Many promises are being made for what will be one of the great tourist onslaughts of the century—local officials are estimating as many as 30 million visitors to the capital over the year. Just whether the city will get its act together in time remains to be seen.

Art and Architecture

The Etruscans

Although Rome stood on the fringes of the Etruscan world, the young city could hardly help being overwhelmed by the presence of a superior culture almost on its doorstep. Along with much of its religion, customs and its engineering talent, early Rome owed its first art to the enemies from the north. Thanks to the Villa Giulia Museum, Rome can show you much of the best of Etruscan art. Enigmatic, often fantastical, and always intensely vital, Etruria's artists stole from every Greek style and technique, and turned it into something uniquely their own.

The Romans Learn Building and Just Can't Stop

The Romans learned how to build roads and bridges from the Etruscans, perfected the art, and built works never dreamed of before. Speaking strictly of design, the outstanding fact of Roman building was its conservatism. Under the Republic, Rome adopted Greek architecture, with a predilection for the more delicate Corinthian order. When the money started rolling in, the Romans began to build in marble. But for 400 years, until the height of Empire under

Trajan and Hadrian, very little changed. As Rome became the capital of the Mediterranean, its rulers introduced new building types to embellish it: the series of *Imperial Fora*, variations on the Greek *agora*, the first of which was begun by Julius Caesar; *public baths*, a custom imported from Campania; *colonnaded streets*, as in Syria and Asia Minor; and *theatres*.

Concrete may not seem a very romantic subject, but in the hands of Imperial builders it changed both the theory and practice of architecture. Volcanic sand from the Bay of Naples, used with rubble as a filler, allowed the Romans to cover vast spaces cheaply. First in the palaces, and later in the Pantheon's giant concrete dome and in the huge public baths, an increasingly sophisticated use of arches and vaults was developed. Concrete seating made the Colosseum and the vast theatres possible, and allowed *insulae*—Roman apartment blocks—to climb six storeys and occasionally more. Near the Empire's end, the tendency towards gigantism becomes an enduring symptom of Roman decadence; the clumsy forms of late monsters like Diocletian's Baths and the Basilica of Maxentius show a technology far outstripping art.

Roman Sculpture, Painting and Mosaics

Even after the conquests of the 2nd century BC and the looting of the cultured East, it was a long time before Rome produced anything of its own. As in architecture, the other arts were dependent for centuries on the Greeks. Portrait sculpture, inherited from the Etruscans, is the notable exception, with a tradition of almost photographic busts and funeral reliefs. Sculpture, most of all, provides a vivid psychological record of Rome's history. In the 3rd century, as its confidence was undergoing its first crisis at the hands of German and Persian invaders, sculpture veers slowly towards the introverted and strange. Under the late Antonines the tendency is apparent, with grim, realistic battle scenes on Marcus Aurelius' column, and troubled portraits of the Emperor himself. Later portraits are even more unsettling, with rigid features and staring eyes, concerned more with psychological depth than outward appearances.

During the 3rd and 4th centuries there was little public art at all. There was a brief revival under Constantine, and no work better evokes the Rome of the psychotic, totalitarian late Empire than his weird, immense head in the Capitoline Museum. Gigantism survived the final disappearance of individuality and genuinely civic art, while the Imperial portraits freeze into eerie icons. Painting and mosaics were present from at least the 1st century BC, but Romans considered them little more than decoration, rarely entrusting to them any serious subjects.

Early Christian and Medieval Art

Almost from the beginning, Rome's Christians sought to express their faith in art. On dozens of finely carved sarcophagi and statues the figure of Christ is represented as the 'Good Shepherd', a beardless youth with a lamb slung over his shoulder. Occasionally he wears a Roman toga. Familiar New Testament scenes are common, along with figures of the early martyrs. The 4th-century building programme financed by Constantine filled Rome with imposing Christian basilicas, though little remains. Through the 5th and early 6th centuries, Christian art—now the only art permitted—changed little in style but broadened its subject matter, including scenes from the Old Testament and the Passion of Christ.

An impressive revival of Roman building came in the late 8th century, with peace, relative prosperity, and enlightened popes such as Hadrian, Leo III and Paschal I. New churches went up, decorated with mosaics by Greek artists. The return of hard times after the collapse of the Carolingian Empire put an end to this little Renaissance. When Rome began building again, it was largely with native artists, and stylistically there was almost a clean break with the past. The **Cosmati**, perhaps originally a single family, but eventually a name for a whole school, ground up fragments of coloured glass and precious stone and turned them into intricate pavements, altars, candlesticks and pulpits, geometrically patterned in styles derived from southern Italy, and ultimately from the Muslim world. Perhaps the greatest Roman artist of the Middle Ages was **Pietro Cavallini** (c. 1250–1330), whose freedom in composition and talent for expressive portraiture make him a genuine precursor of the Renaissance, equally at home in mosaics and fresco painting.

The Renaissance in Rome

Rome's High Renaissance begins with Julius II (1503–13). **Michelangelo Buonarroti** had already arrived, to amaze the world of art with his *Pietà* in St Peter's (1499), but the true inauguration of Rome's greatest artistic period was the arrival of **Donato Bramante**. This new marriage of the Renaissance and ancient Rome can best be seen at Bramante's *Tempietto* at S. Pietro in Montorio (1503), or at his cloister for S. Maria della Pace (1504).

For painting and sculpture, the High Renaissance meant a greater emphasis on emotion, dynamic movement and virtuosity. **Raphael**, following in Bramante's footsteps, arrived from Florence in 1508 and was the most influential painter of his time, with a virtuosity and sunny personality that patrons found irresistible. In the frescoes in the Vatican Stanze, he combined the grand manner from antique sculpture and the ancient approach to decoration from Nero's recently unearthed Golden House to create one of the definitive achievements of the age, and also excelled at portraiture, mythological frescoes, and even almost visionary religious work.

The Sack of Rome in 1527 rudely interrupted artistic endeavours, and many artists left Rome for ever. Among those who returned to Rome was, of course, Michelangelo, who in 1536 began the *Last Judgement* in the Sistine Chapel, whose sombre tones and subject matter illustrate more clearly than any other work the change in mood that had come over Roman art.

The Art of the Counter-Reformation

The Counter-Reformation and the Inquisition put a chill on the Italian imagination that would never really be dispelled. In 1563 the Council of Trent decreed the new order for art: it was to be conformist and naturalistic, propaganda entirely in the service of the totalitarian Church, with a touch of Spanish discipline and emotionalism. Rome was to become the symbol of the Church resurgent, the most modern and beautiful city in the world. Under Sixtus V, **Domenico Fontana** and other architects planned a scheme to unite the sprawling medieval city with a network of straight avenues sighted on obelisks in the major piazzas.

The Age of Baroque

During this period art was reduced to mere decoration, forbidden to entertain any thoughts that might be politically dangerous or subversive to Church dogma. But in this captive art there was still talent and will enough for new advances to be made, particularly in architecture. Plenty of churches, fountains and palaces were built, and there was every opportunity for experimentation. In sculpture it meant a new emphasis on cascading drapery and exaggerated poses, typecasting emotion, saintliness or virtue in a way the Renaissance would have found slightly trashy. Here **Bernini** led the way, with such works as his early *David* in the Galleria Borghese (1623). Painting however was on a definite downward spiral, though one usually had to look up to see it. Decorative ceiling frescoes, such as those of **Pietro da Cortona**, were all the rage, though few artists could bring anything like Cortona's talent to the job.

The Last of Roman Art

From Rome, the art of the High Baroque reached out to all Europe—just as the last traces of inspiration were dying out in the city itself. After the death of Pope Alexander VII (1667) there was less money and less intelligent patronage, and by this time, a more introspective Rome was looking backwards. Meaningful sculpture and painting were gone for ever.

In the 19th century art in Rome continued to lose ground. After 1870 the fathers of the new Italy believed that liberation and Italian unity would unleash a wave of creativity, and they spent tremendous sums to help it along. They were mistaken. The sepulchral, artless monuments they imposed on Rome helped ruin the fabric of the city and provided an enduring reminder of the sterility of the Risorgimento and the subsequent corrupt regimes. Mussolini too wanted his revolution to have its artistic expression. The sort of painting and sculpture his government preferred is best not examined too closely, but his architecture, mashing up Art Deco simplicity with historical pomposity, now and then reached beyond the level of the ridiculous. Rome today is moribund as an art centre, and even architecture has not recovered. There are no first-rate contemporary buildings. Not few—none. Efforts at planning the city's post-War growth resulted in confusion and concrete madness, and the hideous apartment and office blocks of the suburbs. Until recently it seemed impossible that Rome could ever again produce inspired architecture. However, Paolo Portoghesi's mosque, a playful postmodern extravaganza out near the Villa Ada, could be a sign that the tide is about to turn.

A Little Orientation

two walls

Of Rome's earliest wall, built by King Servius Tullius before the republic was founded, little remains; you can see one of the last surviving bits right outside Stazione Termini. The second, built by Aurelian in AD 275, is one of the wonders of Rome. With its 19km length and 383 towers, it is one of the largest ever built in Europe—and certainly the best-preserved of antiquity. In several places you can see almost perfectly preserved bastions and monumental gates.

three Romes

Classical Rome began on the Monte Palatino, and all through its history its business and administrative centre stayed nearby, in the original Forum and the great Imperial Fora. Many of the busiest parts of the city lay to the south. After Rome's fall these areas were never really rebuilt, and even now substantial ruins like Trajan's Baths remain unexcavated. The Second Rome, that of the popes, had its centre in the Campus Martius, the plain west and north of the Monte Capitolino, later expanding to include the 'Leonine City' around St Peter's and the new Baroque district around Piazza del Popolo and the Spanish Steps. The Third Rome, capital of united Italy, has expanded in all directions, its centre the Via del Corso.

seven hills

Originally they were much higher; centuries of building, rebuilding and river flooding have made the ground level in the valleys much higher, and various emperors and popes have shaved bits off the tops. The **Monte Capitolino**, smallest but most important, now has Rome's city hall, the Campidoglio, roughly on the site of ancient Rome's greatest temple, that of Jupiter Greatest and Best. The **Palatino** was originally the most fashionable district, and eventually got entirely covered by the palaces of the emperors. The usually plebeian **Aventino** lies to the south, across from the Circus Maximus. Between the Colosseum and the Stazione Termini, the **Esquilino**, the **Viminale** and the **Quirinale** stand in a row. The Quirinale was

Rome

Galleria Nazionale d'Arte Moderna
Museo Nazionale di Villa Giulia
Villa
Stazione Roma-Viterbo
Piazzale Clodio
Piazza G. Mazzini
Largo Trionfale
Piazzale degli Eroi
Piazzale Flaminio
Monte Pincio
Pza. del Popolo
S. Maria Del Popolo
Villa Medici
Spanish Steps
Trinità del Monte
Piazza del Risorgimento
Musei Vaticani
Castel S.Angelo
Piazza Cavour
Mausoleum of Augustus
Ara Pacis
Pza Silvestro
Palazzo di Montecitorio
Fontana di Trevi
CITTÀ DEL VATICANO
Basílica di San Pietro
Piazza S. Pietro
Ospedale di S. Spirito
Tévere (Tiber)
Palazzo Madama
Piazza della Rotonda
Piazza Colonna
Borsa
S. Ignazio
S. Onofrio
Chiesa Nuova
Piazza Navona
Pantheon
Palazzo Doria Pamphili
Chiesa del Gesù
Vittoriano
Piazza Venezia
Teatro di Pompeo
Palazzo Farnese
Palazzo Spada
Piazza Campo de'Fiori
S. Maria d. Quercia
Palazzo Venezia
S. Maria in Aracoeli
Musei Capitolini
Galleria Corsini
Villa Farnesina
Sinagoga
Teatro di Marcello
Monte Capitolino
AURELIO
Villa Abamelek
Piazzale Giuseppe Garibaldi
S. Pietro in Montorio
Pza. S. Maria in Trast.
Pza. G. Belli
Torre di Anguillara
Isola Tiberina
Piazza Bocca della Verità
Villa Doria Pamphili
Villa Aurelia
S.Maria in Trastevere
Pza. S. Cosimato
S. Crisogano
S. Cecelia
S. Sabina
Villa Doria Pamphili
Ponte Sublicio
Prioria delle Cav. di Malta
S. Prisca
S. Alessio
Monte Aventino
Piazza Albania
Tévere
Monte Testaccio
Cimitero Protestante
Piramide
Piazza Porta S. Paolo
Porto S. Paolo
Stazione Roma-Lido di Ostia
Airport Bus Stop
Stazione Roma-Ostiense
Stazione Trastevere (100 metres)

········ Metropolitana

1 km

½ mile

N

72

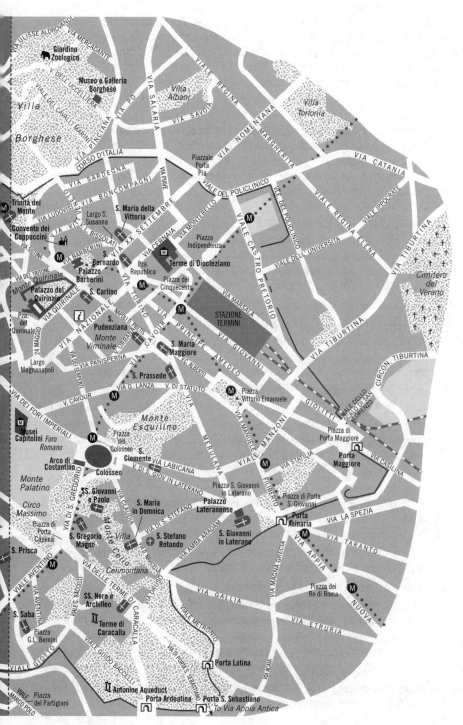

the residence of the popes, and later of the Italian kings. The **Monte Celio**, south of the Colosseum, is now a charming oasis of parkland and ancient churches in the centre of Rome. Rome has other hills not included in the canonical seven: **Monte Vaticano**, from which the Vatican takes its name, **Monte Pincio**, including the Villa Borghese, Rome's biggest park, and the **Gianicolo**, the long ridge above Trastevere the ancients called the Janiculum.

Getting Around

Looking at the map, Rome seems to be a city made for getting around on foot. This may be so in the *centro storico* around Piazza Navona, but elsewhere it's deceptive— it will always take you longer than you think to walk anywhere. If you fancy more of a stroll, head for the old districts west of the Corso, around the Tiber Island, in the old parts of Trastevere and around the Monte Celio.

by Metro

The two Metro lines, A and B, cross at Stazione Termini; one or the other will take you to the Colosseum, around the Monte Aventino, to Piazza di Spagna, St John Lateran, St Paul's outside the walls, Piazza del Popolo, or within eight blocks of St Peter's. Single tickets (*L1500*), also good for city buses—within 75mins of valida- tion—are available from Metro stations and tobacconists, bars and newspaper kiosks.

by bus and tram

Buses are by far the best way to get around. Pick up a map of the bus routes from the **ATAC** (city bus company) information booth outside Stazione Termini. Bus tickets cost L1500, and are good for travel on any ATAC city bus or tram and one Metro ride; they must be stamped in the machines in the back entrance of buses or trams or in the Metro turnstiles. There are also special-price full-day, weekly and monthly passes.

by taxi

It's easiest to get official taxis (painted yellow or white) at a rank (in most of the main piazzas). To phone for a taxi, call ✆ 06 3570, or ✆ 06 4994; there's no specific surcharge, but expect to pay for the time it takes for it to reach you.

Tourist Information

EPT: main office: Via Parigi 5, ✆ 06 4889 9253 (*open Mon–Fri 8.15–7.15, Sat 8.15–1.30*); also Stazione Termini, Fiumicino Airport, the Colosseum, Castel Sant'Angelo and Via Nazionale next to Palazzo Esposizione (*all slightly varying hours*).

Two weeklies available from news-stands, *Roma c'e'* (with a short English section at the back) and *Time Out* (in Italian) have listings for arts, culture and entertainment.

General emergencies, 113.

24-hour pharmacies: Piram, Via Nazionale 228, ✆ 06 488 0754; **Arenula**, Via Arenula 73, ✆ 06 6880 3278. Duty pharmacists are listed outside all pharmacies.

Outside banking hours money can be exchanged at **American Express**, Piazza di Spagna 38, ✆ 06 67641 (*open Mon–Fri 9–5.30, Sat 9–12.30*); **Thomas Cook**, Via della Conciliazione 23–25, ✆ 06 6830 0435 (*open Mon–Sat 8.30–6, Sun 9–1.30*).

Main post office: Piazza San Silvestro, ✆ 06 6771 (*open Mon–Fri 8.30–6, Sat and Sun 8.30–2; other branches generally open 8.30–1.30*).

Piazza Venezia

This traffic-crazed, thoroughly awful piazza may be a poor introduction to Rome, but it makes a good place to start, with the ruins of old Rome on one side and the boutiques and bureaucracies of the new city on the other. The piazza takes its name from the **Palazzo Venezia**, built for Pope Paul II in 1455, but long the Embassy of the Venetian Republic. Mussolini made it his residence, leaving a light on all night to make the Italians think he was working. His famous balcony, from which he would declaim to the 'oceanic' crowds in the square (renamed the Forum of the Fascist Empire in those days) still holds its prominent place, a bad memory for the Italians. Nowadays the palazzo holds a **museum** of Renaissance and Baroque decorative arts (*open Tues–Sat 9–1.30, Sun 9–1; adm exp*).

Long ago the southern edge of this piazza had approaches up to the Capitoline Hill. The hill is still there, though it's now entirely blocked out by the mammoth white bulk of the **Altar of the Nation** (also known as the *Vittoriano*, the Vittorio Emanuele Monument or, less respectfully, the 'Wedding Cake' or the 'Typewriter'), Risorgimento Italy's own self-inflicted satire and one of the world's apotheoses of kitsch.

The Capitoline Hill

Behind the *Vittoriano*, two stairways lead to the top of the hill. This is a fateful spot; in 121 BC the great reformer Tiberius Gracchus was murdered here by what today would be called a 'right-wing death squad'. Almost a millennium and a half later Cola di Rienzo was trying to escape Rome in disguise when an enraged mob recognized him by the rings on his fingers and tore him to pieces. Rienzo built the left-hand staircase, and was the first to climb it. It leads to the church of **Santa Maria in Aracoeli**, begun in the 7th century over the temple of Juno Moneta—the ancient Roman Mint was adjacent to it. The Aracoeli, which in Rienzo's time served as a sort of council hall for the Romans, is one of the most revered of Roman churches.

The second stairway takes you to the real heart of Rome, Michelangelo's **Piazza del Campidoglio**, passing on the way a rather flattering statue of Rienzo set on a bronze pedestal. At the top, bordering the piazza, a formidable cast of statues includes the Dioscuri, who come from Pompey's Theatre, and Marforio (in the Capitoline Museum courtyard), a river god once employed as one of the 'talking statues' of Rome, decorated with graffiti and placards commenting on current events. The great 2nd-century bronze equestrian statue of the benign and philosophical emperor **Marcus Aurelius**, that stood on the plinth in the middle of the piazza from the 16th century until 1981, has been fully restored and regilded and is now on show in the security of the Capitoline Museums. Fortunately enough, since it was an old Roman saying that the world would end when all the original gold flaked off. The Christians of old only refrained from melting him down for cash because they believed he was not Marcus Aurelius, but Constantine. A copy of the original now stands at the centre of the piazza.

The Capitoline Museums

Michelangelo's original plans may have been adapted and tinkered with by later architects, but nevertheless his plan for the Campidoglio has come out as one of the triumphs of Renaissance design. The centrepiece, the **Palazzo Senatorio**, Rome's city hall, with its distinctive stairway and bell tower, is built over the ruins of the Roman *tabularium*, the state archive. At the base of the stair note the statue of Minerva, in her aspect as the allegorical goddess Roma.

Flanking it, Michelangelo redesigned the façade of **Palazzo dei Conservatori** (on the right), and projected the matching building across the square, **Palazzo Nuovo**, built in the early 18th century. Together they make up the **Capitoline Museums**. Founded by Pope Clement XII in 1734, and so the oldest true museum in the world, the Capitoline (*open Tues–Sun 9–7; adm*) displays both the heights and depths of ancient society and culture. For the heights, there are the reliefs from the triumphal arch of Marcus Aurelius—first-class work in scenes of the emperor's clemency and piety, and his triumphal receptions in Rome. Marcus always looks a little worried in these, perhaps considering his good-for-nothing son Commodus, and the empire he would inherit, sinking into corruption and excess. What was to come is well illustrated by the degenerate art of the 4th century, like the colossal bronze head, hand and foot of Constantine, parts of a colossal statue in the Basilica of Maxentius (now in the courtyard).

In between these extremes come roomfuls of statuary, including the famous *Capitoline She-Wolf*, the very symbol of Rome; statues of most of the emperors, busts of Homer, Sophocles and Pythagoras; the voluptuous *Capitoline Venus*; a big baby Hercules (who may have inspired Donatello's famous *Amor* in Florence); and the *Muse Polyhymnia*, one of the most delightful and beautiful statues of antiquity. Later works include lots of papal paraphernalia, a statue of Charles of Anjou by Florence's Arnolfo di Cambio and—in a small **Pinacoteca** in the Palazzo dei Conservatori—some dignified Velázquez gentlemen looking scornfully at the other paintings and two major works by Caravaggio, the *Fortune Teller* and *John the Baptist*. There are also some lovely, though at times silly, 18th-century porcelains—orchestras of monkeys in powdered wigs, and such.

From behind the Palazzo Senatorio a stairway leads down, offering the best overview of the Forum; the entrance is a little further down Via dei Fori Imperiali. The southern end of the Capitol, one of the quietest corners of Rome, was the site of Jupiter Optimus Maximus (Greatest and Best), a temple built originally by the Etruscan kings. At the time it was the largest in Italy, testimony to Rome's importance as far back as 450 BC. Along the southern edge of the hill, the cliffs you see are the somewhat reduced remains of the **Tarpeian Rock**, from which traitors and other malefactors were thrown in Rome's early days.

Along the Tiber

The early emperors did their best to import classical Greek drama to Rome, and for a while, with the poets of the Latin New Comedy, it seemed the Romans would carry on the tradition. Great theatres were built in Rome, like the **Theatre of Marcellus** at the foot of the Capitoline, begun by Caesar and completed by Augustus. By the 2nd century AD, however, theatre had already begun to degenerate into music-hall shows, lewd performances with naked actresses and grisly murders (condemned prisoners were sometimes butchered on stage), and shows by celebrity actors probably much like some unseemly spectacles of our own time. Marcellus' theatre (Augustus named it after his favourite nephew) survived into the Middle Ages, when the Orsini family converted it into their palace-fortress, the strongest in Rome after the Castel Sant'Angelo. Today it presents one of Rome's more curious sights, the tall arches of the circumference surmounted by the rough medieval walls of the Orsini.

The streets to the west contain a mix of some of Rome's oldest houses with new buildings; the latter have replaced the old walled **ghetto**, demolished only a century ago. There has been a sizeable Jewish community in Rome since Pompey and Titus first brought them to Rome as slaves. They helped finance the career of Julius Caesar, who would prove to be their greatest benefactor. For centuries they lived near this bend in the river and in Trastevere. Paul IV took time off from burning books and heretics to wall them into the tiny ghetto in 1555; at the same time he forced them to wear orange hats, attend Mass on Sunday, and limited them to the rag and old iron trades. Tearing down the ghetto walls was one of the first acts of the Italian kingdom after the entry into Rome in 1870. The exotic, eclectic main **synagogue** was built in 1904, after the last of the ghetto was demolished.

Opposite the synagogue, the **Tiber Island** is joined to both sides of the river by surviving ancient bridges. In Imperial times, the island was sacred to Aesculapius, god of healing; a legend records how some serpents brought from the god's shrine in Greece escaped and swam to the spot, choosing the site by divine guidance. Now, as in ancient times, most of the lovely island is taken up by a hospital, the Ospedale Fatebenefratelli; in place of the Temple of Aesculapius, there is also the church of **San Bartolomeo**, most recently rebuilt in the 1690s.

Piazza Bocca della Verità

Tourists almost always overlook this beautiful corner along the Tiber, but here you can see two well-preserved Roman temples. Both have probably been conventionally misnamed, the round **Temple of Vesta**, used as an Armenian church in the Middle Ages, and the **Temple of Fortuna Virilis**—it now seems almost certain that they were actually dedicated to Hercules Victor and Portunus (the god of harbours) respectively. Some bits of an exotic, ornate Roman cornice are built into the brick building opposite, part of the **House of the Crescenzi**, a powerful family in the 9th century, descended from Theodora Senatrix. Look over the side of the Tiber embankment here, and you can see the outlet of the **Cloaca Maxima**, the great ancient sewer begun by King Tarquin. Big enough to drive two carriages through, it is still in use today. Just upstream, past the Palatine Bridge, a single arch decorated with dragons in the middle of the river is all that remains of the ancient *Pons Aemilius*. Originally built in the 2nd century BC, it collapsed twice and was last restored in 1575 by Gregory XIII, only to fall down again 20 years later. Now it is familiarly known as the 'broken bridge', or **Ponte Rotto**.

Across from the temples, the handsome medieval church with the lofty campanile is **Santa Maria in Cosmedin**, built over an altar of Hercules in the 6th century and given to Byzantine Greeks escaping from the Iconoclast heretic emperors in the 8th. The name (like 'cosmetic') means 'decorated', but little of the original art has survived; most of what you see is from the 12th century, including some fine Cosmatesque work inside. In the portico, an ancient, ghostly image in stone built into the walls has come down in legend as the Bocca della Verità—the 'Mouth of Truth'. Medieval Romans would swear oaths and close business deals here; if you tell a lie with your hand in the image's mouth he will most assuredly bite your fingers off. Try it.

The Heart of Ancient Rome

In the 1930s Mussolini built the **Via dei Fori Imperiali**, a grand boulevard between the Vittoriano and the Colosseum designed to ease traffic congestion and show off the ancient sites, and named after the Imperial Fora which it partly covers. The **Imperial Fora** of Augustus, Nerva and Trajan were built to relieve congestion in the original Roman Forum. **Trajan's Forum**, built with the spoils of his conquest of Dacia (modern Romania), was perhaps the grandest architectural and planning conception ever built in Rome, a broad square surrounded by colonnades, with a huge basilica flanked by two libraries and a covered market outside. A large part of **Trajan's Market** still stands, with entrances on Via IV Novembre and down the stairs just to the side of the Trajan Column (*open Tues–Sun 9–one hour before sunset; adm*).

Behind it, you can see Rome's own leaning tower, built in the 12th century and called the **Torre delle Milizie**. All that remains of Trajan's great square is some paving and its centre-piece, the **Trajan Column**. The spiralling bands of sculptural reliefs, illustrating the Dacian Wars, reach to the top, some 100ft high. They rank with the greatest works of Roman art. Plaster casts taken during a lengthy restoration are on display at the Museum of Roman Civilization in the EUR suburb. Behind the column, the church of **Santa Maria di Loreto** is a somewhat garish High Renaissance bauble, built by Bramante and Antonio da Sangallo the Younger, starting in 1501. The Romans liked it so much they built another one just like it next door, the **Santissimo Nome di Maria**, from the 1730s. Scanty remains of the **Forum of Caesar** and the **Forum of Augustus** can be seen along the boulevard to the south.

The Roman Forum

For a place that was once the centre of the Mediterranean world, there is surprisingly little to see; centuries of use as a quarry have seen to that. The word *forum* originally meant 'outside' (like the Italian *fuori*), a marketplace outside the original Rome that became the centre of both government and business as the city expanded around it. The entrances are on the Via dei Fori Imperiali at Via Cavour, and at the end of the ramp that approaches the Forum from the Colosseum side (*open April–Oct daily 9–one hour before sunset; May–Sept Mon–Sat 9–3, Sun 9–1*).

The **Via Sacra**, ancient Rome's most important street, runs the length of the Forum. At the end of it beneath the Capitol you will be facing the **Arch of Septimius Severus** (AD 203), with reliefs of some rather trivial victories over the Arabs and Parthians; conservative Romans of the time must have strongly resented this upstart African emperor planting his monument in such an important spot. The arch also commemorated Septimius' two sons, Geta and Caracalla; when the nasty Caracalla did his brother in, he had his name effaced from it. In front of it, the **Lapis Niger**, a mysterious stone with an underground chamber beneath it, is the legendary tomb of Romulus. The inscription down below—a threat against the profaning of this sacred spot—is one of the oldest ever found in the Latin language. The famous Golden Milestone also stood here, the 'umbilicus' of Rome and the point from which all distances in the Empire were measured. To the right is the **Curia** (the Senate House), heavily restored after centuries' use as a church (the good Baroque church behind it is **SS. Luca e Martina**, built by Pietro di Cortona in the 1660s). To the left of the arch the remains of a raised stone area were the **Rostra**, the speakers' platform in public assemblies under the republic, decorated with ships' prows (*rostra*) taken in a sea-battle about

320 BC. Of the great temples on the Capitol slope only a few columns remain; from left to right, the **Temple of Saturn**, which served as Rome's treasury, the **Temple of Vespasian** (three columns standing) and the **Temple of Concord**, built by Tiberius to honour the peace—so to speak—that the emperors had enforced between the patricians and plebeians.

Behind the Rostra, in the open area once decorated with statues and monuments, the simple standing **column** was placed by the Romans in honour of Phocas, Byzantine Emperor in 608—the last monument ever erected in the Forum, and they had to steal the column from a ruined building. Just behind it a small pool once marked the spot of one of ancient Rome's favourite legends. In 362 BC, according to Livy, an abyss suddenly opened across the Forum, and the sibyls predicted that it would not close unless the 'things that Rome held most precious' were thrown in. A consul, Marcus Curtius, took this as meaning a Roman citizen and soldier. He leapt in fully armed, horse and all, and the crack closed over him.

This section of the Forum was bordered by two imposing buildings, the **Basilica Aemilia** to the north and the **Basilica Julia** to the south, built by Caesar with the spoils of the Gallic Wars. The **Temple of Caesar** closes the east end, built by Augustus as a visual symbol of the new Imperial mythology. The adjacent **Temple of the Dioscuri** makes a good example of how temples were used in ancient times. This one was a meeting hall for men of the equestrian class (the knights, though they were really more likely to be businessmen); they had safe-deposit boxes in the basement, where the standard weights and measures of the Empire were kept. Between them, the round pedestal was the foundation of the small **Temple of Vesta**, where the sacred hearth-fire was kept burning by the Vestal Virgins; ruins of their extensive apartments can be seen next door.

Two more Christian churches stand in this part of the Forum. **SS. Cosma e Damiano** was built on to the **Temple of Antoninus Pius and Faustina** in the 6th century; most of the columns of the temple survive, with a fine sculptural frieze of griffons on top. **Santa Francesca Romana** is built over a corner of ancient Rome's largest temple, that of **Venus and Rome**. The temple, built by Hadrian, was a curious, double-ended shrine to the state cult; one side devoted to the goddess Roma and the other to Venus—in the Imperial mythology she was the ancestress of the family of the Caesars. The church entrance is outside the Forum, but the adjoining convent, inside the monumental area, houses the **Antiquarium Forense**, with a small collection of Iron Age burial urns and other paraphernalia from the Forum excavations. Between the two churches the mastodonic **Basilica of Maxentius**, finished by Constantine, remains the largest ruin of the Forum, its clumsy arches providing an illustration of the ungainly but technically sophisticated 4th century.

Near the exit the **Arch of Titus** commemorates the victories of Titus and his father Vespasian over the rebellious Jews (AD 60–80), one of the fiercest struggles Rome ever had to fight. The reliefs on the arch show some of the booty being carted through Rome in the triumphal parade—including the famous seven-branched golden candlestick from the holy of holies in the Temple at Jerusalem. South of the arch a path leads up to the **Palatine Hill** (*open April–Oct daily 9–one hour before sunset; May–Sept Mon–Sat 9–3, Sun 9–1; adm*). Here, overlooking the little corner of the ancient world that gave our language words like *senate*, *committee*, *rostrum*, *republic*, *plebiscite* and *magistrate*, you can leave democracy behind and visit the etymological birthplace of *palace*. The ruins of the imperial *Palatium* once covered the entire hill. As with the Forum, almost all the stone has been cannibalized, and there's little to see of what was once a palace complex three-quarters of a kilometre long, to which a dozen of the emperors contributed. There are good views across the Circus Maximus from just above what was once a big portico from which the Emperor could watch the races. Don't miss the chance to take a stroll through the gardens planted by the Farnese family over what were the Imperial servants' quarters—one of the most peaceful spots in the city.

The Colosseum

Its real name was the Flavian Amphitheatre, after the family of emperors who built it, beginning with Vespasian in AD 72; Colosseum refers to the *Colossus*, a huge gilded statue of Nero (erected by himself, of course) that had formerly stood in the square in front. There doesn't seem to be much evidence that Christians were literally thrown to lions here—there were other places for that—but what did go on was perhaps the grossest and best-organized perversity in all history. Gladiatorial contests began under the Republic, designed to make Romans better soldiers by rendering them indifferent to the sight of death. Later emperors introduced new displays—men versus animals, lions versus elephants, women versus dwarfs, sea-battles (the arena could be flooded at a moment's notice), public tortures of condemned criminals, and even genuine athletics, a Greek import the Romans never much cared for. In one memorable day of games, 5000 animals were slaughtered, about one every 10 seconds. The native elephant and lion of North Africa and Arabia are extinct thanks to such shenanigans.

However hideous its purpose, the Colosseum ranks with the greatest works of Roman architecture and engineering; all modern stadiums have copied most of its general plan. One surprising feature was a removable awning that covered the stands. A detachment of sailors from Cape Misenum was kept to operate it; they also manned the galleys in the mock sea-battles. Originally there were statues in all of the arches and a ring of bronze shields all around the cornice. The concrete stands have eroded away, showing the brick structure underneath. Renaissance and Baroque popes hauled away half the travertine exterior—enough to build the Palazzo Venezia, the Palazzo Barberini, a few other palaces and bridges and part of St Peter's. Almost all of the construction work under Vespasian and Titus was performed by Jewish slaves, brought here for the purpose after the suppression of their revolt (*open Tues–Sat 9–one hour before sunset, Sun and Mon 9–2; adm*).

Just outside the Colosseum, the **Arch of Constantine** marks the end of the ancient Triumphal Way (now Via di San Gregorio) where victorious emperors and their troops would parade their captives and booty. The arch, with a coy inscription mentioning Constantine's 'divine inspiration' (the Romans weren't sure whether it was yet respectable to mention Christianity), is covered with reliefs stolen from older arches and public buildings—a sad commentary on the state of art in Constantine's day.

San Clemente

This church, a little way to the east of the Colosseum on Via San Giovanni in Laterano, is one of the more fascinating remnants of Rome's many-layered history. One of the first substantial building projects of the Christians in Rome, the original basilica of *c.* 375 burned along with the rest of the quarter during a sacking by the Normans in 1084. It was rebuilt soon afterwards with a new Cosmatesque pavement, and the 6th-century choir screen—a rare example of sculpture from that ungifted time—saved from the original church. The 12th-century mosaic in the apse represents the *Triumph of the Cross*, and the chapel at the entrance contains a beautiful series of quattrocento frescoes by Masolino, partly uncovered after restoration. From a vestibule, nuns sell tickets to the **Lower Church** (*open daily 9–12 and 3.30–6.30; adm*).

This is the lower half of the original San Clemente, and there are remarkable, though deteriorated, frescoes from the 900s and the 12th century, some of the oldest medieval paintings to have survived anywhere in Italy. The plaque from Bulgaria, mentioned on p.62, commemorates SS. Cyril and Methodius, who went from this church to spread the Gospel among the Slavs; they translated the Bible into Old Slavonic, and invented the first Slavic alphabet (Cyrillic) to do it.

From here, steps lead down to the lowest stratum, 1st- and 2nd-century AD buildings divided by an alley; this includes the **Mithraeum**, the best-preserved temple of its kind after the one in Capua. The larger, neighbouring building was filled with rubble to serve as a foundation for the basilica, and the apse was later added over the Mithraeum. Father Mulhooly of Boston started excavating in the 1860s, and later excavations have revealed a Mithraic antechamber with a fine stuccoed ceiling, the Mithraic school with an early fresco, and the temple proper, a small cavern-like hall with benches for the initiates to share a ritual supper.

Mithraism was a mystery religion, full of secrets closely held by the initiates (all male, and largely soldiers) and it is difficult to say what else went on down here. Two altars were found, each with the usual image of the Persian-import god Mithras dispatching a white bull, including a snake, a scorpion and a crow, and astrological symbolism in the decorative scheme. Underneath all this, there is yet a fourth building level, some foundations from the Republican era. At the end of the 1st-century building you can look down into an ancient sewer or underground stream, one of a thousand entrances to the surreal sub-Roma of endless subterranean caves, buildings, rivers and lakes, mostly unexplored and unexplorable. A century ago a schoolboy fell in the water here; they found him, barely alive, in open country several kilometres from the city.

Along Corso Vittorio Emanuele

This street, chopped through the medieval centre of Rome in the 1880s, still hasn't quite been assimilated into its surroundings; nevertheless, this ragged, smoky traffic tunnel will come in handy when you find yourself lost in the tortuous, meandering streets of Rome's oldest quarter. Starting west from Piazza Venezia, the church of the **Gesù** (1568–84) was a landmark for a new era and the new aesthetic of cinquecento Rome. The transitional, pre-Baroque fashion was often referred to as the 'Jesuit style', and here in the Jesuits' head church architects Vignola and della Porta first laid down Baroque's cardinal principle: an intimation of Paradise for the impressionable through decorative excess. It hasn't aged well, though at the time it must have seemed to most Romans a perfect marriage of Renaissance art and a reformed, revitalized faith. St Ignatius, the Jesuits' founder, is buried in the left transept right under the altar, Spanish-style; the globe incorporated in the sculpted Trinity overhead is the biggest piece of lapis lazuli in the world. A little way further west the street opens into a ghastly square called Largo Argentina. Remains of several Republican-era temples, unearthed far below ground level, can be seen in the square's centre.

One of the earliest and best of the palaces on Corso Vittorio Emanuele, the delicate **Piccola Farnesina** by Antonio da Sangallo the Younger, houses another little museum, a collection of ancient sculpture called the **Museo Barracco** (*open Tues–Sat 9–7, Sun 9–1.30; adm*). A third museum—not a well-known one—is just around the corner from Sant'Andrea on Via Sudario. The **Burcardo Theatre Museum** (*open by appointment, call the custodian, © 06 684 0001*) is a collection of fascinating old relics from the Roman theatrical tradition.

The biggest palace on the street, attributed to Bramante, is **Palazzo della Cancelleria**, once the seat of the papal municipal government. St Philip Neri, the gifted, irascible holy man who is patron saint of Rome, built the **Chiesa Nuova** near the eastern end of the Corso (1584). Philip was quite a character, with something of the Zen Buddhist in him. He forbade his followers any sort of philosophical speculation or dialectic, but made them sing and recite poetry; two of his favourite pastimes were insulting popes and embarrassing new initiates— making them walk through Rome with a foxtail sewn to the back of their coat to learn humility. As was common in those times, sincere faith and humility were eventually translated into flagrant Baroque. The Chiesa Nuova is one of the larger and fancier of the species. Its altarpiece is a *Madonna with Angels* by Rubens. Even more flagrant, outside the church you can see the curved arch-Baroque façade of the **Philippine Oratory** by Borromini. The form of music called the *oratorio* takes its name from this chapel.

Campo de' Fiori

Around Campo de' Fiori, one of the spots dearest to the hearts of Romans themselves, you may think yourself in the middle of some scruffy south Italian village. Rome's market square, disorderly, cramped and chaotic, is easily the liveliest corner of the city, full of market barrows, buskers, teenage bohemians and the folkloresque types who have lived here all their lives—the least decorous and worst-dressed crowd in Rome. During papal rule the old square was also used for executions—most notoriously the burning of Giordano Bruno in 1600. This well-travelled philosopher was the first to take Copernican astronomy to its logical extremes— an infinite universe with no centre, no room for heaven, and nothing eternal but change. The Church had few enemies more dangerous. Italy never forgot him; the statue of Bruno in Campo de' Fiori went up only a few years after the end of papal rule.

Just east of the square, the heap of buildings around Piazzetta di Grottapinta is built over the cavea of **Pompey's Theatre**, ancient Rome's biggest. This complex included a *curia*, where Julius Caesar was assassinated in 44 BC. Walk south from Campo de' Fiori, and you will be thrown back from cosy medievalism into the High Renaissance with the **Palazzo Farnese**, one of the definitive works of that Olympian style. The younger Sangallo began it in 1514, and Michelangelo contributed to the façades and interiors.

The building now serves as the French Embassy, and it isn't easy to get in to see it. Most of the palaces that fill up this neighbourhood have one thing in common—they were made possible by someone's accession to the papacy, the biggest jackpot available to any aspiring Italian family. Built on the pennies of the faithful, they provide the most outrageous illustration of Church corruption at the dawn of the Reformation. Alessandro Farnese, who as Paul III was a clever and effective pope—though perhaps the greatest nepotist ever to decorate St Peter's throne—managed to build this palace 20 years before his election, with the income from his 16 absentee bishoprics.

Palazzo Spada, just to the east along Via Capo di Ferro, was the home of a mere cardinal, but its florid stucco façade (1540) almost upstages the Farnese. Inside, the **Galleria Spada** (*open Tues–Sat 9–7, Sun 9–1; adm*) is one of Rome's great collections of 16th- and 17th-century painting. Guido Reni, Guercino and the other favourites of the age are well represented. To the south, close to the Tiber, **Via Giulia** was laid out by Pope Julius II: a famous and pretty thoroughfare lined with churches and palazzi from that time. Many artists (successful ones) have lived here, including Raphael.

Piazza Navona

In 1477 the area now covered by one of Rome's most beautiful piazzas was a half-forgotten field full of huts and vineyards, tucked inside the still-imposing ruins of the Stadium of Domitian. A redevelopment of the area covered the long grandstands with new houses, but the decoration had to wait for the Age of Baroque. In 1644, with the election of Innocent X, it was the Pamphili family that won the papal sweepstakes. Innocent, a great grafter and such a villainous pope that when he died no one—not even his newly wealthy relatives—would pay for a proper burial, built the ornate **Palazzo Pamphili** (now the Brazilian Embassy) and hired Borromini to complete the gaudy church of **Sant'Agnese in Agone**, begun by Carlo and Girolamo Rainaldi.

Borromini's arch-rival, Bernini, got the commission for the piazza's famous fountains; the central **Fountain of the Four Rivers** is Bernini's masterpiece, Baroque at its flashiest and most likeable. Among the travertine grottoes and fantastical flora and fauna under the obelisk, the four colossal figures represent the Ganges, Danube, Rio de la Plata and Nile (with the veiled head because its source was unknown). Bernini also designed the smaller fountain, the **Fontana del Moro**, at the southern end. Off the southern end of the piazza, at the back of Palazzo Braschi, **Pasquino** is the original Roman 'talking statue', embellished with placards and graffiti ('pasquinades') since the 1500s—one of his favourite subjects in those days was the insatiable pigginess of families like the Farnese; serious religious issues were usually too hot to touch, even for a statue.

The Pantheon

When we consider the fate of so many other great buildings of ancient Rome we begin to understand what a slim chance it was that allowed this one to come down to us. The first Pantheon was built in 27 BC by Agrippa, Emperor Augustus' son-in-law and right-hand man, but was destroyed by fire and replaced by the present temple in 119–28 by the Emperor Hadrian, though, curiously, retaining Agrippa's original inscription on the pediment. Its history has been precarious ever since. In 609 the empty Pantheon was consecrated to Christianity as 'St Mary of the Martyrs'. Becoming a church is probably what saved it, though the Byzantines hauled away the gilded bronze roof tiles soon after, and for a while in the Middle Ages the portico saw use as a fish market. The Pantheon's greatest enemy, however, was Gian Lorenzo Bernini. He not only 'improved' it with a pair of Baroque belfries over the porch (demolished in 1887), but he had Pope Urban VIII take down the bronze covering on the inside of the dome to use the metal for his *baldacchino* over the altar at St Peter's. Supposedly there was enough left over to make the Pope 60 cannons.

Looking at the outside you may notice the building seems perilously unsound. There is no way a simple vertical wall can support such a heavy, shallow dome (steep domes push downwards, shallow ones outwards). Obviously the walls will tumble at any moment. That is a little joke the Roman architects are playing on us, for here they are showing off their engineering virtuosity as shamelessly as in the Colosseum, or the aqueduct with four storeys of arches that used to run up to the Palatine Hill. The wall that looks so fragile is really 25ft thick and the dome on top isn't a dome at all; the real, hemispherical dome lies underneath, resting easily on the walls inside. The ridges you see on the upper dome are courses of cantilevered bricks, effectively almost weightless.

The real surprise, however, lies behind the enormous original bronze doors, an interior of precious marbles and finely sculpted details, the grandest and best-preserved building to have survived from the ancient world (*open Mon–Sat 9–6.30 and Sun 9–1*). The movie directors who made all those Roman epics in the 1950s and '60s certainly took many of their settings from this High Imperial creation of Hadrian's time, just as architects from the early Middle Ages onwards have tried to equal it. Brunelleschi learned enough from it to build his dome in Florence, and a visit here will show you at a glance what Michelangelo and his contemporaries were trying so hard to outdo. The coffered dome, the biggest cast-concrete construction ever made before the 20th century, is the crowning audacity, even without its bronze plate. At 140ft in diameter it is probably the largest in the world (St Peter's dome is almost 7ft less, though much taller). Standing in the centre and looking at the clouds through the 30ft *oculus*, the hole at the top, is an odd sensation you can experience nowhere else.

Inside, the niches and recesses around the perimeter were devoted to statues of the Pantheon's 12 gods, plus those of Augustus and Hadrian; in the centre, illuminated by a direct sunbeam at midsummer noon, stood Jove. All these are gone, of course, and the interior decoration is limited to an *Annunciation*, to the right of the door, attributed to Melozzo da Forlì, and the tombs of eminent Italians such as Kings Vittorio Emanuele II and Umberto I, as well as those of Raphael and other artists. The Pantheon simply stands open, with no admission charges, probably fulfilling the same purpose as in Hadrian's day—no purpose at all, save that of an unequalled monument to art and the builder's skill. The Cult of the Twelve Gods, a Greek import from Augustus' time, never attracted many followers in Rome—even though many of the individual gods were present in Roman religion from the earliest times.

Via del Corso

Campus Martius, the open plain between Rome's hills and the Tiber, was the training ground for soldiers in the early days of the Republic. Eventually the city swallowed it up and the old path towards the Via Flaminia became one of the most important thoroughfares, Via Lata ('Broad Street'). Not entirely by coincidence, the popes of the 14th and 15th centuries laid out a grand new boulevard almost in the same place. **Via del Corso**, or simply the Corso, has been the main axis of Roman society ever since. Goethe recorded a fascinating account of the Carnival festivities held here in Rome's benignly decadent 18th century; the horse races that were held as the climax of the Carnival gave the street its name. Much of its length is taken up by the overdone palaces of the age, such as the Palazzo Doria (1780), where the **Galleria Doria Pamphili** (*open Fri–Wed 10–5; visits to the apartments at 10.30 and 12.30; adm*), still wholly owned by the Pamphili, has a fine painting collection with Velázquez' *Portrait of Innocent X*, Caravaggio's *Flight into Egypt*, and works by Rubens, Titian, Brueghel and more.

Continuing northwards, the palaces have come down in the world somewhat, tired-looking blocks that now house banks and offices. Look on the side-streets for some hidden attractions: **Sant'Ignazio**, on Via del Seminario, is another Jesuit church with spectacular *trompe l'œil* frescoes on the ceiling; a block north, columns of the ancient **Temple of Hadrian** are incorporated into the north side of the city's tiny Stock Exchange (Milan is Italy's financial capital). **Piazza Colonna** takes its name from the column of Marcus Aurelius, whose great military victories are remembered in a column (just like those of Trajan); atop this column is a statue of St Paul. The obelisk in adjacent Piazza di Montecitorio once marked the hours on a gigantic sundial in Emperor Augustus' garden; **Palazzo Montecitorio**, begun by Bernini, now houses the Italian Chamber of Deputies.

A little way east of Piazza Colonna is the **Trevi Fountain**, into which you can throw your coins to guarantee your return trip to Rome. The fountain, completed in 1762, was originally planned to commemorate the restoration of Agrippa's aqueduct by Nicholas V in 1453. The source was called the 'Virgin Water' after Virgo, a young girl who had showed thirsty Roman soldiers the hidden spring. It makes a grand sight—enough to make you want to come back; not many fountains have an entire palace (the Palazzo Poli) for a stage backdrop. The big fellow in the centre is Oceanus, drawn by horses and tritons through cascades of travertine and blue water. Across from the fountain, the little church of **SS. Vicenzo and Anastasio** has the distinction of caring for the pickled hearts and entrails of several dozen popes; an odd custom. They're kept down in the crypt.

Piazza di Spagna

The shuffling crowds of tourists who congregate here at all hours of the day are not a recent phenomenon; this irregular but supremely sophisticated piazza has been a favourite with foreigners ever since it was laid out in the early 16th century. The Spaniards came first, as their embassy to the popes was established here in 1646, giving the square and the steps their name. Later, the English Romantic poets made it their headquarters in Italy; typical Romantic mementoes—locks of hair, fond remembrances, mortal remains, death masks—are awaiting your inspired contemplation at the **Keats-Shelley Memorial House** at no.26 (*open April–Sept Mon–Fri 9–1 and 3–6; Oct–Mar Mon–Fri 9–1 and 2.30–5.30; adm*). Almost every artist, writer or musician of the last century spent some time in the neighbourhood, but today the piazza often finds itself bursting at the seams with refreshingly philistine gawkers and wayward youth from all over Europe, America and Japan, caught between the charms of McDonald's (the first one built in Rome) and the fancy shops on and around nearby Via Condotti.

All these visitors need somewhere to sit, and the popes obliged them in 1725 with the construction of the **Spanish Steps**, an exceptionally beautiful and exceptionally Baroque ornament about which it is hard to be cynical. The youth of today who loll about here are taking the place of the hopeful artists' models of the more picturesque centuries, who once crowded the steps, striking poses of antique heroes and Madonnas, waiting for some easy money. At the top of the stairs the simple but equally effective church of **Trinità dei Monti** by Carlo Maderno (early 16th century) was paid for by the King of France. At the southern end of Piazza di Spagna a Borromini palace housed the papal office called the *Propaganda Fide*, whose job was just what the name implies. The column in front (1856) celebrates the proclamation of the Dogma of the Immaculate Conception, one of their hardest tasks. Via del Babuino, a street named after a siren on a fountain so ugly that Romans called her the 'baboon', connects Piazza di Spagna with Piazza del Popolo. Besides its very impressive and equally expensive antique shops, the street carries on the English connection, with All Saints' Church, a sleepy neo-pub and an English bookshop just off it.

Piazza del Popolo

If you have a choice of how you enter Rome, this is the way to do it, through the gate in the old Aurelian wall and into one of the most successful of all Roman piazzas, copied on a smaller scale all over Italy. Valadier, the Pope's architect after the Napoleonic occupation, gave the piazza the form it has today, but the big obelisk of Pharaoh Ramses II punctuating the view down the boulevards arrived in the 1580s. It is 3200 years old but, like all obelisks, it looks mysteriously brand-new; Augustus brought it to Rome from Heliopolis and planted it in the Circus Maximus, and it was transferred here by Pope Sixtus V. The two domed churches designed by Rainaldi, set like bookends at the entrance to the three boulevards, are from the 1670s, part of the original plan for the piazza.

Emperor Nero's ashes were interred in a mausoleum here, at the foot of the Monte Pincio. The site was planted with walnut trees and soon everyone in Rome knew the stories of how Nero's ghost haunted the grove, sending out demons—in the forms of flocks of ravens that nested there—to perform deeds of evil. About 1100 Pope Paschal II destroyed the grove and scattered the ashes; to complete the exorcism he built a church on the site, **Santa Maria del Popolo**. Rebuilt in the 1470s, it contains some of the best painting in Rome: Caravaggio's stunning *Crucifixion of St Peter* and *Crucifixion of St Paul* (in the left transept), and frescoes by Pinturicchio around the altar. Raphael designed the Chigi Chapel, off the left aisle, and contributed the designs for its mosaics.

Villa Borghese

From Piazza del Popolo a winding ramp leads up to Rome's great complex of parks. Just by coincidence this was mostly parkland in ancient times. The **Monte Pincio** once formed part of Augustus' Imperial gardens, and the adjacent **Villa Medici** occupies the site of the Villa of Lucullus, the 2nd-century BC philosopher and general who conquered northern Anatolia and first brought cherries to Europe. Now the home of the French Academy, the Villa Medici was a posh jail of sorts for Galileo during his Inquisitorial trials. The Pincio, redesigned by Valadier as a lovely formal garden, offers rare views over Rome. It is separated from the **Villa Borghese** proper by the Aurelian wall and the modern sunken highway that borders it; its name, Viale del Muro Torto, means 'crooked wall', and refers to a section of the Roman wall that collapsed in the 6th century and was left as it was because it was believed to be protected by St Peter.

Exploring the vast spaces of Villa Borghese, you will come across charming vales, woods and a pond (rowing boats for rent), an imitation Roman temple or two, Rococo avenues where the bewigged dandies and powdered tarts of the 1700s came to promenade, bits of ancient aqueduct and the dated **Zoological Garden** (*open daily 8–2 hours before sunset; adm*). On the northern edge of the park is a ponderous boulevard called **Viale delle Belle Arti**, setting for several academies, each set up by a foreign government to stimulate cultural exchange. The **National Gallery of Modern Art** (*open Tues–Sun 9–7; adm exp*) makes its home here in one of Rome's biggest and most inexcusable buildings (1913), but the collection includes some of the best works of Modigliani and the Futurists, as well as a fair sampling of 19th- and 20th-century artists from the rest of Europe.

From there, gingerly skirting the Romanian Academy, you come to the **Villa Giulia Museum** (*open Tues–Sat 9–7, Sun 9–2; adm exp*). If you cannot make it to Tarquinia, this is the best place to get to know the Etruscans. Some of their best art has been collected here, as well as laboriously reconstructed terracotta façades to give you some idea of how an Etruscan temple looked. As usual the compelling attraction of the art here is the Etruscans' effortless, endearing talent for portraiture: expressive faces that help bridge the gap between the centuries can be seen in terracotta ex-votos (some of children), sarcophagi and even architectural decoration. The museum building and its courts and gardens are attractions in themselves.

The Borghese family collected an impressive hoard of ancient and modern art. Much of it was shipped off to the Louvre in the 1800s, to please Napoleon, but later generations did their best to rebuild the collection, and the **Museo and Galleria Borghese** (*open Tues–Sun 9–7; adm; tickets by reservation, call © 06 328 101, Mon–Fri 9.30–6*) today offers an intriguing mix of great art and Roman preciosity.

Via Veneto and the Quirinale

This chain of gardens was once much bigger, but at the end of the last century many of the old villas that hemmed in Rome were lost to the inevitable expansion of the city. Perhaps the greatest loss was the Villa Ludovisi, praised by many as the most beautiful of all Rome's parks. Now the choice 'Ludovisi' quarter, it has given the city one of its most famous streets, Via Veneto, the long winding boulevard of grand hotels, cafés and boutiques that stretches down from Villa Borghese to Piazza Barberini. A promenade for the smart set in the 1950s, it wears something of the forlorn air of a jilted beau now that fashion has moved on. Pull yourself away from the passing show on the boulevard to take in the unique spectacle provided by the **Convento dei Cappuccini** at the southern end of the street, just up from Piazza Barberini (*entrance halfway up the stairs of Santa Maria della Concezione; open Fri–Wed 9–12 and 3–6; adm*). Unique, that is, outside Palermo, for, much like the Capuchin convent there, the Roman brethren have created a loving tribute to Death. In the cellars 4000 dead monks team up for an unforgettable *danse macabre* of bones and grinning skulls, carefully arranged by serious-minded Capuchins long ago to remind us of something we know only too well.

On the other side of Piazza Barberini, up a gloomy Baroque avenue called Via delle Quattro Fontane, you'll find the Palazzo Barberini, one of the showier places in Rome, decorated everywhere with the bees from the family arms. Maderno, Borromini and Bernini all worked on it, with financing made possible by the election of a Barberini as Pope Urban VIII in 1623. Currently it houses the **National Museum of Ancient Art** (*open Tues–Sun 9–7; adm*)—a misleading title, since this is a gallery devoted to Italian works of the 12th–18th centuries.

San Carlino (*currently closed for restoration*), on the corner of Via delle Quattro Fontane and Via Quirinale, is one of Borromini's best works—and his first one (1638), a purposely eccentric little flight of fancy built exactly the size of one of the four massive pillars that hold up the dome in St Peter's. Follow **Via Quirinale** to reach the summit of that hill, covered with villas and gardens in ancient times, and abandoned in the Middle Ages. Then even the name Quirinale had been forgotten, and the Romans called the place 'Montecavallo' after the two big horses' heads projecting above the ground. During the reign of Sixtus V they were excavated to reveal monumental Roman statues of the **Dioscuri** (Castor and Pollux), probably copied from Phidias or Praxiteles. Together with a huge basin found in the Forum, they make a centrepiece for Piazza del Quirinale. Behind it, stretching for a dreary half-kilometre along the street, is the **Palazzo del Quirinale** (*open 8.30–1.30 on the second and fourth Sun of each month; adm exp*), built in 1574 to symbolize the political domination of the popes, later occupied by the kings of Italy, and now the official residence of the country's president.

Further along the Via XX Settembre, the **Santa Maria della Vittoria**, on Piazza San Bernardo, is home to one of the essential works of Baroque sculpture, the disconcertingly erotic *St Teresa in Ecstasy* by Bernini (in a chapel off the left aisle).

The Patriarchal Basilicas: Santa Maria Maggiore

Besides St Peter's there are three patriarchal basilicas, ancient and revered churches under the care of the Pope that have always been a part of the Roman pilgrimage. Santa Maria Maggiore, St Paul's outside the Walls and St John Lateran are all on the edges of the city, away from the political and commercial centre; by the Middle Ages they stood in open countryside, and only recently has the city grown outwards to swallow them once more.

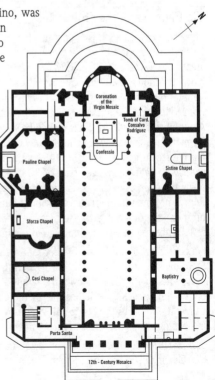

Santa Maria Maggiore, on the Monte Esquilino, was probably begun about 352, when a rich Christian saw a vision of the Virgin Mary directing him to build a church; Pope Liberius had received the same vision at the same time, and the two supposedly found the site marked out for them by a miraculous August snowfall. With various rebuildings over the centuries the church took its current form in the 1740s, with a perfectly elegant façade by Fernando Fuga and an equally impressive rear elevation by other architects; the obelisk behind it came from the Mausoleum of Augustus. Above everything rises the tallest and fairest **campanile** in Rome, an incongruous survival from the 1380s. Inside, the most conspicuous feature is the coffered ceiling by Renaissance architect Giuliano da Sangallo, gilded with the first gold brought back from the New World by Columbus, a gift from King Ferdinand and Queen Isabella of Spain. In the apse there are splendid but faded mosaics from 1295 of the *Coronation*

of the Virgin. Mosaics from the 5th century can be seen in the nave and in the triumphal arch in front of the apse. Santa Maria has a prize relic—nothing less than the genuine manger from Bethlehem, preserved in a sunken shrine in front of the altar; in front, kneeling in prayer, is a colossal, rather grotesque statue of Pope Pius IV added in the 1880s.

St John Lateran

Where is Rome's cathedral? It isn't St Peter's, and never has been. The true seat of the Bishop of Rome, and the end of a Roman pilgrimage, is here in the shadow of the Aurelian wall, a church believed to have been established by Constantine himself. The family of Plautius Lateranus, according to ancient records, had their property here confiscated after a failed coup against Nero in AD 66. It eventually became part of the imperial real estate and Constantine and his wife Fausta (whom he later executed) once kept house in the Lateran Palace. Later he donated it to Pope Miltiades as a cult centre for the Christians of Rome. Almost nothing remains of the original basilica; the sacks of the Vandals and Normans, two earthquakes and several fires have resulted in a jigsaw of bits and pieces from each of the last 16 centuries.

Like Santa Maria Maggiore, this church has an 18th-century exterior that is almost miraculously good, considering other Italian buildings from that age, with a west front by Alessandro Galilei (1736) that confidently and competently reuses the High Renaissance architectural vernacular. The equally fine north façade is older, done by Domenico Fontana in 1586, and incorporating the twin medieval bell towers into the design. Entering at the west front you pass an ancient statue of Constantine, found at the baths he built on the Quirinale; the bronze doors in the central portal once graced the entrance to the Senate House in the Forum. Inside, the nave is dominated by giant, impressive statues of the Apostles (*c.* 1720), glaring down like Roman emperors of old. There is some carefree and glorious Baroque work in the side chapels—also remains of a fresco by Giotto, behind the first column on the right. Near the apse, decorated with 13th-century mosaics (of a reindeer worshipping the cross, an odd conceit probably adapted from older mosaics in Ravenna), the Papal Altar supposedly contains the heads of Peter and Paul. Below floor level is the tomb of Pope Martin V; for some reason pilgrims drop flowers and telephone tokens on him for good luck.

Rome in the later Middle Ages had evolved an architectural style entirely its own, strangely uninterested in Gothic or reviving classicism, or, for that matter, anything else that was going on in the rest of Italy. Sadly, almost all of it disappeared in the Renaissance and Baroque rebuildings. The towers of Santa Maria in Cosmedin and Santa Maria Maggiore are good examples of it, as well as the expressive mosaics of Pietro Cavallini and his school and the intricate, geometrical Cosmatesque pavements in this church and so many others. Perhaps the most striking survival of this lost chapter in art is the Lateran **Cloister** (*open daily 9–6, until 5 in winter; adm exp*), with its pairs of spiral columns and 13th-century Cosmatesque mosaics; it completely upstages everything else in the church. All around the cloister walls, fragments from the earlier incarnations of the basilica have been assembled, a hoard of broken pretty things that includes an interesting tomb of a 13th-century bishop, which may be the work of Arnolfo di Cambio.

The Lateran's **Baptistry** is no ordinary baptistry—nothing less than the first one in Christendom, converted from an older temple by Constantine; its octagonal form has been copied in other baptistries all over Italy. Fortunately the damage done by a Mafia bombing in 1993 has been restored. Inside there are unusual pairs of bronze doors on either side: one from 1196 with scenes of how the Lateran basilica appeared at that time, and the other from the Terme di Caracalla, 'singing' doors that make a low, harmonic sound when you open them slowly. Built around the baptistry are three venerable chapels with more mosaics from the early Middle Ages. The entrance to the baptistry is in Piazza San Giovanni in Laterano, behind the **Lateran Palace**, rebuilt in 1588 over the original building that had served as home of the popes for 1000 years (4th–14th centuries).

Across the piazza, with the obligatory obelisk at its centre, you will see the **Scala Santa** (*open daily 6.30–12 and 3–6.30*), supposedly the stairs of Pilate's palace in Jerusalem, ascended by Christ on his way to Judgement and brought to Rome by Constantine's mother, St Helena. The more serious pilgrims ascend them on their knees. The Chapel of San Lorenzo at the top of the stairs, a part of the medieval Papal Palace, contains two miraculous portraits of Jesus, painted by angels.

While you're here, you have a good opportunity to explore the Aurelian wall. The stretch of it behind the Lateran probably looks much as it did originally, and the nearby **Porta Asinara** (next to Porta San Giovanni) is one of the best-preserved monumental ancient gateways.

The Via Appia: Rome's Catacombs

Rome's 'Queen of Roads', the path of trade and conquest to Campania, Brindisi and the East, was begun in 312 BC by Consul Appius Claudius. Like most of the consular roads outside Rome, over the centuries it became lined with cemeteries and the elaborate mausolea of the wealthy: ancient Roman practice, inherited from the Etruscans, prohibited any burials within the *pomerium*, the sacred ground of the city itself. Later the early Christian community built some of its most extensive catacombs here—the word itself comes from the location, *ad catacumbas*, referring to the dip in the Via Appia near the suburban Circus of Maxentius. The Via Appia Antica (as distinguished from the modern Via Appia Nuova to the east) makes a pleasant excursion outside the city, especially on Sundays when the road is closed to traffic all the way back to Piazza Venezia.

The road passes under the Aurelian wall at **Porta San Sebastiano**, one of the best-preserved of the old gates. It houses the **Museum of the Walls** (*open Tues–Sun 9–one hour before sunset; adm*), a very thorough exhibition on the history of Rome's walls, admission to which also gives you access to a well-preserved section of the 4th-century wall alongside it. Continuing along the road, after about ½km, with some ruins of tombs along the way, there is the famous church of **Domine Quo Vadis**, on the spot where Peter, fleeing from the dangers of Rome, met Christ coming the other way. 'Where goest thou, Lord?' Peter asked. 'I am going to be crucified once more,' was the reply. As the vision departed the shamed apostle turned back, soon to face his own crucifixion in Rome.

Another kilometre or so takes you to the **Catacombs of St Calixtus**, off on a side road to the right (*open 8.30–12 and 2.30–5; closed Wed and Nov; guided tours only; adm*). Here the biggest attraction is the Crypt of the Popes, burial places of 3rd- and 4th-century pontiffs with some well-executed frescoes and inscriptions. A word about catacombs: popular romance and modern cinema notwithstanding, these were never places of refuge from persecution or anything else, but simply burial grounds. The word 'catacombs' was only used after the 5th century; before that the Christians simply called them 'cemeteries'. The burrowing instinct is harder to explain. Few other Mediterranean cities have catacombs (Naples, Syracuse, Malta and the Greek island of Milos are among them). One of the requirements for catacombs seems to be tufa, or some other stone that can be easily excavated. Even so, the work involved was tremendous, and not explainable by any reasons of necessity. Christians were still digging them after they had become a power in Rome, in Constantine's time. No one knows for certain what sort of funeral rites were celebrated in them, just as no one knows much about any of the prayers or rituals of the early Christians; we can only suspect that a Christian of the 4th century and one of the 16th would have had considerable difficulty recognizing each other as brothers in the faith.

Most catacombs began small, as private family cemeteries; over generations some grew into enormous termitaries extending for miles beneath the surface. Inside, most of the tombs you see will be simple *loculi*, walled-up niches with only a symbol or short inscription scratched in to identify the deceased. Others, especially the tombs of popes or the wealthy, may have paintings of scriptural scenes, usually very poor work that reflects more on the dire state of the late Roman imagination than on the Christians.

Monte Aventino

Every now and then, whenever left-wing parties walk out on negotiations or talks to establish a government coalition, Italian newspapers may call it an 'Aventine Secession', an off-the-cuff reference to events in Rome 2500 years ago. Under the Roman Republic the Monte Aventino was the most solidly plebeian quarter of the city. On several occasions, when legislation proposed by the Senate and consuls seriously threatened the rights or interests of the people, they retired *en masse* to the Aventino and stayed there until the plan was dropped. Rome's unionists today often keep the city tied up in knots, but most are probably unaware that their ancestors had the honour of inventing the general strike.

The Aventino had another distinction in those times. In its uninhabited regions—the steep, cave-ridden slopes and parks towards the south—Greek immigrants and returning soldiers introduced the midnight rituals of Dionysus and Bacchus. Though secret, such goings-on soon came to the attention of the Senate, which saw the orgies quite rightly as a danger to the state and banned them in 146 BC. However, they cannot have died out completely and, in the Middle Ages, the Aventino had a reputation as a haunt of witches. The early Christian community also prospered here, and some of their churches are the oldest relics on the Aventino today.

Coming up from the Circus Maximus along Via Santa Sabina, the church of **Santa Sabina** is a simple, rare example of a 5th-century basilica, with an atrium at its entrance like a Roman secular basilica, and an original cypress door carved with scriptural scenes. This has been the head church of the Dominicans ever since a 13th-century pope gave it to St Dominic. Both S. Sabina and the church of **Sant'Alessio**, down the street, have good Cosmatesque cloisters.

At the end of this street, one of the oddities only Rome can offer stands on its quiet square, oblivious of the centuries: the **Priory of the Sovereign Order of Malta**, a fancy Rococo complex designed by Giambattista Piranesi. The Knights of Malta—or more properly, the Knights Hospitallers of St John—no longer wait for the popes to unleash them against Saracen and Turk. Mostly this social club for old nobles bestirs itself to assist hospitals, its original job during the Crusades. The headquarters is presently at a fancier address in Rome, but the order's ambassadors to Italy and the Vatican live here.

St Paul's Outside the Walls

Paul was beheaded on a spot near the Ostia road; according to legend the head bounced three times, and at each place where it hit a fountain sprang up. The Abbazia delle Tre Fontane, near EUR, occupies the site today. Later, Constantine built a basilica alongside the road as a fitting resting place for the saint. Of the five patriarchal basilicas, this one has had the worst luck. Today it sits in the middle of the unprepossessing neighbourhood of Ostiense, full of factories, gasworks and concrete flats. Once it was the grandest of them all; 9th-century chroniclers speak of the separate walled city of 'Giovannipolis' that had grown up around St Paul's, connected to the Aurelian wall by a 1½km-long colonnade built by Pope John VIII in the 870s.

The Norman sack of 1084, a few good earthquakes, and finally a catastrophic fire in 1823 wiped Giovannipolis off the map, and left us with a St Paul's that for the most part is barely more than a century old. Still, the façade of golden mosaics and sturdy Corinthian columns is pleasant to look at, and some older features survive—the 11th-century door made in Constantinople, a Gothic *baldacchino* over Paul's tomb by Arnolfo di Cambio, a beautiful 13th-century Cosmatesque cloister (almost a double of the one in the Lateran), and 5th-century mosaics over the triumphal arch in front of the apse, the restored remains of the original mosaics from the façade, contributed by Empress Galla Placidia. Art Deco is not what you would expect from those times, but Americans at least will have a hard time believing these mosaics were not done by President Roosevelt's WPA. The apse itself has some more conventional mosaics from the 13th-century Roman school, and the nave is lined with the portraits of all 263 popes. According to Roman tradition, when the remaining eight spaces are filled, the world will end.

Castel Sant'Angelo

Though intended as a resting place for a most serene emperor, this building has seen more blood, treachery and turmoil than any in Rome. Hadrian, it seems, designed his own mausoleum three years before his death in 138, on an eccentric plan consisting of a huge marble cylinder surmounted by a conical hill planted with cypresses. The marble, the obelisks and the gold and bronze decorations did not survive the 5th-century sacks, but in about 590, during a plague, Pope Gregory the Great saw a vision of St Michael over the mausoleum, ostensibly announcing the end of the plague, but perhaps also mentioning discreetly that here, if anyone cared to use it, was the most valuable fortress in Europe.

There would be no papacy, perhaps, without this castle—at least not in its present form. Hadrian's great cylinder is high, steep and almost solid—impregnable even after the invention of artillery. With rebellions of some sort occurring on average every two years before 1400, the popes often had recourse to this place of safety. It last saw action in the sack of 1527, when Clement VII withstood a siege of several months while his city went up in flames around him. The popes also used Castel Sant'Angelo as a prison; famous inmates included Giordano Bruno, Cellini and Beatrice Cenci (better known to the English than the Italians, thanks to Shelley's verse drama). Tosca throws herself off the top at the end of Puccini's opera.

Inside the castle (*open daily 9–7; closed the second and fourth Tues of each month; adm*), the recently restored spiral ramp leads up to the **Papal Apartments**, decorated as lavishly by 16th-century artists as anything in the Vatican. The **Sala Paolina** has frescoes by Perin del Vaga depicting events in the history of Rome, and the **Sala di Apollo** is frescoed with grotesques attempting to reproduce the wall decorations of the ancient palaces, perhaps like

Nero's Golden House. Above everything, a mighty statue of Michael commemorates Pope Gregory's vision.

The three central arches of the **Ponte Sant'Angelo** were built by Hadrian, although the statues added in 1688 steal the show; at once dubbed Bernini's Breezy Maniacs, they battle a never-ending Baroque hurricane to display the symbols of Christ's Passion.

The Vatican

St Peter's

Along Borgo Sant'Angelo, leading towards the Vatican, you can see the famous **covered passageway,** used by the popes since 1277 to escape to the castle when things became dangerous. The customary route, however, leads up **Via della Conciliazione,** a broad boulevard laid out under Mussolini over a tangled web of medieval streets. Critics have said it spoils the surprise, but no arrangement of streets and buildings could really prepare you for Bernini's Brobdingnagian **Piazza San Pietro.** Someone has calculated there is room for about 300,000 people in the piazza, with no crowding. Few have ever noticed Bernini's little joke on antiquity; the open space almost exactly meets the size and dimensions of the Colosseum. Bernini's **Colonnade** (1656), with 284 massive columns and statues of 140 saints, stretches around it like 'the arms of the Church embracing the world'—perhaps the biggest cliché in Christendom by now, but exactly what Bernini had in mind. Stand on either of the two dark stones at the foci of the elliptical piazza and you will see Bernini's forest of columns resolve into neat rows, a subtly impressive optical effect like the hole in the top of the Pantheon. Flanked by two lovely fountains, the work of Maderno and Fontana, the Vatican **obelisk** seems nothing special as obelisks go, but is actually one of the most fantastical relics in all Rome. This obelisk comes from Heliopolis, the Egyptian city founded as a capital and cult centre by Akhnaton, the half-legendary pharaoh and religious reformer who, according to Sigmund Freud and others, founded the first monotheistic religion, influencing Moses and all that came after. Caligula brought it over to Rome in AD 37 to decorate the now-disappeared Circus Vaticanus (later referred to as the Circus of Nero) where it would have overlooked Peter's martyrdom. In the Middle Ages it was placed to the side of the basilica, but Sixtus V moved it to where it now stands in 1586.

It may be irreverent to say so, but the original St Peter's, begun over the apostle's tomb by Constantine in 324, may well have been a more interesting building, a richly decorated basilica full of gold and mosaics with a vast porch of marble and bronze in front and a lofty campanile, topped by the famous golden cockerel that everyone believed would some day crow to announce the end of the world. This St Peter's, where Charlemagne and Frederick II received their imperial crowns, was falling to pieces by the 1400s, conveniently in time for the popes and artists of the Renaissance to plan a replacement. Nicholas V, in about 1450, conceived an almost Neronian building programme for the Vatican, ten times as large as anything his ancestors could have contemplated. It was not until the time of Julius II, however, that Bramante was commissioned to demolish the old church and begin the new. His original plan called for a great dome over a centralized Greek cross. Michelangelo, who took over the work in 1546, basically agreed, and if he had had his way St Peter's might indeed have become the crowning achievement of Renaissance art that everyone hoped it would be.

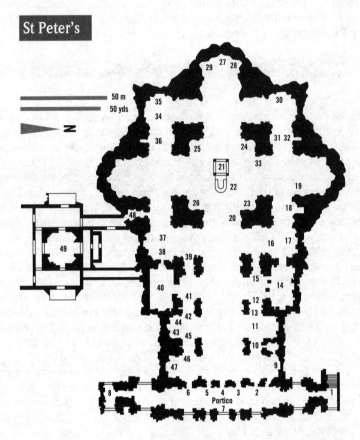

St Peter's

50 m
50 yds

N

29 27 28

35
34
36
25
24
31 32
33
21
22
19
26
23
18
20
16 17
37
38
39
15 14
40
41
12
42 13
44 11
43 45
10
46
9
47
48
49
8 6 5 4 3 2 1
Portico
7

1 Statue of Constantine / Scala Regia
2 Holy Door
3 Crocetti's Door
4 Filarete's Door
5 Manzù Door
6 Minguzzi's Door
7 Giotto's Navicella
8 Statue of Charlemagne
9 Michelangelo's Pietà
10 Queen Christina Monument
11 Cappella di S. Sebastiano
12 Countess Matilda Monument
13 Innocent XII Monument
14 Cappella del Smo. Sacramento
15 Gregory XIII Monument
16 Cappella Gregoriana
17 Madonna del Soccorso
18 Lift up to Dome

19 Altar of St Wenceslas
20 Statue of St Peter
21 High Altar / Bernini's
   Baldacchino
22 Confessio
23 St Longinus / Entrance
   to Grottoes
24 St Helen
25 St Veronica
26 St Andrew
27 Tribune / Cathedra of St Peter
28 Urban VIII Monument
29 Paul III Monument
30 Guercino's St Petronilla
31 Altar of the Navicella
32 Clement XIII Monument
33 St Bruno
34 Cappella della Colonna

35 Leo the Great Tomb
36 Alexander VII Monument
37 Cappella Clementina
38 Pius VII Monument
39 Leo XI Monument
40 Cappella del Coro
41 Innocent VIII Monument
42 Pius X Monument
43 Cappella della Presentazione
44 John XXIII Monument
45 Clementina Sobieska Monument / stairs
   and down lift from dome
46 Monument to the Last Stuarts
47 Baptistry
48 Pius VIII Monument / entrance to
   St Peter's Treasury
49 Sacristy

Unfortunately over the 120 years of construction too many popes and too many artists got their hand in—Rossellino, Giuliano da Sangallo, Raphael, Antonio da Sangallo, Vignola, Ligorio, della Porta, Fontana, Bernini and Maderno all contributed something to the tremendous hotchpotch we see today. The most substantial tinkering came in the early 17th century, when a committee of cardinals decided that a Latin cross was desired, resulting in the huge extension of the nave that blocks the view of Michelangelo's dome from the piazza. Baroque architects, mistaking size and virtuosity for art, found perfect patrons in the Baroque popes, less interested in faith than the power and majesty of the papacy. Passing though Maderno's gigantic façade seems like entering a Grand Central Station full of stone saints and angels, keeping an eye on the big clocks overhead as they wait for trains to Paradise. All along the nave, markers showing the length of other proud cathedrals prove how each fails miserably to measure up to the Biggest Church in the World. This being Rome, not even the markers are honest—Milan's cathedral is actually 65ft longer.

The best is on the right: Michelangelo's *Pietà*, now restored and kept behind glass to protect it from future madmen. This work, sculpted when he was only 25, helped make Michelangelo's reputation. Its smooth and elegant figures, with the realities of death and grief sublimated on to some ethereal plane known only to saints and artists, were a turning point in religious art. From here the beautiful, unreal art of the religious Baroque was the logical next step. Note how Michelangelo has carved his name in small letters on the band around the Virgin's garment; he added this after overhearing a group of tourists from Milan who thought the *Pietà* the work of a fellow Milanese. Not much else in St Peter's really stands out. In its vast spaces scores of popes and saints are remembered in assembly-line Baroque, and the paintings over most of the altars have been replaced by mosaic copies. The famous bronze statute of St Peter, its foot worn away by the touch of millions of pilgrims, is by the right front pier. Stealing the show, just as he knew it would, is Bernini's great, garish **baldacchino** over the high altar, cast out of bronze looted from the Pantheon roof.

Many visitors head straight for Michelangelo's **dome** (*open May–Sept daily 8–6; Oct–April daily 8–5; adm*). To be in the middle of such a spectacular construction is worth the climb itself. You can walk out on the roof for a view over Rome, but even more startling is the chance to look down from the interior balcony over the vast church 250ft below. In the **Sacristy** (*open April–Sept daily 9–6; Oct–Mar daily 9–5; adm exp*), built in the 18th century, there are a number of treasures—those the Saracens, the imperial soldiers of 1527, and Napoleon couldn't steal. The ancient bronze cockerel from the old St Peter's is kept here, along with ancient relics, Baroque extravaganzas and a gown that belonged to Charlemagne.

Do not pass up a descent to the **Sacred Grottoes**, the foundation of the earlier St Peter's converted into a crypt. Dozens of popes are buried here, along with distinguished friends of the Church like Queen Christina of Sweden and James III, the Stuart pretender. Perhaps the greatest work of art here is the bronze tomb of Sixtus IV, a definitive Renaissance confection by Pollaiuolo, though the most visited is undoubtedly the simple monument to John XXIII.

The Vatican Museums

The admission (*currently L15,000*) may be the most expensive in Italy, but for that you get about 10 museums in one, with the Sistine Chapel and the Raphael rooms thrown in free. Altogether almost 7km of exhibits fill the halls of the Vatican Palace, and unfortunately for you there isn't much dull museum clutter that can be passed over lightly. Seeing this infinite, exasperating hoard properly would be the work of a lifetime. On the bright side, the Pope sees to it that his museum is managed more intelligently and thoughtfully than anything run by the Italian state. A choice of colour-coded itineraries, depending on the amount of time you have to spend, will get you through the labyrinth in 90 minutes, or five hours.

Near the entrance (with a branch of the Vatican Post Office), the first big challenge is a large **Egyptian Museum**—one of Europe's best collections—and then some rooms of antiquities from the Holy Land and Syria, before the **Museo Chiaramonti**, full of Roman statuary (including famous busts of Caesar, Mark Antony and Augustus) and inscriptions. The **Pio Clementino Museum** contains some of the best-known statues of antiquity: the dramatic *Laocoön*, dug up in Nero's Golden House and mentioned in the works of many classical authors, and the *Apollo Belvedere*. No other ancient works recovered during the Renaissance had a greater influence on sculptors than these two. A 'room of animals' captures the more fanciful side of antiquity, and the 2nd-century Baroque tendency in Roman art comes out clearly in a giant group called *The Nile*, complete with sphinxes and crocodiles—it came from a Roman temple of Isis. The bronze papal fig-leaves that protect the modesty of hundreds of nude statues are a good joke at first—it was the same spirit that put breeches on the saints in Michelangelo's *Last Judgement*, a move ordered, in Michelangelo's absence, by Pius IV.

The best things in the **Etruscan Museum** (*open Tues*) are Greek, a truly excellent collection of vases imported by discriminating Etruscan nobles that includes the famous picture of *Oedipus and the Sphinx*. Beyond that, there is a hall hung with beautiful high-medieval tapestries from Tournai (15th century), and the long, long **Map Room**, lined with carefully painted town views and maps of every corner of Italy; note the long scene of the 1566 Great Siege of Malta at the entrance. Anywhere else, with no Michelangelos to offer competition, Raphael's celebrated frescoes (*recently restored*) in the **Stanze della Segnatura** would be the prime destination on anyone's itinerary. The *School of Athens* is too well known to require much of an introduction, but here is a guide to some of the figures: on Aristotle's side, Archimedes and Euclid surrounded by their disciples (Euclid, drawing plane figures on a slate, is supposedly a portrait of Bramante); off to the right, Ptolemy and Zoroaster hold the terrestrial and celestial globes. Raphael includes himself among the Aristotelians, standing between Zoroaster and the painter Il Sodoma. Behind Plato stand Socrates and Alcibiades, among others, and to the left, Zeno and Epicurus. In the foreground, a crouching Pythagoras writes while Empedocles and the Arab Averroes look on. Diogenes sprawls philosophically on the steps, while isolated near the front is Heraclitus—really Michelangelo, according to legend; Raphael put him in at the last minute after seeing the work in progress in the Sistine Chapel.

Across from this apotheosis of philosophy, Raphael painted a triumph of theology to keep the clerics happy, the *Dispute of the Holy Sacrament*. The other frescoes include the *Parnassus*, a vision of the ancient Greek and Latin poets, the *Miracle of Bolsena*, the *Expulsion of Heliodorus*, an allegory of the triumphs of the Counter-Reformation papacy, the *Meeting of Leo I and Attila* and, best of all, the solemn, spectacularly lit *Liberation of St Peter*. Nearby, there is the **Loggia** of Bramante, also with decoration designed by Raphael, though executed by other artists (*only visitable with written permission*), and the **Chapel of Nicholas V**, with frescoes by Fra Angelico. The **Borgia Apartments**, a luxurious suite built for Pope Alexander VI, have walls decorated with saints, myths and sibyls by Pinturicchio. These run into the **Gallery of Modern Religious Art**, a game attempt by the Vatican to prove that such a thing really exists.

The Vatican Museums

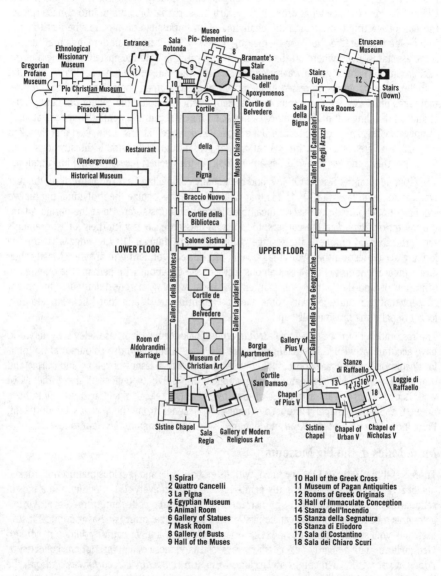

1 Spiral
2 Quattro Cancelli
3 La Pigna
4 Egyptian Museum
5 Animal Room
6 Gallery of Statues
7 Mask Room
8 Gallery of Busts
9 Hall of the Muses

10 Hall of the Greek Cross
11 Museum of Pagan Antiquities
12 Rooms of Greek Originals
13 Hall of Immaculate Conception
14 Stanza dell'Incendio
15 Stanza della Segnatura
16 Stanza di Eliodoro
17 Sala di Costantino
18 Sala dei Chiaro Scuri

The Sistine Chapel

To the sophisticated Sixtus IV, building this ungainly barn of a chapel may have seemed a mistake in the first place. When the pushy, despotic Julius II sent Michelangelo up, against his will, to paint the vast ceiling, it might have turned out to be a project as hopeless as the tomb Julius had already commissioned. Michelangelo spent four years of his life on the Sistine Ceiling. No one can say what drove him to turn his surly patron's whim into a masterpiece: the fear of wasting those years, the challenge of an impossible task, or maybe just to spite Julius—he exasperated the Pope by making him wait, and refused all demands that he hire some assistants. Everywhere on the Sistine Ceiling you will note the austere blankness of the backgrounds. Michelangelo always eschewed stage props; one of the tenets of his art was that complex ideas could be expressed in the portrayal of the human body alone. With sculpture, that takes time. Perhaps the inspiration that kept Michelangelo on the ceiling so long was the chance of distilling out of the Book of Genesis and his own genius an entirely new vocabulary of images, Christian and intellectual. Like most Renaissance patrons, Julius had merely asked for virtuoso interior decoration. What he got was nothing like simple illustrations from Scripture; this is the way the Old Testament looks in the deepest recesses of the imagination.

The fascination of the Sistine Ceiling, and the equally compelling **Last Judgement** on the rear wall, done much later (1534–41), is that while we may recognize the individual figures we still have not captured their secret meanings. Hordes of tourists stare up at the heroic Adam, the mysterious *ignudi* in the corners, the Russian masseuse sibyls with their longshoremen's arms, the six-toed prophets, the strange vision of Noah's deluge. They wonder what they're looking at, a question that would take years of inspired wondering to answer. Mostly they direct their attention to the all-too-famous scene of the Creation, with perhaps the only representation of God the Father ever painted that escapes being merely ridiculous. One might suspect that the figure is really some ageing Florentine artist, and that Michelangelo only forgot to paint the brush in his hand.

The restoration of the ceiling and *Last Judgement*, paid for by a Japanese television network, have accurately revealed Michelangelo's true colours—jarring, surprise colours that no interior decorator would ever choose, plenty of sea-green, with splashes of yellow and purple and dramatic shadows. No new paint is being applied, only solvents to clear off the grime. Most visitors overlook the earlier frescoes on the lower walls, great works of art that would have made the Sistine Chapel famous by themselves: scenes from the *Exodus* by Botticelli, Perugino's *Donation of the Keys*, and Signorelli's *Moses Consigning his Staff to Joshua*.

More Miles in the Big Museum

There's still the **Vatican Library** to go, with its endless halls and precious manuscripts tucked neatly away in cabinets. The brightly painted rooms contain every sort of oddity: thousands of reliquaries and an entire wall of monstrances, a memorable collection of medieval ivories, gold-glass medallions from the catacombs, every sort of globe, orrery and astronomical instrument. If you survive this, the next hurdle is the new and beautifully laid out **Museo Gregoriano**, with a hoard of excellent classical statuary, mosaics and inscriptions collected by Pope Gregory XVI. Then comes a **Carriage Museum** (*currently closed for restoration*), the **Pius Christian Museum** of early Christian art and, finally, one of the most interesting of all, though no one has time for it: the **Ethnological Museum**, with wonderful art from peoples of every continent, brought home by Catholic missionaries over the centuries.

By itself the Vatican **Pinacoteca** would be by far the finest picture gallery in Rome, a representative sampling of Renaissance art from its beginnings, with some fine works of Giotto (*Il Redentore* and the *Martyrdoms of Peter and Paul*) and contemporary Sienese painters, as well as Gentile da Fabriano, Sano di Pietro and Filippo Lippi. Don't overlook the tiny but electrically surreal masterpiece of Fra Angelico, the *Story of St Nicolas at Bari*, or the *Angelic Musicians* of Melozzo da Forlì, set next to Melozzo's famous painting of Platina being nominated by Sixtus IV to head the Vatican Library—a rare snapshot of Renaissance humanism. Venetian artists are not well represented, but there is a *Pietà* by Bellini and a *Madonna* by the fastidious Carlo Crivelli. Perhaps the best-known paintings are the recently restored *Transfiguration of Christ*, Raphael's last work, and the *St Jerome* of Da Vinci.

Vatican Practicalities

The **museums** are open Nov–Feb Mon–Sat 8.45–1.45 (last admission 12.45); the rest of the year Mon–Sat 8.45–4.45 (last admission 3.45); adm; closed Sun, except the last Sun of each month and religious holidays 8.45–1.45 (last admission 12.45); free. The entrance is rather far from St Peter's Square, to the north on Viale Vaticano. **St Peter's** is open daily 7–7; Oct–Mar till 6; the basilica is closed when there are official ceremonies in the piazza, although visitors are allowed during Mass. The dress code—no shorts, short skirts or sleeveless dresses—is strictly controlled by the papal gendarmes.

The **Vatican Information Office**, © 06 6988 4466, in St Peter's Square (*open daily 8–7*) is very helpful, and there are Vatican post offices on the opposite side of the square and inside the Vatican Museums for distinctive postcards home (it is rumoured to be a much more reliable mail service than that offered by the Italian post). The information office arranges 2hr-long morning tours of the **Vatican Gardens**, easily Rome's most beautiful park, with a remarkable Renaissance jewel of a villa inside, the **Casino of Pius IV** by Pietro Ligorio and Peruzzi (1558–62) (*open May–Sept Mon–Sat; Oct–April once a week; L18,000 per person; reserve in advance through the information office*). Underneath the crypt of St Peter's, archaeologists in the 1940s discovered a **street of Roman tombs**, perfectly preserved with many beautiful paintings and mosaics (*open Mon–Sat 9–5; adm; tours can be arranged through the Uffizio degli Scavi, just to the left of St Peter's; in summer book early as fragile conditions permit only 15 people at a time*). The rest of the Vatican is strictly off limits, patrolled by genuine Swiss Guards (still recruited from the three Catholic cantons).

Michelangelo also designed the **defensive wall** that since 1929 has marked the Vatican boundaries. Behind them are things most of us will never see: several small old churches, a printing press, the headquarters of *L'Osservatore Romano* and Vatican Radio (run, of course, by the Jesuits), a motor garage, a *palazzo di giustizia* and even a big shop—everything the world's smallest nation could ever need. Modern popes, in glaring contrast to their predecessors, do not take up much space. The current Papal Apartments are in a corner of the Vatican Palace overlooking Piazza San Pietro; John Paul II usually appears to say a few electrically amplified words from his window at noon on Sundays. For tickets to the Wednesday morning **papal audience**, usually held at 11am in the piazza (*May–Sept*) or in the Nervi Auditorium (*Oct–April*), apply in advance at the Papal Prefecture—through the bronze door in the right-hand colonnade of Piazza San Pietro (*open Mon and Tues 9–1, © 06 6988 3217*).

Rome on the whole isn't as exciting for big-game shoppers as Milan, though when it comes to clothing you will find all the major designers and labels well represented. Rome is not famous for any particular artisanal craft, save the religious items and priestly garb, sold near the Vatican and along Via dei Cestari near the Pantheon. There is no shortage of shops selling **antiques**, a great number of them clustered together between the Tiber and Piazza Navona; look especially off Via Monserrato, Via dei Coronari and Via dell'Anima. For old prints, generally inexpensive, try **Casali**, Piazza Rotonda 81A; **Alinari**, Via Alibert 16/a is a good address for artistic black and white pictures of old Rome. **L'Art Nouveau**, Via dei Coronari 221, offers just what its name implies. Antiques also show up in Rome's large and celebrated Sunday morning flea market at **Porta Portese**, as well as anything else you can imagine, all lumped together in often surreal displays. It starts just after dawn and closes gradually around noon; beware the pickpockets.

The most **fashionable shopping** is on the streets between Piazza di Spagna and the Corso. Some special items: **Massoni**, Largo Goldoni 48, near Via Condotti, much frequented by film stars, sells some of Rome's finest jewellery; for menswear, **Testa,** Via Borgognona 13 and Via Frattina 42, or **Valentino Uomo**, Via Condotti 13, or for custom tailoring, **Battistoni**, Via Condotti 61/a; for womenswear try Rome's outlets of the great designers like **Missoni**, Via del Babuino 96, **Giorgio Armani**, Via Condotti 77 and Via del Babuino 102, **Mila Schöen**, Via Condotti 51, or the Rome-based **Fendi**, Via Borgognona nos.8, 10, 12 and 39. For leather, the **Gucci** outlet is at Via Condotti 8, and do not miss **Fausto Santini**, Via Frattina 120.

For a special bottle of **wine**, try **Enoteca Costantini**, Piazza Cavour 16, for a wide selection. If you wish to stock up on Italian **coffee**, **Tazza d'Oro**, Via degli Orfani 84, has special bags of the city's best, the 'Aroma di Roma'.

Rome ✉ *00100*   ***Where to Stay***

For a city that has been entertaining crowds of visitors for the last 2000 years, Rome does not seem to have acquired any special flair for accommodating them. From Belle Epoque palaces on Via Veneto to grimy hovels on the wrong side of Stazione Termini, there will always be something for you to come home to after a hard day's sight-seeing, although places with a history, a famous view or quiet gardens to shut out the city noise are rare; all things considered this is not the place to make the big splurge.

In the 1890s when the Stazione Termini district was the newest and choicest part of Rome, the streets around the station spawned hundreds of hotels, some quite elegant. Today a great part of the city's accommodation is still here. Unfortunately it has gone the way of all such 19th-century toadstool neighbourhoods: overbuilt, dingy and down-at-heel, and not at all the place to savour the real Rome. It's also inconvenient for most of the sights.

Rooms can be difiicult to find on short notice, but the free Hotel Reservation Service, © 06 699 1000, will do the looking for you.

★★★★★ **Hassler-Villa Medici**, Piazza Trinità dei Monti 6, ✆ 06 699 340, 📠 06 678 9991, is one of Rome's best hotels, with a fine location at the top of the Spanish Steps and wonderful views over the city for those who book far enough in advance. Around for over a century, it seems to have regained its position as the élite hotel of Rome, with a beautiful garden courtyard, deferential service and large wood-panelled rooms.

★★★★★ **Excelsior**, Via V. Veneto 125, ✆ 06 47081, 📠 06 482 6205, is also located in a choice area, though lacking the aura of glamour it had in the 1950s. The reception areas have thicker carpets, bigger chandeliers and more gilded plaster than anywhere in Italy, and most of the rooms are just as good—don't let them give you one of the modernized ones. There are saunas, boutiques, a famous bar and as much personal attention as you could ask for.

very expensive

★★★★ **D'Inghilterra**, Via Bocca di Leone 14, ✆ 06 69981, 📠 06 6992 2243, is another favourite in the Piazza di Spagna area. Parts of this building date from the 15th century, when it served as a prince's guesthouse; in its career as a hotel, since 1850, it has played host to most of the literati and artists of Europe and America. Recent restorations have left it looking more palatial than ever, although some rooms are a biton the small side.

★★★★ **Forum**, Via Tor de' Conti 25, ✆ 06 679 2446, 📠 06 678 6479, is the only real luxury establishment near the ancient Forum, a somewhat worn hotel, but with unbeatable views from the roof terrace.

expensive

★★★★ **Cardinal**, Via Giulia 62, ✆ 06 6880 2719, 📠 06 678 6376, in the heart of the *centro storico*, is perhaps the best place to experience Renaissance Rome in style—in a building attributed to Bramante, which has been completely restored inside, but without spoiling the atmosphere.

★★★ **Fontana**, Piazza di Trevi 96, ✆ 06 678 6113, 📠 06 679 0024, would be a good hotel anywhere, and it is also right across the street from the Trevi Fountain—something to look at out of your window that will guarantee nice dreams.

★★★ **Gregoriana**, Via Gregoriana 18, ✆ 06 679 4269, 📠 06 678 4258, close to the Spanish Steps but reasonably priced, is small, tasteful and gratifyingly friendly, with a devoted regular clientele—there are only 19 rooms, so book early.

★★★ **La Residenza**, Via Emilia 22, ✆ 06 488 0789, 📠 06 485 721, near the Via Veneto, stands out as a very pleasant base, with beautifully appointed rooms in an old town house, and some luxuries more common to the most expensive hotels.

★★★ **Villa Florence**, Via Nomentana 28, ✆ 06 440 3036, 📠 06 440 2709, near the Porta Pia and the British Embassy, is a 19th-century villa with a garden, which has been thoroughly restored inside, and is now very well-run and friendly.

moderate

★★★ **Hotel Sant'Anselmo**, Piazza Sant'Anselmo 2, ✆ 06 578 3214, 📠 06 578 3604, up on the Monte Aventino, is a very peaceful hotel with a garden and comfortable rooms.

★★ **Abruzzi**, Piazza della Rotonda 69, ✆ 06 679 2021, is a budget hotel with views over the Pantheon; none of the rooms has private bath.

★★ **Campo de' Fiori**, Via del Biscione 6, ✆ 06 6880 6865, 🖷 06 687 6003, is a good, cheap alternative with small comfortable rooms and a roof terrace.

★★ **Sole**, Via del Biscione 76, ✆ 06 6880 6873, 🖷 06 689 3787, is a large old hotel with lots of character, just off the Campo de' Fiori. Ask for one of the larger rooms.

cheap

★ **Campo Marzio**, Piazza Campo Marzio 7, ✆ 06 6880 1486, is just north of the Pantheon; none of the rooms has private bath.

★ **Fiorella**, Via del Babuino 196, ✆ 06 361 0597, in a good location just off Piazza del Popolo, has simple rooms, none with private bath.

The area around Stazione Termini offers a wide choice of cheap hotels; **Via Principe Amedeo** is also a good place to look, particularly at nos.62, 76, 82 and 79.

★ **Tony**, Via Principe Amedeo 79, ✆ 06 446 6887, 🖷 06 485 721, is a friendly above-average-quality budget hotel.

★ **Katty**, Via Palestro 35, ✆ 06 444 1216, 🖷 06 444 1261, is simple and clean, on a street on the east side of the station which has a number of other cheap hotels.

Eating Out

Unlike many other Italians, the Romans aren't afraid to try something new. Lately, for example, Chinese restaurants have been appearing in numbers that culinary conservatives find alarming, not to mention Arab, Korean and macrobiotic places and the occasional hamburger stand.

Of course, there is also a grand old tradition of Roman cooking, with such specialities as *saltimbocca* (literally 'jump in the mouth'), tender veal *scalope* cooked with ham, *stracciatella* (a soup with eggs, parmesan cheese and parsley), fried artichokes called *carciofi alla giudia* and veal *involtini*. On a genuine Roman menu in the less expensive places you are likely to encounter such favourites as *baccalà* (salt cod), *bucatini all' amatriciana* (in a tomato and bacon sauce) or *alla carbonara* (with egg and bacon), tripe and *gnocchi*. Unless you ask for something different, the wine will probably come from the Castelli Romani—light, fruity whites of which the best come from Frascati and Velletri.

very expensive

Perched high above the city is **La Pergola dell'Hotel Hilton**, Via Cadlolo 4, ✆ 06 3509 2211, currently Rome's most celebrated restaurant for first-rate *alta cucina* served in elegant surroundings with all of Rome at your feet. *Closed Sun and Mon; open for dinner only; reserve well ahead.*

For fish, head to **La Rosetta**, Via della Rosetta 8, near the Pantheon, ✆ 06 686 1002, Rome's best fish-only restaurant. If the menu posted outside the door seems too expensive, step in anyway just to admire the heap of shiny, coloured fish, oysters and sea-urchin arranged on the marble slab in the hall. *Closed Sun; reserve well ahead.*

There is no better place to try *carciofi alla giudia* than right on the edge of the old ghetto at **Piperno**, Via Monte de' Cenci 9, ✆ 06 6880 6629, Rome's most famous purveyor of Roman-Jewish cooking—simple dishes on the whole, but prepared and served with refinement. *Closed Sun eve and Mon.*

Across the river, Trastevere, with its attractive piazzas with space for tables outside, has long been one of the most popular corners of the city for dining. Many of its restaurants specialize in fish, most notably **Alberto Ciarla**, Piazza San Cosimato 40, ✆ 06 581 8668, some way south of Santa Maria in Trastevere. The French-trained owner, proud enough to put his name on the sign, sees to it that everything is delicately and perfectly done, and graciously served: oysters, seafood ravioli and quite a few adventurous styles of *pesce crudo* (raw fish) are among the most asked for. *Dinner only; closed Sun.* Not far away, **Sabatini**, Piazza Santa Maria in Trastevere 13, ✆ 06 581 2026, has been a Roman tradition for many a year, as much for the cuisine (again, lots of seafood) as for the tables outside, which face the lovely piazza and its church. *Closed Tues in winter, Wed in summer.*

If you find yourself anywhere around Porta San Paolo and the Testaccio district at dinnertime, don't pass up a chance to dine at the acknowledged temple of old Roman cooking, **Checchino dal 1887**, Via di Monte Testaccio 30, ✆ 06 574 6318, which has been owned by the same family for 107 years—the longest family record in Rome. Both the fancy and humble sides of Roman food are well represented, with plenty of the powerful offal dishes that Romans have been eating since ancient times, and the setting is unique—on the edge of Monte Testaccio, with one of Rome's best cellars excavated underneath the hill. *Closed Sun eve and Mon.*

moderate

Dal Toscano, Via Germanico 58, ✆ 06 397 25717, is perhaps your best option in the tourist-trap Vatican area: family-run and very popular with Roman families, this restaurant offers well-prepared Tuscan specialities like *pici* (rough, fresh spaghetti rolled by hand) in game sauce and *fiorentina* steak—save room for the good homemade desserts. Reserve. *Closed Mon.* Another Tuscan place off the Via Veneto, also family-run but slightly fancier and more expensive, is **Papà Baccus**, Via Toscana 33, ✆ 06 4274 2808, which has remarkably good *prosciutto* sliced by hand, delicious potato ravioli and, in winter, baked fish (called *rombo* in Italian) with artichokes, along with the more strictly regional soups and *fiorentina*. Reserve. *Closed Sat lunch and Sun.*

Only in Rome would you find a good French restaurant run by a Catholic lay missionary society—*sole meunière* and onion soup in the well-scrubbed and righteous atmosphere of **L'Eau Vive**, Via Monterone 85, ✆ 06 6880 1095, not far from the Pantheon. A nourishing meal at a modest price, served with serenity, will have you joining in a prayer to the Virgin Mary before dessert; the fixed lunch menu at *L25,000* is a great bargain. *Closed Sun.*

The Piazza di Spagna area is not as promising for restaurants as it is for hotels, but there are a few, of which the best, perhaps, is **Nino**, Via Borgognona 11, ✆ 06 678 6752, with an attractive flask full of cannellini beans simmering in the window, the signpost for true, well-prepared Tuscan cuisine. *Closed Sun.* **Dal Bolognese**, Piazza del Popolo 1, ✆ 06 361 11426, with tables outside on the grand piazza and a view of the Pincio, is the place to go to sample Emilian specialties—don't miss the tortellini or any other fresh pasta dish, and finish with *fruttini*, a selection of real fruit shells each filled with its own sorbet flavour. *Closed Mon.*

At **Paris**, Piazza San Calisto 7/a, ✆ 06 581 5378, just beyond Piazza Santa Maria in Trastevere, you get classic Roman-Jewish cuisine; particularly good is the *minestra di arzilla* (skate soup). *Closed Sun eve and Mon.*

The quarters just outside the Aurelian wall and north and east of the Villa Borghese are more good places to look for res-taurants. **Le Coppedè**, Via Taro 28/a, between Via Nomentana and Villa Ada, ✆ 06 841 1772, is a pleasant neighbourhood restaurant totally devoted to Pugliese cuisine, which is lighter than typical Roman fare. **Semidivino**, Via Alessandria 230, ✆ 06 4425 0795, is a classy and intimate wine bar which is also good for a first-rate meal based on excellent salads, an interesting selection of cheese and *salumi* (cured meats) and comforting soups at reasonable prices. *Closed Sat lunch and Sun.*

cheap

Roman Lounge de l'Hotel d'Inghilterra, Via Bocca di Leone 14, ✆ 06 699 81500, is an elegant retreat in the heart of the shopping district at the foot of the Spanish Steps, which at lunchtime offers an interesting *piatto unico* (one-dish menu) for *L35,000*; if you like their style you can return for a very expensive dinner. **Armando al Pantheon**, Salita de' Crescenzi 31, ✆ 06 6880 3034, not far from the Pantheon, is an authentic Roman trattoria famous for spaghetti *cacio e pepe* (with pecorino cheese and black pepper) or *all'amatriciana*, *saltimbocca* (veal topped with sage and prosciutto) and a delicious ricotta tart. *Closed Sat eve and Sun.*

In Trastevere there's a small family trattoria, **Da Lucia**, Vicolo del Mattonato, ✆ 06 580 3601, two streets north of Piazza Santa Maria, that offers local cooking in a typical setting. If you are near the Vatican, an area with little more than forgettable tourist restaurants, venture a little way north to the **Antico Falcone**, Via Trionfale 60, ✆ 06 3974 3385, a simple place housed in what's left of a 15th-century farmhouse, for tasty *rigatoni alla nasona* (pasta with melted cheese and tomato sauce), *melanzane alla parmigiana* (baked eggplants topped with mozzarella, tomato and parmesan) and, in season, well-fried *carciofi alla giudia. Closed Tues.*

pizzerias

Roman pizza tends to be crisp and thin; most traditional wood-oven pizzerias have tables outside and are open only for dinner, often until 2am. **Da Baffetto**, Via del Governo Vecchio 11, ✆ 06 686 1617, is a beloved institution not far from Piazza Navona, as is **Panattoni**, Viale Trastevere 53, ✆ 06 580 0919, perhaps the best place to see *pizzaioli* at work, *closed Wed*. Nearby **Dar Poeta**, Vicolo del Bologna 45, ✆ 06 588 0516, is more on the verge of Neapolitan pizza, and perhaps the only pizzeria in town with a pizza dessert, the *calzone di ricotta* (filled with ricotta and chocolate) and a non-smoking room. *Closed Mon.* For strictly Neapolitan pizza, head to the pricy **Al Forno della Soffitta**, Via dei Villini 1/e, off the Via Nomentana, ✆ 06 440 4692, where they also have delicious pastry delivered daily from Naples. *Closed Sun.*

Entertainment and Nightlife

The best entertainment in Rome is often in the passing cosmopolitan spectacle of its streets; as nightlife goes, the capital can be a real snoozer compared with other European cities, though if you don't expect too much you'll have a good time.

To keep up with any area of entertainment in Rome you would do well to buy a copy of *Romac'e'* (from news-stands) which has comprehensive listings and a small section at the back in English. Another source is the weekly *Time Out*, with listings and articles (in Italian).

opera, classical music, theatre and film

From November until May you can take in a performance at the **Teatro dell'Opera di Roma**, Via Firenze 72 (box office, ✆ 06 4816 0255, information, ✆ 06 481 601). Other concerts and chamber music are performed at and by the **Accademia Nazionale di Santa Cecilia**, in the auditorium on Via della Conciliazione 4 (box office, ✆ 06 6880 1044, information, ✆ 06 361 1064), and by the **Accademia Filarmonica** at the **Teatro Olimpico**, Piazza Gentile da Fabriano 17 (box office, ✆ 06 323 4936, information, ✆ 06 323 4890). Medieval music, Baroque music, chamber music and choral music are frequently performed at the **Oratorio del Gonfalone**, Via del Gonfalone 32/a, ✆ 06 687 5952.

If you want to go to any concerts in Rome, try to get tickets as soon as possible to avoid disappointment. **Orbis**, Piazza Esquilino 37, ✆ 06 474 4776, is a reliable concert and theatre ticket agency (*open Mon–Sat 9.30–1 and 4–7.30*).

Despite the Italian tendency to dub all foreign films, you can find films in *versione originale* at the **Alcazar**, Via Cardinal Merry del Val 14 (*Mon*), at the **Nuovo Sacher**, Largo Ascianghi 1 (*Mon and Tues*), at the **Majestic**, Via SS. Apostoli 20 (*Tues*), and at the **Pasquino**, on Piazza Sant'Egidio, near Piazza Santa Maria in Trastevere, ✆ 06 580 3622 (*daily*).

cafés and bars

When you're tired of window-shopping you can rest your legs at Rome's oldest café, the **Antico Caffé Greco**, Via Condotti 86 (1760), and fantasize that you are sitting perhaps in the very place where Keats or Casanova was wont to do. The headquarters for visiting poets in the Romantic era, the Greco is now the average tourist's cheapest chance for a 20-minute dose of *ancien régime* luxury in Rome. Another of the city's *grand cafés* is the **Caffé Rosati**, in Piazza del Popolo, an elegant place founded in 1922, and traditionally popular with the Roman intelligentsia, no doubt attracted by its extravagant ice-creams. Other cafés can be dignified, historic or crazily expensive—for example, the 150-year-old **Babington's Tea Rooms**, on Piazza di Spagna, for scones and tea or a full lunch in the proper Victorian atmosphere. At trendy **Sant'Eustachio**, Piazza Sant'Eustachio, near Piazza Navona, tell them to mind the sugar.

Another kind of Roman bar is represented by the ultra-hip **Bar della Pace**, Via della Pace 3, supposedly much frequented by celebrities and a place for serious posing. A more funky and friendly atmosphere can be found most evenings at **La Vineria**, Campo de' Fiori 15, a relaxed traditional wine bar/shop with tables outside.

It's not hard to find *gelato* on nearly every corner in Rome, but hold out for the best the city has to offer, at the celebrated **Il Gelato di San Crispino**, Via della Panetteria 42, near the Trevi Fountain. Another novelty in Rome are sweets from **Il Forno del Ghetto** (*closed Sat*), the Jewish bakery at the west end of Via del Portico d'Ottavia (note the incredible building it's in—a recycled ancient structure covered with reliefs and inscriptions).

rock, jazz and clubs

Rome has a select band of clubs with live music almost every night—*Romac'e'* will have details of current programmes at the folk-oriented **Folkstudio**, Via Frangipane 42, ✆ 06 487 1063, the mainly-rock venues such as **Big Mama**, Vicolo San Francesco a Ripa 18, in Trastevere, ✆ 06 581 2551, and a blues club, **Alpheus**, Via del Commercio 36–38, in Ostiense, ✆ 06 574 9826. Also for jazz venues—which have a strong Roman following—like the suave **Alexanderplatz**, Via Ostia 9, in Prati, ✆ 06 3974 2971, and the **New Mississippi Jazz Club**, Borgo Angelico 18/a, near San Pietro, ✆ 06 6880 6348.

For serious dancing try **Alien**, Via Velletri 13, near Piazza Fiume, ✆ 06 841 2212, **Alpheus**, Via del Commercio 36, off Via Ostiense, ✆ 06 574 7826, or the less juvenile (jacket required) **Gilda**, Via Mario de' Fiori 97, close to the Spanish Steps, ✆ 06 678 4838.

Venice

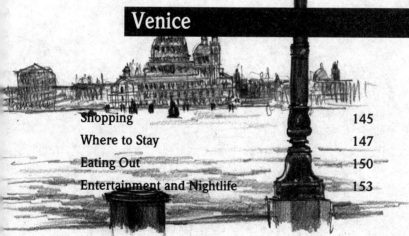

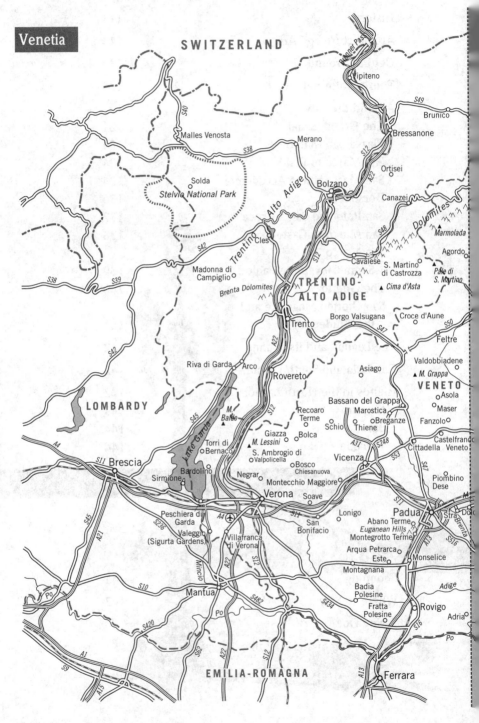

Venetia

SWITZERLAND

Brenner Pass

Vipiteno

Brunico

S49

Malles Venosta

Merano

Bressanone

S12

Ortisei

A22

Solda

Stelvio National Park

Bolzano

Canazei

S40

S38

Dolomites

Marmolada

Trentino

Alto Adige

Cles

S42

Agordo

Cavalese

S. Martino di Castrozza

Pale di S. Martino

Madonna di Campiglio

S38

S39

Brenta Dolomites

TRENTINO-ALTO ADIGE

Cima d'Asta

S42

Borgo Valsugana

Croce d'Aune

S50

Trento

S47

Feltre

A22

Valdobbiadene

Riva di Garda

Arco

Asiago

M. Grappa

VENETO

Rovereto

Bassano del Grappa

Asola

S42

S45

M. Baldo

S12

Recoaro Terme

Marostica

Maser

Breganze

Fanzolo

LOMBARDY

Giazza

Schio

Thiene

A31

S248

Castelfranco Veneto

Torri di Bernaco

M. Lessini

Bolca

Cittadella

Veneto

Lake Garda

S. Ambrogio di Valpolicella

Vicenza

S53

A4

S11

Brescia

Bardolino

Negrar

Bosco Chiesanuova

Piombino Dese

Sirmione

Montecchio Maggiore

S11

Verona

Soave

Padua

M

Peschiera di Garda

A4

Lonigo

Abano Terme

Stra

Brenta

Dolo

S45

S236

Villafranca di Verona

San Bonifacio

Euganean Hills

A13

S516

A21

Valeggio (Sigurta Gardens)

S12

Montegrotto Terme

Mincio

A22

Arqua Petrarca

Este

Monselice

S10

Montagnana

Adige

Po

Mantua

S434

Badia Polesine

S482

Po

Fratta Polesine

Rovigo

Adria

S420

S62

A15

A22

S12

A13

Ferrara

S16

Po

A1

S9

EMILIA-ROMAGNA

108

Venetia, sometimes known as the Three Venetias, is one of Italy's ripest showpieces and most chic holiday playgrounds, bursting at the seams with brilliant art, palaces, villas and beautiful cities. To these add some of Europe's most ravishing mountains, alpine lakes and sophisticated winter sports facilities; add too a few of Italy's most famous wines, delicious seafood and a very noticeable cultural diversity and richness.

Venetia encompasses roughly the region controlled by Venice from the 14th and 15th centuries until the conquest of Napoleon. It includes three modern Italian regions—the Veneto itself, and the autonomous regions of Trentino-Alto Adige (Trento and Bolzano provinces) and Friuli-Venezia Giulia (Trieste, Udine, Pordenone and Gorizia)—stretching from the Po to the Dolomites, from Lake Garda to the border of Slovenia.

Venice

Venice seduces, Venice irritates, but Venice rarely disappoints. She is a golden fairy-tale city floating on the sea, a lovely mermaid with agate eyes and the gift of eternal youth. On the surface she is little changed from the days when Goethe called her the 'marketplace of the Morning and the Evening lands', when her amphibious citizens dazzled the world with their wealth and pageantry, their magnificent fleet, their half-oriental doges, their crafty merchant princes, their splendidly luminous art, their lack of scruples, their silken debauchery, and their long decline and fall into a seemingly endless carnival.

One can easily imagine Julius Caesar bewildered by modern Rome, or Romeo and Juliet missing their rendezvous in the traffic of modern Verona, but Marco Polo, were he to return from Cathay today, could take a familiar gondola up the familiar Grand Canal to his house in the Rialto, astonished more by the motor-boats than anything else. Credit for this unique preservation must go to the Lagoon and the canals, the amniotic fluid of Venice's birth and the formaldehyde that has pickled her more thoroughly than many more venerable cities on the mainland, where Fiats and industry have not feared to tread.

For a thousand years Venice called herself the 'Most Serene Republic' (*la Serenissima*), and at one point she ruled 'a quarter and a half' of the Roman Empire. The descent to an Italian provincial capital was steep, if gracefully bittersweet; and sensitive souls find gallons of melancholy, or, like Thomas Mann, even death, brewed into the city's canals that have nothing to do with the more flagrant microbes. In the winter, when the streets are silent, Venice can be so evocative that you have to kick the ghosts out of the way to pass down the narrower alleys.

But most people (some million of them a year) show up in the summer and, like their ancestors, have a jolly good time. For Venice is a most experienced old siren in her boudoir of watery mirrors. International organizations pump in the funds to keep her petticoats out of the water as well as smooth the worst of her wrinkles.

Notices posted throughout the city acknowledge that she 'belongs to everybody', while with a wink and swivel of her fascinating hips she slides a knowing hand deep into your pocket. Venice has always lived for gold, and you can bet she wants yours—and you might just as well give it to her, in return for the most enchanting, dream-like favours any city can grant.

History

Venice has always been so different, so improbable, that one can easily believe the legend that once upon a time the original inhabitants sprang up from the dew and mists on the muddy banks of their Lagoon. Historians who don't believe in fairies prefer to think that Venice was born of adversity: the islands and treacherous shallows of the Lagoon provided the citizens of the Veneto a refuge from Attila the Hun and the damning heresies sweeping the mainland. Twelve Lagoon townships grew up between modern Chioggia and Grado; when Theodoric the Great's secretary visited them in 523 he wrote that they were 'scattered like sea-birds' nests over the face of the waters'.

In 697 the 12 townships united to elect their first duke, or doge. Fishing, trading—in slaves, among other things—and their unique knowledge of the Lagoon brought the Venetians their first prosperity, but their key position in between the Byzantine Empire of the East and the 'barbarian' kings on the mainland also made them a bone of contention. Early Venice grew up helped by Byzantine patronage, but towards the end of the 8th century the Franks, who had defeated the Lombards in the name of the Pope and claimed dominion over the whole of northern Italy, turned their attention to the obstinate Venetians, hoping to add their islands to their possessions. In 810 they expected to achieve their goal when the Doge, Obelario de'Antenori, who was engaged in a bitter internal feud with other Venetian factions, invited Charlemagne's son Pepin to send his army into the city.

The Venetians, until then undecided amongst themselves whether to support Rome or Constantinople, united in response to the approach of Pepin's fleet, deposing the reviled Doge, defiantly declaring for Byzantium, and entrenching themselves on the islands of the Rialto. The shallows and queer humours of the Lagoon confounded Pepin, and after a gruelling six-month siege he gave up. It was there on the Rialto that the city-republic of Venice was born, and a subsequent treaty between the Franks and the Eastern Emperor Nicephorus (814) recognized the city as a subject of Byzantium, with all-important trading concessions. Byzantine authority over the city was, though, a matter of pure theory, so from then on Venice was effectively independent.

The Venetians lacked only a dynamic spiritual protector; their frumpy, obscure St Theodore with his crocodile was too low in the celestial hierarchy to fulfil the destiny they had in mind. In 829 some Venetian merchants, supposedly on secret orders from the Doge, carried off one of the republic's greatest coups when they purloined the body of St Mark from Alexandria; they smuggled him past the Egyptian authorities by claiming that the saint was a shipment of pickled pork, so that the Muslim guards turned away in disgust. To acquire an Evangelist for themselves was, in itself, a demonstration of the Venetians' ambition.

Marriage to the Sea

As the East–West trade grew in importance, the Venetians designed their domestic and external policies to accommodate it. At home they required peace and stability, and by the beginning of the 11th century had squelched aristocratic notions of an hereditary dogeship by exiling the most over-ambitious families; Venice would never have the despotic *signori* who plagued the rest of Italy.

The raids of Dalmatian pirates spurred the Venetians to fight their first major war in 997, when the great Doge Pietro Orseolo captured the pirates' coastal strongholds. The Venetians were so pleased with this first victory that they celebrated the event with a splendidly arrogant ritual every Ascension Day, the *Sensa* or 'Marriage of the Sea', in which the Doge would sail out to the Lido in his sumptuous barge, the *Bucintoro*, and cast a diamond ring into the sea, proclaiming, 'We wed thee, O sea, in sign of our true and perpetual dominion'.

Venice, because of her location and her mighty fleet, supplied a great deal of the transport for the first three Crusades, and in return received her first important trading concessions in the Middle East. Arch-rival Genoa became increasingly envious, and in 1171 convinced the Byzantine Emperor to all but wipe out Constantinople's Venetian quarter. Rashly the Doge Vitale Michiel II set off with a fleet himself to launch a revenge attack upon the Empire, which was an utter failure; on his return he was killed by an angry mob (Venetians were always sore losers), and the Great Council, the *Maggior Consiglio*, was brought into being to check the power of the Doge and avert future calamities.

Vengeance stayed on the back-burner until the next doge, the spry and cunning old Enrico Dandolo, was contracted to provide transport for the Fourth Crusade. When the Crusaders turned up without the Venetians' fee, Dandolo offered to forgo it in return for certain services: first, to reduce Venice's rebellious satellites in Dalmatia, and then, in 1204, to take Constantinople itself. Aged 90 and almost blind, Dandolo personally led the attack; Christendom was scandalized, but Venice had gained not only a glittering hoard of loot but also three-eighths of Constantinople and 'a quarter and a half' of the Roman Empire—enough islands and ports to control the trade routes in the Adriatic, Aegean, Asia Minor and Black Sea.

To ensure their dominance at home, in 1297 the merchant princes limited membership in the *Maggior Consiglio* to themselves and their heirs (an event known in Venetian history as the *Serrata*), inscribing their names in the famous *Golden Book*. The doges were slowly reduced to honorary chairmen of the board, bound up by a complex web of laws and customs to prevent any dictatorial ambitions.

A Rocky 14th Century

First the people (1300) and then the snubbed patricians (the 1310 Tiepolo Conspiracy) unsuccessfully rose up against their disenfranchisement under the republic's government. The latter threat was serious enough that a committee of public safety was formed to hunt down the conspirators, and in 1335 this committee became a permanent institution, the infamous Council of Ten. Because of its secrecy and speedy decisions, the Council of Ten took over much of Venice's government; in later years it was streamlined into a Council of Three. Membership was for one year, and over the centuries the Council (and especially its offshoot, the State Inquisition, set up in 1539) developed a reputation that dripped with terror. Its techniques—inviting private denunciations, torture, secret trials and executions, all supported by a network of spies and informers—have often been compared to those of a modern police state.

Away from home the 14th century was marked by a fight to the death with Genoa over Eastern trade routes. Each city annihilated the other's fleet on more than one occasion before things came to a head in 1379, when the Genoese, fresh from a victory over the Venetian commander Vittor Pisani, captured Chioggia and waited for Venice to starve, boasting that they had come to 'bridle the horses of St Mark'.

As was their custom, the Venetians had imprisoned Pisani for his defeat, but the republic was now in such a jam, with half of its fleet far away, that he was released to lead what remained of their navy. A brilliant commander, Pisani exploited his familiarity with the Lagoon and in turn blockaded the Genoese in Chioggia. When the other half of Venice's fleet came dramatically racing home, the Genoese surrendered (June 1380) and never recovered in the East.

Fresh Prey on the Mainland

After Genoa's defeat, Venice was determined never to feel hungry again, and set her sights on the mainland—not only for the sake of farmland, but to control her trade routes into the West that were being increasingly harried and taxed by the *signori* of the Veneto. Opportunity came in 1402 with the death of the Milanese duke Gian Galeazzo Visconti, whose conquests became the subject of a great land grab. Venice snatched Padua, Bassano, Verona and Belluno in the first round, and in 1454 added Treviso, Ravenna, Friuli and Bergamo. In 1489 the republic reached its furthest extent when it was presented with Cyprus, a gift from the King's widow, a Venetian noblewoman named Caterina Cornaro.

But just as Venice expanded, Fortune's wheel gave a creak and conspired to squeeze her back into her Lagoon. The Ottoman Turks captured Constantinople in 1453 and, although the Venetians tried to negotiate trading terms with the sultans (as they had previously done with the infidel Saracens, to the opprobrium of the West), they soon found themselves fighting and losing three centuries' worth of battles for their Eastern territories. Far graver to Venice's merchants was Vasco da Gama's voyage around the Cape of Good Hope to India, blazing a cheaper and easier route for Venice's markets that broke her monopoly of oriental luxuries.

On the mainland, Venice's rapid expansion had excited the fear and envy of Italy's potentates, who responded by forming the League of Cambrai (1508) with the sole aim of humbling the proud Venetians. They snatched her possessions after her defeat at Agnadello in 1509, but quarrelled amongst themselves afterwards, and before long all the territories they had conquered voluntarily returned to Venice. The republic, however, never really recovered, and although her renowned arsenal produced a warship a day, and her captains won a glorious victory over the Turks at Lepanto (1571), she was increasingly forced to retreat.

A Most Leisurely Collapse

The odds were stacked against her, but in her golden days Venice had accumulated enough wealth and verve to cushion her fall. Her noble families retired into the country, consoling themselves in the classical calm of Palladio's villas, while the city was adorned with the solace of great masterpieces of Venice's golden age of art. Carnival, ever longer, ever more licentious, was sanctioned by the state to bring in moneyed visitors like Lord Byron, who dubbed it 'the revel of the earth, the masque of Italy'. In the 1600s the city had 12,000 courtesans, many of them dressed as men to whet the Venetians' passion.

By the time of the French Revolution the Lion of St Mark had lost his remaining teeth, and Napoleon, declaring he would be 'an Attila for the Venetian state', took it with scarcely a whimper in 1797, neatly ending the story of the world's most enduring republic, in the reign of its 120th doge. Napoleon took the horses of St Mark to Paris as his trophy, and replaced the old *Pax tibi, Marce, Evangelista Meus* inscribed in the book the lion holds up on Venice's coat-of-arms with 'The Rights of Men and Citizens'. Reading it, a gondolier made the famous remark, 'At last he's turned the page'.

Napoleon gave Venice to Austria, whose rule was confirmed by the Congress of Vienna after the Emperor's defeat in 1815. The Austrians' main contribution was the railway causeway linking Venice irrevocably to the mainland (1846). Two years later, in the revolutionary year of 1848, Venice gave its last gasp of independence, when a patriotic revolt led by Daniele Manin seized the city and re-established the republic, only to fall to the Austrian army once again after a heroic one-year siege.

Modern Venice

The former republic did, however, finally join the new kingdom of Italy—the last of the great Italian cities to do so—in 1866, after Prussia had conveniently defeated the Austrians. Already better known as a magnet to foreign visitors than for any activity of its own, Venice played a quiet role in the new state, though the economy did begin to change, particularly under Mussolini, when the industrial zones of Mestre and Marghera were begun on the mainland and a road was added to the railway causeway. Luckily the city escaped damage in the two World Wars, despite heavy fighting in the environs; according to one legend, when the Allies finally occupied Venice in 1945 they arrived in a fleet of gondolas.

But Venice was soon to engage in its own private battle with the sea. From the beginning the city had manipulated nature's waterways for her own survival and defence, diverting a major outlet of the Po, the Brent, the Piave, the Adige and the Sile Rivers to keep her Lagoon from silting up. All but three outlets to the sea were blocked; and most famously, in 1782, Venice completed the *murazzi*, the 4km-long, 20ft-high sea walls to protect the Lagoon. But on 4 November 1966 a combination of wind, torrential storms, high tides and giant waves breached the *murazzi*, wrecked the Lido and left Venice under record *acque alte* (high water) for 20 hours, with disastrous results to the city's architecture and art. The catastrophe galvanized the international community's efforts to save Venice. Even the Italian state, notorious for its indifference to Venice (historical grudges die slowly in Italy), passed a law in 1973 to preserve the city, and contributed to the construction of a new flood barricade similar to the one on the Thames.

This giant sea gate, known as 'Moses', has now been completed, but arguments continue over whether it will ever be effective if needed, and what its ecological consequences might be. Venice today is perennially in crisis, permanently under restoration, and seemingly threatened by a myriad potential disasters—the growth of algae in the Lagoon, the effects of the outpourings of Mestre on its foundations, the ageing of its native population, and perhaps most of all the sheer number of its tourists. Fears of an environmental catastrophe have, though, receded of late; somehow the city contrives to survive, as unique as ever, and recent proposals to give it more of a function in the modern world, as, for example, a base for international organizations, may serve to give it new life as well.

Architecture

At once isolated on her islands but deeply linked to the traditions of East and West, Venice developed her own charmingly bastard architecture, adopting only the most delightfully visual elements from each tradition. Ruskin's *The Stones of Venice* is the classic work on the city's buildings, which harsher critics—and Ruskin was one—disparage for being all artifice and show, devoid of any proper theories and conceptional ideals. The Venetians inherited the Byzantines' fondness for colour, mosaics, rare marbles and exotic effects, epitomized in the magnificently garish **St Mark's**. Venetian Gothic is only slightly less elaborate, and achieved its most notable products in the great palaces, most notably the **Palazzo Ducale** and the **Ca' d'Oro**, with their ogival windows and finely wrought façades.

The Renaissance arrived in Venice relatively late, and its early phase is called Lombardesque, after the **Lombardo** family (Pietro and sons Tullio and Antonio) who designed the best of it, including the small but flawless **Santa Maria dei Miracoli** and the rich **Scuola di San Marco**. Later Renaissance architects brought Venice into the mainstream of the classical revival, and graced Venice with the arcaded **Piazza San Marco**, the **Libreria** of Sansovino, the **San Michele** of Mauro Codussi (also named Coducci), and two of **Palladio**'s finest churches, which stand out in clear contrast to the exuberant jumble that surrounds them. Venice's best Baroque works are by **Longhena**, the spiritual heir of Palladio.

To support all this on the soft mud banks, the Venetians drove piles of Istrian pine 16ft into the solid clay—over a million posts hold up the church of Santa Maria della Salute alone. If Venice tends to lean and sink (an eighth of an inch a year, according to the tourist office), it's due to erosion of these piles by the salty Adriatic, pollution and the currents and wash caused by the deep channels dredged into the Lagoon for the large tankers sailing to Marghera. Or, as the Venetians explain it, the city is a giant sponge.

Most Venetian houses are between four and six storeys high. On the tops of some you can see the wooden rooftop loggias, or *altane*, where the Renaissance ladies of Venice were wont to idle, bleaching their hair in the sun; they wore broad-brimmed hats to protect their complexions, and spread their tresses through a hole cut in the crown.

Art

Though a late bloomer in painting, Venice is rivalled only by Florence when it comes to the artistic treasures she has to offer. Before the 14th century the Venetians excelled primarily in mosaic, an art they learned from the Byzantines and produced most memorably in the cathedrals of Torcello and St Mark's. But change was in the air: in 1306 Giotto was working on his great series of paintings in the Scrovegni Chapel in Padua, and his influence can be seen in the works of **Paolo Veneziano**, the first Venetian painter of note (14th century). Byzantine and Gothic tendencies, however, remained strong for a long period, especially in the works of later Venetians, the **Vivarini** dynasty of Murano and **Jacobello del Fiore**.

All of these gave way in the 15th century before the advanced styles of two great Veneto masters. **Andrea Mantegna** (1431–1506), trained in Padua, influenced generations of artists and sculptors with his strong interest in antiquity and powerful sculptural figures, while the long career of his brother-in-law, **Giovanni Bellini** (1440?–1516) marked the transition in Venice from the Early to the High Renaissance. Giovanni's father, **Jacopo Bellini**, instilled a love of nature and the senses in his son, who was later influenced by the luminous oil painting techniques of **Antonello da Messina** (who visited Venice in 1475). The light and colour that are the hallmarks of Venetian painting were first explored by Giovanni Bellini, and his sweet

Madonnas are one of the delights of the Italian Renaissance. Other noteworthy artists of the Venetian quattrocento include **Vittore Carpaccio** (1470–1523), the charming master of narrative painting, and **Carlo Crivelli** (1432–93), a lover of clear detail—and cucumbers—who spent his later career in the Marches.

The Cinquecento

The 16th century is often called the golden age of Venetian art. While the rest of Italy followed the artists in Rome in learning drawing and anatomy, the Venetians went their own way, obsessed with the dramatic qualities of atmosphere. **Giorgione of Castelfranco** (1475–1510), a pupil of Bellini, was the seminal figure in this new manner; his *Tempest* in the Accademia is a remarkable study in brooding tension. Giorgione is also credited with inventing 'easel painting'—art that served neither Church nor state nor the vanity of a patron, but stood on its own for the pleasure of the viewer.

Giorgione's pupil, Tiziano Vecellio, or **Titian** (1477–1576), was another major transitional figure in Venetian art; while his early works are often confused with his master's, his later career is marked by dramatic, often spiralling compositions and striking tonal effects produced by large brushstrokes. His contemporary, **Tintoretto** (1518–94), took these Mannerist tendencies to unforgettable extremes, while *trompe l'œil* master **Paolo Veronese** (1528–88), originally of Verona, painted visually lavish canvases that are the culmination and epitome of all that Venice had to teach.

Other outstanding Venetians of the period include **Cima da Conegliano**, creator of some of Venice's loveliest landscapes, and **Palma il Vecchio**, Titian's rival, fond of depicting luscious blonde Venetian goddesses.

Venetian painting, from Titian on, was the international style of its day, and it enjoyed a healthy revival in the 18th century when demand was high in Venice and abroad. **Giambattista Tiepolo** (1696–1770) and his son **Giandomenico** were the masters of a huge school of theatrical, buoyant ceiling art and narrative frescoes, while **Antonio Canaletto** (1697–1768) and **Francesco Guardi** (1712–93) produced countless views of Venice that were the rage among travellers on the Grand Tour; even today the majority of their works are in Britain and France. **Pietro Longhi**, their contemporary, devoted himself to genre scenes that offer a delightful insight into the Venice of 200 years ago.

Getting Around

The historic centre of Venice stands on 117 islets, divided by over 100 canals that are spanned by some 400 bridges. The open sea is about 2km across the Lagoon, beyond the protective reefs of *lidi* formed by centuries of river silt and the Adriatic current.

The Grand Canal, Venice's incomparable main street, was originally the bed of a river that fed the Lagoon. The other canals, its tributaries (called *rio*, singular, or *rii*, plural), add up to 45km of watery thoroughfares. A warren of 2300 alleys, or *calli*, handle Venice's pedestrian-only traffic, and they come with a colourful bouquet of names—a *rio terrà* is a filled-in canal; a *piscina* a filled-in pool; a *fondamenta* or *riva* a quay; a *salizzada* a street that was paved in the 17th century; a *ruga* one lined with shops; a *sottoportico* passes under a building. A Venetian square is a *campo*, recalling the days when they were open fields; the only square dignified with the title of *piazza* is San Marco, though the two smaller squares flanking the basilica are called *piazzette*.

The *rii* and *calli* are divided into six quarters or *sestiert*: **San Marco** (by the piazza), **Castello** (by the Arsenal) and **Cannaregio** (by the Ghetto), all on the northeast bank of the Grand Canal; and **San Polo** (by the church), **Santa Croce** (near the Piazzale Roma) and **Dorsoduro**, the 'hard-back' by the Accademia, all on the southwest bank. Besides these, the modern *comune* of Venice includes the towns on the Lagoon islands, the Lido, and the mainland townships of Mestre and Marghera where most Venetians live today.

vaporetti *and* motoscafi

Public transport in Venice means by water, by the grunting, canal-cutting *vaporetti* (the all-purpose water-buses), or the sleeker, faster *motoscafi*, run by the ACTV (✆ 041 528 7886). Note that the only canals served by public transport are the Grand Canal, the Rio Nuovo, the Canale di Cannaregio and the Rio dell'Arsenale; between them, you'll have to rely on your feet, which is not as gruelling as it sounds, as Venice is so small you can walk across it in an hour.

Single **tickets** (a flat rate of L6000) should be purchased and validated in the machines at the landing-stages (random inspections aren't very frequent, but if you get caught without a validated ticket you'll have to pay a L30,000 fine on the spot). As some landing-stages don't sell tickets, it's best to stock up (most *tabacchi* sell them in blocks of ten). Or, if you intend being on a boat at least three times in a given day, purchase a **24-hour tourist pass**, for L18,000, valid for unlimited travel on all lines, or the **3-day pass**, for L35,000. If you plan to spend more than a few days in Venice, the cheapest option is to buy a *tesserino di abbonamento* from the ACTV office at Piazzale Roma (L10,000) and a passport photo—there's a machine at the Ferrovia) which is valid for three years and entitles you to buy monthly season tickets (L45,000) or single tickets at greatly reduced rates.

water-taxis

These are really more tourist excursion boats—they work like taxis, but their fares are de luxe. Stands are at the station, Piazzale Roma, Rialto, San Marco, Lido and the airport. These jaunty motor-boats can hold up to 15 passengers, and fares are set for destinations beyond the historic centre, or you can pay L150,000 per hour. Within the centre the minimum fare for up to four people is L50,000; additional passengers are up to L10,000 each, and there are surcharges for baggage, holiday or nocturnal service (after 10pm), and for using a radio taxi (✆ 041 522 2303).

gondolas

Gondolas, first mentioned in the city's annals in 1094, have a stately mystique that commands all other boats to give way. Shelley and many others have compared them to a funeral barque or the soul ferry to Hades, and not a few gondoliers share the infernal Charon's expectation of a solid gold tip for their services. Like Model Ts, gondolas come in any colour as long as it's black, still obeying the Sumptuary Law of 1562, though nowadays hardly any gondolas have their traditional cabins, once notorious for clandestine trysts.

Venice Transport

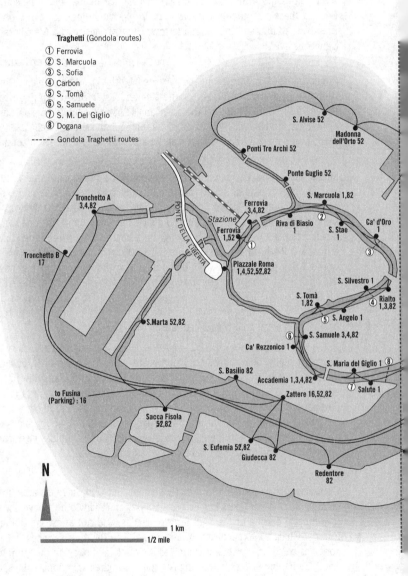

Traghetti (Gondola routes)

① Ferrovia
② S. Marcuola
③ S. Sofia
④ Carbon
⑤ S. Tomà
⑥ S. Samuele
⑦ S. M. Del Giglio
⑧ Dogana

------ Gondola Traghetti routes

S. Alvise 52

Madonna dell'Orto 52

Ponti Tre Archi 52

Ponte Guglie 52

Tronchetto A 3,4,82

Ferrovia 3,4,82

Stazione

S. Marcuola 1,82

Ferrovia 1,52

Riva di Biasio 1

S. Stae 1

Ca' d'Oro 1

②

③

①

Tronchetto B 17

Plazzale Roma 1,4,52,52,82

PONTE DELLA LIBERTA

S. Silvestro 1

S. Tomà 1,82

Rialto 1,3,82

④

S.Marta 52,82

S. Angelo 1

⑤

S. Samuele 3,4,82

⑥

Ca' Rezzonico 1

S. Maria del Giglio 1 ⑧

S. Basilio 82

Accademia 1,3,4,82

Salute 1

⑦

to Fusina (Parking) : 16

Zattere 16,52,82

Sacca Fisola 52,82

S. Eufemia 52,82

Giudecca 82

Redentore 82

N

1 km

1/2 mile

Regular Lines

1: *(accelerato)* Piazzale Roma–Ferrovia–Grand Canal–San Marco–Lido: stops every where; around the clock, every 10min (20mins after 9pm). The entire one-way journey takes an hour.

6: *(diretto motonave)* S. Zaccaria–Lido; every 20mins.

11: (the 'mixed' line) Lido–Alberoni (by bus)–Pellestrina (by boat)–Chioggia (by boat); about once an hour. (Not shown.)

12: Fondamente Nuove–Murano–Torcello–Burano–Treporti; about once an hour.

13: Fondamente Nuove–Murano–Vignole–S. Erasmo; about once an hour.

14: S. Zaccaria–Lido–Punta Sabbioni–Treporti–Burano–Torcello (every half-hour).

17: (car ferry) Tronchetto (Piazzale Roma)–Giudecca–Lido–Punta Sabbione; every 50mins.

5̶2: (red 'barred') *(motoscafo)* Piazzale Roma–Giudecca–S. Zaccaria–Campo della Tana (the Arsenale)–Fondamente Nuove–Murano (all six stops)–S. Michele; every 20mins.

52: (green) *(motoscafo)* Lido–S. Zaccaria–Zattere–Piazzale Roma–Ferrovia–Fondamente Nuove–Murano; every 20mins.

82: (orange) *(diretto)* S. Zaccaria (S. Marco)–Lido–Giudecca–S. Giorgio Maggiore; a speedy circular tour; every 10min during the day, approx. once an hour at night.

82: (green) *(diretto)* S. Zaccaria–S. Giorgio Maggiore–Giudecca–Zattere–S. Marta; every 10mins.

N: *(servizio notturno)* Lido–S. Zaccaria–Accademia–S. Toma–Rialto–Piazzale Roma–Zattere–Zitelle–S. Giorgio Maggiore; every 20mins from about 11pm all night.

Summer only

3: Tronchetto–Grand Canal–S. Zaccaria–Tronchetto

4: S. Zaccaria–Grand Canal–Tronchetto–S. Zaccaria

16: (private service *L8000*) Zattere–Fusina car park; every 50mins.

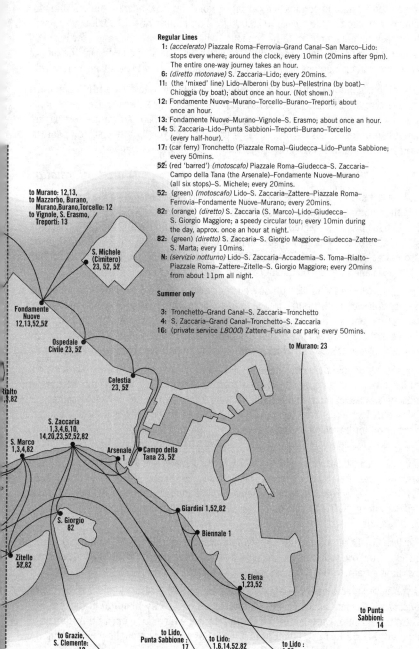

to Murano: 12,13,
to Mazzorbo, Burano,
Murano,Burano,Torcello: 12
to Vignole, S. Erasmo,
Treporti: 13

S. Michele
(Cimitero)
23, 52, 5̶2

Fondamente
Nuove
12,13,52,5̶2

Ospedale
Civile 23, 5̶2

Celestia
23, 5̶2

Rialto
,3,82

S. Zaccaria
1,3,4,6,10,
14,20,23,5̶2,52,82

S. Marco
1,3,4,82

Arsenale
1

Campo della
Tana 23, 5̶2

to Murano: 23

Giardini 1,52,82

Biennale 1

S. Giorgio
82

Zitelle
5̶2,82

S. Elena
1,23,52

to Punta
Sabbioni:
14

to Grazie,
S. Clemente:
10

to Lido,
Punta Sabbione :
17

to Lido:
1,6,14,52,82

to Lido :
1,52

Once used by all and sundry like carriages, gondolas now operate quite frankly for tourists who can pay the official L120,000 for a 50-minute ride (L150,000 after 8pm). Before setting out, agree with the gondolier where you want to go and how long you expect it to take, to avoid any unpleasantness later. The above prices are the official tariff, but many gondoliers (especially in high season) will try to negotiate a premium.

In addition, gondolas retired from the tourist trade are used for **gondola traghetti** services across the Grand Canal at various points between its three bridges—your only chance to enjoy an economical, if brief, gondola ride for L700. *Traghetto* crossings are signposted in the streets nearby. For appearances' sake you'll have to stand up for the short but precarious experience: only sissies ever sit down on *traghetti.*

Tourist Information

The main information office is in one corner of Piazza San Marco, to the far left as you face the square (Ascensione 71/c, © 041 522 6356). Branch offices are at Palazzetto Selva, right by the S. Marco *vaporetto* stop (© 041 529 8730), the railway station (© 041 529 8727) and the bus station in Piazzale Roma (© 041 522 7402). There are also offices on the Rotonda Marghera (© 041 937 764), Marco Polo Airport (© 041 541 5887) and on the Lido at Gran Viale 6 (© 041 526 5721).

The main source in English on any current events is the fortnightly magazine *Un Ospite di Venezia*, distributed free at tourist offices. Otherwise, the two local papers *Il Gazzettino* and *Nuova Venezia* both have listings of films, concerts and so on in Venice and the *terraferma*. Another detailed source of information is the monthly city magazine *Marco Polo*, with articles written in Italian but summarized in English.

For L5000, people between the ages of 14 and 29 can buy a *Rolling Venice* card, which gives discounts on the city's attractions, from films at the Film Festival to museums, hostels, shops and restaurants (and free access to the university canteen in Palazzo Badoer, Calle del Magazen 2840). It also allows you to buy a special reduced-price ticket for travelling on the *vaporetti*.

Apply at one of these three associations: the Assessorato alla Gioventù, Corte Contarina 1529, San Marco, © 041 274 7650/1 (*Mon–Fri 9.30–1, Tues and Thurs also 3–5*); Agenzia Arte e Storia, Corte Canal 659, Santa Croce, © 041 524 0232 (*Mon–Fri 9–1 and 3.30–7*); or Associazione Italiana Alberghi per la Gioventù, Calle del Castelforte 3101, San Polo, © 041 520 4414 (*Mon–Sat 8–2*). Take a photo and your passport.

For less urgent enquiries, the *Carabinieri* barracks is in Piazzale Roma, © 041 523 5333. If you lose something in the city, try the Municipio, © 041 274 8111; or if you lost it on a train, © 041 785 238; or on a *vaporetto*, © 041 780 310.

If you have an accident or become seriously ill, go to the casualty (first aid) or *Pronto Soccorso* (Accident and Emergency) department of the **city hospital** in Campo Santi Giovanni e Paolo, Castello, or the **Ospedale del Mare**, Lungomare d'Annunzio 1, Lido (© 041 529 4111); if you need a doctor at night or on public holidays ring the *Guardia Medica*, © 041 529 4060.

Italian pharmacists are trained to diagnose minor ills and can give you prescription drugs. Several *farmacie* are open all night on a rotating basis: the addresses are in the window of each, or you can ring ✆ 041 523 0573 for a list, or find them in *Un Ospite di Venezia*.

Places that exchange money outside normal banking hours include:

American Express: S. Moisè 1471, ✆ 041 520 0844 (*open April–Oct Mon–Sat 8–8*).

CIT: Piazza S. Marco 4850, ✆ 041 528 5480 (*open Mon–Sat 8–6*).

INTRAS: Piazza S. Marco, at the corner of the Procuratie Nuove and the clock tower (*open Mon–Sat 8.30–6*).

World Vision: (Thomas Cook), Calle delle Ostreghe 2457, S. Marco.

The **main post office** is in the Fóndaco dei Tedeschi, near the Ponte Rialto (*open Mon–Sat 8.15–7.25*). There are also smaller offices at the foot of Piazza San Marco (Calle dell'Ascensione) and at the western end of the Zattere, although you can buy stamps at any tobacco shop.

Around the City

The Grand Canal

A ride down Venice's bustling and splendid main artery is most visitors' introduction to the city, and there's no better one. The Grand Canal has always been Venice's status address, and along its looping banks the aristocrats, or *nobili homini*, as they called themselves, built a hundred marble palaces with their front doors giving on to the water, framed by the peppermint-stick posts where they moored their watery carriages. The oldest palaces, dating back to the 12th century, reveal Byzantine influences, but most are either Venetian Gothic or Lombardesque, or a combination of several periods and styles remodelled over the years.

Connoisseurs of palaces can purchase guides of the Grand Canal that give details of each structure, but in brief the most acclaimed, heading from Piazzale Roma to the Piazza San Marco, are: the **Fóndaco dei Turchi** (on the right after the Station Bridge), formerly the Turkish warehouse and now the Natural History Museum; almost opposite, Mauro Codussi's Renaissance **Palazzo Vendramin-Calergi**, where Richard Wagner died in 1883, now the winter home of the casino. Back on the right bank, just after the San Stae landing, the Baroque **Ca' Pésaro** is adorned with masks by Longhena. And then comes the loveliest of them all, the **Ca' d'Oro**, by its own landing stage, with an elaborate florid Gothic façade, formerly etched in gold, now housing the Galleria Franchetti (*see* p.140).

After the Ca' d'Oro Europe's most famous bridge, the **Ponte di Rialto**, swings into view. 'Rialto' recalls the days when the canal was the Rio Alto; originally it was spanned here by a bridge of boats, then by a 13th-century wooden bridge. When that was on the verge of collapse, the republic held a competition for the design of a new stone structure. The winner, Antonio da Ponte, was the most audacious, proposing a single arch spanning 48m; built in 1592, it has since defied the dire predictions of the day and still stands, even taking the additional weight of two rows of shops. The reliefs over the arch are of St Mark and St Theodore.

To the right stretch the extensive **Rialto Wholesale Markets**, and on the left the **Fóndaco dei Tedeschi** ('German Warehouse'), once the busiest trading centre in Venice, where merchants from all over the north lived and traded. The building (now the post office) was

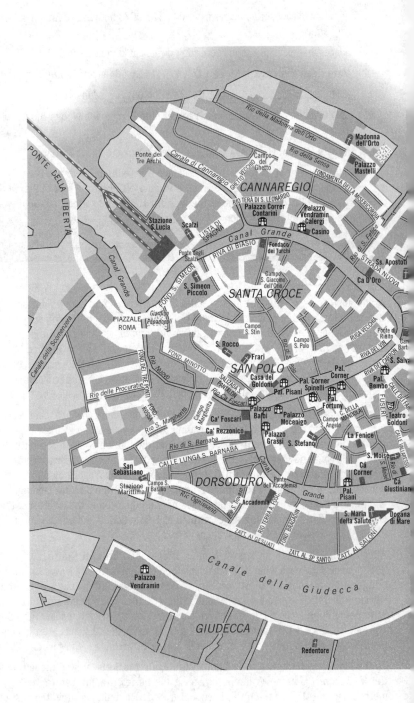

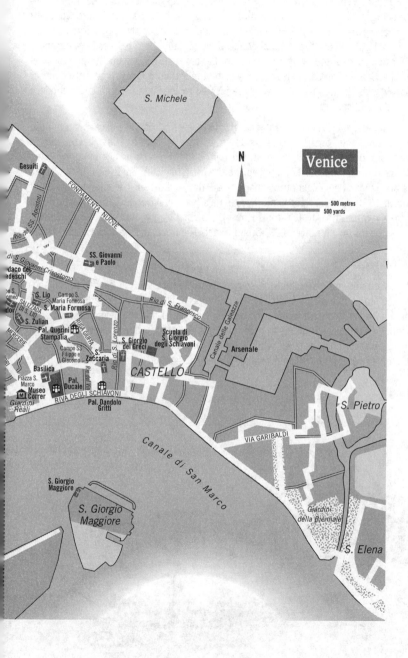

S. Michele

N

Venice

500 metres
500 yards

Gesuiti

FONDAMENTA NUOVE

Rio de SS. Apostoli

Rio di S. Giovanni Crisostomo

daco dei
adeschi

o S.
omeo

S. Lio

Campo S.
Maria Formosa

SALIZZADA
DI S. LIO

S. Maria Formosa

dor

SS. Giovanni
e Paolo

Rio di S. Francesco

S. Zulian

MERCERIE

Pal. Querini
Stampalia

RUGA GIUFFA

Rio di S. Lorenzo

S. Giorgio
dei Greci

Scuola di
S. Giorgio
degli Schiavoni

Canale delle Galeazze

Arsenale

Campo S.
Filippo e
Giacomo

S.
Zaccaria

Basilica

Piazza S.
Marco

Museo
Correr

Pal.
Ducale

Rio del Vin

CASTELLO

RIVA DEGLI SCHIAVONI

Giardini
Reali

RIVA DEGLI SCHIAVONI

Pal. Dandolo
Gritti

S. Pietro

VIA GARIBALDI

Canale di San Marco

S. Giorgio
Maggiore

S. Giorgio
Maggiore

Giardini
della Biennale

S. Elena

123

remodelled in 1505 and adorned with exterior frescoes by Giorgione and Titian, of which only some fragments survive (now in the Ca' d'Oro).

Beyond the Ponte di Rialto are two Renaissance masterpieces: across from the S. Silvestro landing, Sanmicheli's 1556 **Palazzo Grimani**, now the Appeals Court, and Mauro Codussi's **Palazzo Corner-Spinelli** (1510) just before Sant'Angelo landing stage. A short distance further along the left bank are the **Palazzi Mocenigo**, actually three palaces in one, where Byron lived for two years. A little way further on on the same side a space opens up in the wall of buildings, the Campo San Samuele, dominated by the **Palazzo Grassi**, an 18th-century neoclassical residence that has been completely renovated by the Fiat Corporation as a modern exhibition and cultural centre.

On the right bank, just after the bend in the canal, the lovely Gothic **Ca' Foscari** was built in 1437 for Doge Francesco Foscari: two doors down, by its own landing-stage, is Longhena's 1667 **Ca' Rezzonico**, where Browning died. Further on the canal is spanned by the wooden **Ponte dell'Accademia**, built in 1932 to replace the ungainly iron 'English bridge'. On the left bank, before S. Maria del Giglio, the Renaissance **Palazzo Corner** (Ca' Grande) was built by Sansovino in 1550. On the right bank, Longhena's famous Baroque **Santa Maria della Salute** and the **Dogana di Mare** (Customs House), crowned by a golden globe and weather-vane of Fortune, guard the entrance to the Grand Canal. The next landing-stage is San Marco.

Piazza San Marco

Napoleon described this grand asymmetrical showpiece as 'Europe's finest drawing-room' and, no matter how often you've seen it in pictures or in the flesh, its charm never fades. There are Venetians (and not all of them purveyors of souvenirs) who prefer it in the height of summer at its liveliest, when Babylonians from the four corners of the earth outnumber even the pigeons, who swoop back and forth at eye level, while the rival café bands provide a schmaltzy accompaniment. Others prefer it in the misty moonlight, when the familiar seems unreal under hazy, rosy streetlamps.

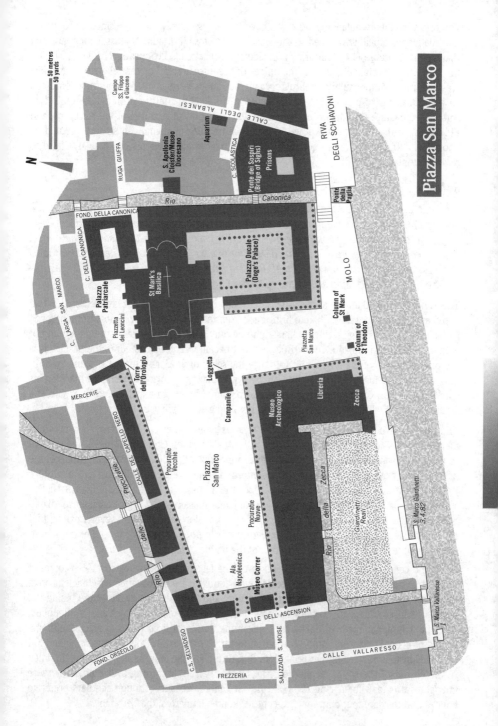

Piazza San Marco

125

The piazza and its two flanking *piazzette* have looked essentially the same since 1810, when the 'Ala Napoleonica' was added to the west end, to close in Mauro Codussi's long, arcaded **Procuratie Vecchie** (1499) on the north side and Sansovino's **Procuratie Nuove** (1540) on the south. Both, originally used as the offices of the 'procurators' or caretakers of St Mark's, are now lined with jewellery, embroidery and lace shops. Two centuries ago they contained an equal number of coffee-houses, the centres of the 18th-century promenade. Only two survive—the **Caffè Quadri** in the Procuratie Vecchie, the old favourite of the Austrians, and **Florian's**, in the Procuratie Nuove, its hand-painted décor unchanged since it opened its doors in 1720, although with coffees at L7000 a head the proprietors could easily afford to remodel it in solid gold.

St Mark's Basilica

> *Open to visitors Mon–Sat 10–4.30, Sun and hols 2–5. Men must wear a shirt and long trousers, women must have their shoulders covered, a minimum of décolletage and no shorts, or risk being peremptorily dismissed from the head of the queue. There are separate admission charges for many of the smaller chapels and individual attractions, and be warned that different sections are frequently closed for restoration. Disabled ramp access from Piazzetta dei Leoncini.*

This is nothing less than the holy shrine of the Venetian state. An ancient law decreed that all merchants trading in the East had to bring back from their voyages a new embellishment for St Mark's. The result is a glittering robbers' den, the only church in Christendom that would not look out of place in Xanadu. Until 1807, when it became Venice's cathedral, the basilica was the private chapel of the doge, built to house the relics of St Mark after their 'pious theft' in 828, a deed sanctioned by a tidy piece of apocrypha that had the good Evangelist mooring his ship in the Rialto on the way from Aquileia to Rome, when an angel hailed him with the famous '*Pax tibi...*', or 'Peace to you, Mark, my Evangelist. Here your body shall lie.'

The present structure, consecrated in 1094, was begun after a fire destroyed a previous St Mark's in 976. Modelled after Constantinople's former Church of the Apostles, five rounded doorways, five upper arches and five round Byzantine domes are the essentials of the exterior, all frosted with a sheen of coloured marbles, ancient columns and sculpture ('As if in ecstasy,' wrote Ruskin, 'the crests of the arches break into marbly foam...'). The spandrils of the arches glitter with gaudy, Technicolor mosaics—the High Renaissance, dissatisfied with the 13th-century originals, saw fit to commission cartoons from several painters for the scenes, leaving intact only the *Translation of the Body of St Mark* on the extreme left, which includes the first historical depiction of the basilica itself.

Front and centre, seemingly ready to prance off the façade, the controversial 1979 copies of the bronze **horses of St Mark** masquerade well enough—from a distance. The ancient originals (cast some time between the 3rd century BC and 2nd century AD, and now inside the basilica's Museo Marciano) were one of the most powerful symbols of the Venetian Republic, part of a 'triumphal quadriga' taken by Constantine the Great from Chios to grace the hippodrome of his new city, only to be carried off in turn by the artful Doge Dandolo in the 1204 sack of Constantinople. Another prize from Byzantium are the four porphyry 'Moors' huddled in the corner of the south façade near the Doge's Palace; according to legend, they were changed into stone for daring to break into St Mark's treasury, though scholars prefer to believe that they are four chummy 3rd-century Roman emperors, the Tetrarchs.

The Interior

The best mosaics, most of them 13th-century originals, cover the six domes of the **atrium**, or narthex, their old gold glimmering in the permanent twilight. The oldest mosaic in St Mark's is that of the *Madonna and Saints* above the central door, part of the original 11th-century decoration of the basilica. A slab of red marble in the pavement marks the spot where the Emperor Barbarossa knelt and apologized to 'St Peter and his pope'—Alexander III, in 1177. This, a favourite subject of Venetian state art, is one of the few gold stars the republic ever earned with the papacy; mistrust and acrimony were far more common.

The interior, in the form of a Greek cross, dazzles the eye with the intricate splendour of a thousand details. The domes and upper vaults are adorned with golden mosaics on the New Testament, the oldest dating back to the 11th century, though there have been several restorations since. Ancient columns of rare marbles, alabaster, porphyry and verdantique, sawn into slices of rich colour, line the lower walls; the 12th-century pavement is a magnificent geometric mosaic of marble, glass and porphyry. Like a mosque, the central nave is covered with Eastern carpets.

The first door on the right leads to the 14th-century **baptistry**, much beloved by John Ruskin and famous for its mosaics on the life of John the Baptist, with a lovely Salome in red who could probably have had just as many heads as she pleased. (*With luck this may have reopened by the time you visit.*) A door from the baptistry leads into the **Cappella Zen**, designed by Tullio Lombardo in 1504 to house the tomb of one Cardinal Zen, who had left a fortune to the republic on condition he be buried in St Mark's. Further along the right transept you can visit the **treasury** (*open 9.45–5; adm L4000*), containing the loot from Constantinople that Napoleon overlooked—fairy-tale-like golden bowls and crystal goblets studded with huge coloured gems.

Near the Altar of the Sacrament, at the end of the right transept, a lamp burns 'eternally' next to one pillar: after the 976 fire, it appeared that the body of St Mark had been lost, but in 1094 (after Bari had beaten Venice to the relics of St Nicolaus) the good Evangelist was made to stage a miraculous reappearance, popping his hand out of the pillar during Mass. St Mark is now said to be buried in a crypt under the high altar, in the **sanctuary** (*open 9.45–5; adm L3000*). The highlight of the sanctuary is the retable of the altar, the fabulous, glowing **Pala d'Oro**, a masterpiece of medieval gold and jewel work. The upper section may originally have been in the Church of the Pantocrator in Constantinople, and the lower section was commissioned in that same city by Doge Pietro Orseolo I in 976. Over the years the Venetians added their own scenes, and the Pala took its present form in 1345.

In the left transept the **Chapel of the Madonna of Nicopeia** shelters a much-venerated 10th-century icon, the *Protectress of Venice*, formerly carried into battle by the Byzantine Emperor. More fine mosaics are further to the left in the Chapel of St Isidore (whose body the Venetians kidnapped from Chios—and in the mosaic he seems happy to go, grinning like a chimp). In the **Chapel of the Madonna dei Máscoli** there are fine mosaics on the *Life of the Virgin* by Andrea Castagno and Michele Giambono (1453) that were among the first harbingers of the Renaissance in Venice.

Before leaving the narthex, climb the steep stone stair near the west door to the **Museo Marciano, Galleria and Loggia dei Cavalli** (*open 9.45–5; adm L3000*), where you can walk through part of the former women's gallery in the basilica for a closer look at the dome

1 *Translation of the Body of St Mark* (1270)

2 *Venice Venerating the Relics of St Mark* (1718)

3 Central door, with magnificent 13th-century carvings in arches

4 *Venice Welcoming the Relics of St Mark* (1700s)

5 *Removal of St Mark's Relics from Alexandria* (1700s)

6 Pietra del Bando, stone from which the Signoria's decrees were read

7 *Scenes from the Book of Genesis* (1200) and 6th-century Byzantine door of S. Clemente

8 *Noah and the Flood* (1200s), tomb of Doge Vitale Falier (d. 1096)

9 *Madonna and Saints* (1060s); red marble slab where Emperor Barbarossa submitted to Pope Alexander III (1177); stair up to the Loggia and Museo Marciano

10 *Death of Noah and the Tower of Babel* (1200s)

11 *Story of Abraham* (1230s)

12 *Story of SS. Alipius and Simon, and Justice* (1200s)

14 Tomb of Doge Bartolomeo Gradenigo (d. 1342)

15 *Story of Joseph*, remade in 19th century

16 Porta dei Fiori (1200s); Manzù's bust of Pope John XXIII

17 *Christ with the Virgin and St Mark* (13th century, over the door)

18 Pentecost Dome (the earliest, 12th century)

19 On the wall: *Agony in the Garden and Madonna and Prophets* (13th century)

20 Baptistry, *Life of St John the Baptist* (14th century) and tomb of Doge Andrea Dandolo

21 Cappella Zen, by Tullio and Antonio Lombardo (1504–22)

22 On the wall: *Christ and Prophets* (13th century)

23 In arch: *Scenes of the Passion* (12th century)

24 Central Dome, the *Ascension* (12th century)

25 Tabernacle of the Madonna of the Kiss (12th century)

26 On wall: *Rediscovery of the Body of St Mark* (13th century)

27 Treasury

28 Dome of S. Leonardo; Gothic rose window (15th century)

29 In arch, *Scenes from the Life of Christ* (12th century)

30 Altar of the Sacrament; pilaster where St Mark's body was rediscovered, marked by marbles

31 Altar of St James (1462)

32 Pulpit where newly elected doge was shown to the people; entrance to the sanctuary

33 Rood screen (1394) by Jacopo di Marco Benato and Jacobello and Pier Paolo Dalle Masegne

34 Singing Gallery and Cappella di S. Lorenzo, sculptures by the Dalle Masegnes (14th century)

35 Dome, *Prophets Foretell the Religion of Christ* (12th century); Baldacchino, with Eastern alabaster columns (6th century?)

36 Pala d'Oro (10th–14th century)

37 Sacristy door, with reliefs by Sansovino (16th century)

38 Sacristy, with mosaics by Titian and Padovanino (16th century) and Church of St Theodore (15th century), once seat of the Inquisition, and now part of the sacristy: both are rarely open

39 Singing Gallery and Cappella di S. Pietro (14th century): note the Byzantine capitals

40 Two medieval pulpits stacked together

41 *Miracles of Christ* (16th century)

42 Dome, with *Life of St John the Evangelist* (12th century)

43 Cappella della Madonna di Nicopeia (miraculous 12th-century icon)

44 Cappella di S. Isidoro (14th-century mosaics and tomb of the Saint)

45 Cappella della Madonna dei Máscoli: *Life of the Virgin* by Andrea del Castagno, Michele Giambono, Jacopo Bellini

46 On wall: *Life of the Virgin* (13th century)

47 Finely carved Greek marble stoup (12th century)

48 *Virgin of the Gun* (13th century—rifle ex-voto from 1850s)

49 Il Capitello, altar topped with rare marble ciborium, with miraculous Byzantine Crucifixion panel

St Mark's Basilica

Note how crooked it is!
In the Middle Ages symmetry was
synonymous with death.

Numbers in *italics* refer to mosaics.

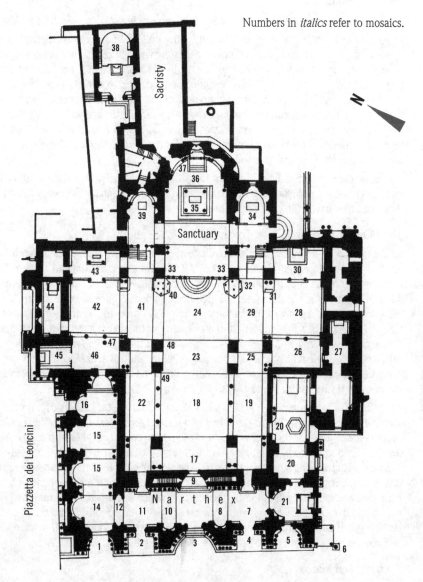

Sacristy

Sanctuary

Narthex

Piazzetta dei Leoncini

Piazza San Marco

mosaics; outside on the loggia, as well as the superb views of the piazza, you can inspect the replica horses and compare them with the excellently restored, gilded, almost alive originals in the museum.

The Campanile

Open summer 9–7.30; winter 9.30–3.30; months in between; adm L8000/4000.

St Mark's bell tower, to those uninitiated in the cult of Venice, is an alien presence, a Presbyterian brick sentinel in the otherwise delicately wrought piazza. But it has always been there, having been begun in 912 and last altered in 1515, and when it gently collapsed into a pile of rubble on 14 July 1902 the Venetians felt its lack so acutely that they began to construct an exact replica, only a few hundred tons lighter and stronger, completed in 1912. It is just shy of 100m tall, and you can take the lift up for a bird's-eye vision of Venice and its Lagoon; from up here the city seems amazingly compact. Though you have to pay for the view, the republic's misbehaving priests had it for free; the Council of Ten would suspend them in cages from the windows.

Under the campanile, Sansovino's elegant **loggetta** adds a graceful note to the brick belfry. Its marbles and sculptures glorifying Venice took it on the nose when the campanile fell on top of them, but they have been carefully restored.

The Museo Correr and Clock Tower

At the far end of the piazza from the basilica, in the Procuratie Nuove, the **Museo Correr** (*open 9–7, last tickets at 6; adm L17,000/10,000—includes entrance to Palazzo Ducale*) contains an interesting collection of Venetian memorabilia—the robes, ducal bonnets and old-maidish nightcaps of the doges, the 20-inch-heeled *zoccoli*, once the rage among Venetian noblewomen, and a copy of the statue of Marco Polo from the Temple of 500 Genies in Canton. Upstairs is a fine collection of Venetian paintings, including two great works by Carpaccio, *Two Venetian Ladies (The Courtesans)* and the *Young Man in a Red Beret*, with his archetypal Venetian face; works by Jacopo Bellini and his sons, Gentile and Giovanni; Antonello da Messina's *Pietà*, one of his best works; and the Bosch-esque *Temptation of St Anthony* by Il Civetta (the 'Little Owl').

At the head of the Procuratie Vecchie two bronze wild men, the 'Moors', sound the hours atop the clock tower, the **Torre dell'Orologio** (*closed for restoration at the time of writing; due to reopen for its 500th anniversary in 1999, when you will again be able to see the interior and climb to the top*), built to a design by Mauro Codussi in 1499 above the entrance to Venice's main shopping street, the Merceria. The old Italians were fond of elaborate astronomical clocks, but none is as beautiful as this, with its richly coloured enamel and gilt face, its Madonna and obligatory lion: the Council of Ten (which encouraged false rumours) supposedly blinded its builders to prevent them creating such a marvel for any other city. Two porphyry lions and a fountain stand in the nearby **Piazzetta Giovanni XXIII** (named after the beloved Venetian patriarch who became Pope), flanking the basilica's north façade.

Piazzetta San Marco

To the south of the basilica, the Piazzetta San Marco was the republic's foyer, where ships would dock under the watchful eye of the Doge. The view towards the Lagoon is framed by two tall Egyptian granite columns, trophies brought to Venice in the 1170s. The Venetians had a knack for converting their booty into self-serving symbols: atop one of the columns several Roman statues were pieced together to form their first patron saint, St Theodore with his crocodile (or dragon, or fish), while on the other stands an ancient Assyrian or Persian winged lion, under whose paw the Venetians slid a book, creating their symbol of St Mark.

Opposite the Doges' Palace stands the **Libreria**, built in 1536 by Sansovino (finished by Scamozzi) and considered by Palladio to be the most beautiful building in the world, one especially notable for the play of light and shadow in its sculpted arcades. Sansovino, trained as a sculptor, was notorious for paying scant attention to architectural details, and the library was scarcely completed when its ceiling collapsed, a miscalculation that cost him a trip to the Council of Ten's slammer. He was only released on the pleading of Titian. In the library scholars with prior permission, obtainable from the director's office, can examine such treasures as the 1501 *Grimani breviary*, a masterwork of Flemish illuminators; Homeric *codices*, the 1459 world map of Fra Mauro, and Marco Polo's will.

Next to the library, at No.17, Venice's **Archaeology Museum** (*closed for restoration at the time of writing; due to reopen later in 1999*) has just been remodelled, and is one of the few museums in the city heated in the winter. It has an excellent collection of Greek sculpture, including a violent *Leda and the Swan* and ancient copies of the famous *Gallic Warriors of Pergamon*, all given to the city by Cardinal Grimani in 1523. On the other side of the Libreria, by the waterfront, is another fine building by Sansovino, the 1547 **Zecca**, or Old Mint, which once stamped out thousands of gold *zecchini*, giving English a new word: 'sequin'.

Palazzo Ducale (Doges' Palace)

Open 15 April–Oct 9–7; winter 8.30–1; other months somewhere in between; adm L17,000/10,000—includes entry to the Museo Correr. Ticket office through Porta della Carta and in the courtyard.

What St Mark's is to sacred architecture, the **Doges' Palace** is to the secular—unique and audacious, dreamlike in a half-light, an illuminated storybook of Venetian history and legend. Like the basilica, it was founded shortly after the city's consolidation on the Rialto, though it didn't begin to take its present form until 1309—with its delicate lower colonnade, its loggia of lacy Gothic tracery, and the massive top-heavy upper floor, like a cake held up by its own frosting. Its weight is partly relieved by the diamond pattern of white Istrian stone and red Verona marble on the façade, which from a distance gives the palace its wholesome peaches-and-cream complexion. Less benign are the two reddish pillars in the loggia (on the Piazzetta façade) said to have been dyed by the blood of Venice's enemies, whose tortured corpses were strung out between them.

Some of Italy's finest medieval sculpture crowns the 36 columns of the lower colonnade, depicting a few sacred and many profane subjects—animals, guildsmen, Turks and Venetians. Beautiful sculptural groups adorn the corners, most notably the 13th-century *Judgement of Solomon*, on the corner nearest the palace's grand entrance, the 1443 **Porta della Carta** (Paper Door), a Gothic symphony in stone by Giovanni and Bartolomeo Bon.

Fires in 1574 and 1577 destroyed much of the palace, and at the time there were serious plans afoot to knock it down and let Palladio start again *à la* Renaissance. Fortunately, however, you can't teach an old doge new tricks, and the palace was rebuilt as it was, with Renaissance touches in the interior. Just within the Porta della Carta, don't miss Antonio Rizzo's delightful arcaded courtyard and his finely sculpted grand stairway, the **Scala dei Giganti**, named for its two Gargantuan statues of *Neptune* and *Mars* by Sansovino.

Visitors enter the palace via another grand stairway, Sansovino's **Scala d'Oro**. The first floor, once the private apartments of the doge, is now used for frequent special exhibitions (*separate adm*), while the golden stairway continues up to the *Secondo Piano Nobile*, from where the Venetian state was governed. After the fire that destroyed its great 15th-century frescoes, Veronese and Tintoretto were employed to decorate the newly remodelled chambers with mythological themes and scores of allegories and apotheoses of Venice—a smug, fleshy blonde in the eyes of these two. These paintings are the palace's chief glory, and signboards in each room identify them. Some of the best works are in the first room, the **Anticollegio** (with Tintoretto's *Bacchus and Ariadne* and Veronese's *Rape of Europa*), and the **Sala del Collegio**, with several masterpieces by both artists. Visiting ambassadors and other foreign official guests would be required to wait in the first of these two rooms before being ushered into the second to be presented to the hierarchy of the Venetian state, and so their decoration had to be suitably impressive.

Tintoretto dominates in the **Sala del Senato**—less lavish, since only Venetians were admitted here—while the main work in the **Sala del Consiglio dei Dieci** is Veronese's ceiling, *Old Man in Eastern Costume with a Young Woman*. Under this the dread Council of Ten deliberated and pored over the anonymous accusations deposited in the *Bocche dei Leoni*—the lions' mouths, the insidious suggestion boxes spread over the city. Next to the Ten's chamber, the old **Armoury** (Sala d'Armi) houses a collection of medieval and Renaissance arms and armour.

From here the visit continues downstairs to the vast and magnificent **Sala del Maggior Consiglio**, built in 1340 and capable of holding the 2500 patricians of the Great Council. At the entrance hangs Tintoretto's crowded, and recently restored, *Paradiso*—the biggest oil painting in the world (23ft by 72ft), looking up at Veronese's magnificent *Apotheosis of Venice* on the ceiling. The frieze along the upper wall portrays the first 76 doges, except for the space that would have held the portrait of Marin Falier (1355) had he not led a conspiracy to take sole power; the dry inscription on the black veil that is there in his stead notes that he was decapitated for treason. The portraits of the last 44 doges, each painted by a contemporary painter, continue around the **Sala dello Scrutinio**, where the votes for office were counted. Elections for doge were Byzantine and elaborate—and frequent; the Maggior Consiglio preferred to choose doges who were old, and wouldn't last long enough to gain a following.

A Doge's Life

Senator in Senate, Citizen in City were his titles, as well as Prince of Clothes, with a wardrobe of gold and silver damask robes and scarlet silks. Once the Doge was dressed, the rest of his procession would fall in line, including all the paraphernalia of Byzantine royalty: a naked sword, six silver trumpets, a damask umbrella, a chair, cushion, candle and eight standards bearing the Lion of St Mark in four colours symbolizing peace, war, truth and loyalty. Yet for all the pomp this was the only man in Venice not permitted to send a private note to his wife, or receive one from her, or from anyone else; nor could he accept any gift beyond flowers or rose-water, or go to a café or theatre, or engage in any money-making activity, while nevertheless having to meet the expenses of his office out of his own pocket. Nor could he abdicate, unless requested to do so.

The office was respected, but often not the man. When a doge died he was privately buried in his family tomb before the state funeral—which used a dummy corpse with a wax mask, after a 16th-century doge had died during a plague. An 'Inquisition of the Defunct Doge' was held over the dummy to discover if the Doge had kept to his *Promissione* (his oath of coronation), if his family owed the state any money, and if it were necessary to amend the *Promissione* to limit the powers of his successor still further. Then the dead Doge's dummy was taken to St Mark's to be hoist in the air nine times by sailors, to the cry of 'Misericordia' ('Mercy'), and then given a funeral service at Santi Giovanni e Paolo.

At the end of the tour the **Bridge of Sighs** (*Ponte dei Sospiri*) takes you to the 17th-century **Palazzo delle Prigioni**, mostly used for petty offenders. Those to whom the republic took real exception were dumped into uncomfortable *pozzi*, or 'wells', in the lower part of the Palazzo Ducale, while celebrities like Casanova got to stay up in the *piombi* or 'leads' just under the roof (*see* below).

In 1984 the section of the palace where the real nitty-gritty business of state took place, a maze of narrow corridors and tiny rooms, was restored and opened to the public. Because the rooms are so small the 1½-hour guided tour, the **Itinerari Segreti** ('Secret Itinerary'), is limited to 20 people, and the reason why it's not better known is that unfortunately it's only available in Italian. The tour begins at the top of the Scala d'Oro, with the snug wood-panelled offices of the **Chancellery** and the 18th-century **Hall of the Chancellors**, lined with cupboards for holding treaties, each bearing the arms of a chancellor. In the justice department is the **Torture Chamber**, where the three Signori della Notte dei Criminali ('judges of the night criminals') would 'put to the question' their suspects, hanging them by the wrists on a rope that is still in place. These practices ended in the early 1700s, when Venice became one of the first states in Europe to abolish torture.

Next is the ornate **Sala dei Tre Capi**, the chamber of the three magistrates of the Council of Ten, who had to be present at all state meetings. As this chamber might be visited by foreign dignitaries, it was lavishly decorated with works by Veronese, Antonello da Messina and Hieronymus Bosch. From here it's up to the notorious **Piombi**, which despite their evil reputation appear downright cosy, as prisons go. Casanova's cell is pointed out, and there's an elaborate exploration of his escape through a hole in the roof.

Near the end of the tour comes one of Venice's marvels: the **attic of the Sala del Maggior Consiglio**, where you can see how the Arsenale's shipwrights made a vast ceiling float unsupported over the room below; built in 1577, it has yet to need any repairs.

San Marco to Rialto

The streets between the piazza and the market district of the Rialto are the busiest in Venice, especially the **Mercerie**, which begin under the clock tower and are lined with some of the city's smartest shops. It was down the Mercerie that Baiamonte Tiepolo led his rebels in 1310, when an old lady cried 'Death to tyrants!' from her window and hurled a brick at his standard-bearer, killing him on the spot, and causing such disarray that Tiepolo was forced to give up his attempted coup. It was a close call that the republic chose never to forget: the site, above the Sottoportego del Capello Nero, is marked by a stone relief of the heroine with her brick.

The Merceria continues to the church of **San Zulian**, redesigned in 1553 by Sansovino, with a façade most notable for Sansovino's statue of its overly proud benefactor, Tommaso Rangone. Sansovino also had a hand in **San Salvatore** in the next campo, adding the finishing touches to its noble Renaissance interior and designing the monument to Doge Francesco Venier. An 89-year-old Titian painted one of his more unusual works for this church, the *Annunciation*, which he signed with double emphasis *Titianus Fecit*—'*Fecit*' ('made it') because his patrons refused to believe that he had painted it. In a chapel north of the altar is the *Supper at the House of Emmaus*, by the school of Giovanni Bellini.

Humming, bustling **Campo San Bartolomeo**, next on the Mercerie, has for centuries been one of the social hubs of Venice, and still gets packed with after-work crowds every evening. Its centre is graced by the **statue of Goldoni**, whose comedies in Venetian dialect still make the Venetians laugh; and by the look on his jolly face, he still finds their antics amusing. Follow the crowds up to the **Ponte di Rialto** (*see* 'The Grand Canal', p.121), the geographical heart of Venice, the principal node of its pedestrian and water traffic.

The city's central markets have been just across the bridge for a millennium, divided into sections for vegetables and for fish. Near the former you may pay your respects to what has traditionally been considered Venice's oldest church, the little **San Giacomo di Rialto**, founded perhaps as long ago as the 5th century and substantially reworked in 1071 and 1601. In the same campo stands a famous Venetian character, the 16th-century granite figure of the hunchback, **Gobbo di Rialto**, who supports a little stairway and marble podium from which the decrees of the republic were proclaimed to the populace.

San Marco to the Accademia

Following the yellow signs 'To the Accademia' from the Piazza San Marco (starting by the tourist office), the first campo belongs to Baroque **San Moisè**, with a grimy opera-buffa façade, rockpile and altarpiece. For more opera and less buffa, take a detour up Calle Veste (the second right after Campo San Moisè) to monumental Campo San Fantin and **La Fenice** (1792), one of Italy's most renowned opera houses, and site of the premieres of Verdi's *Rigoletto* and *La Traviata*. (*At the time of writing the whole theatre is shrouded in scaffolding after the terrible fire which ripped it apart in 1996. Arguments over building contracts are leading to long delays and nobody quite knows when La Fenice will be restored to its former glory.*) Venice has a venerable musical tradition, albeit one that had become more tradition than music by the time of the era of grand opera—even though Lorenzo da Ponte, Mozart's great librettist, was himself a Venetian.

Back on the route to the Accademia, in the next campo stands **Santa Maria Zobenigo** (or del Giglio), on which the Barbaro family stuck a fancy Baroque façade, not for God but for the glory of the Barbaros; the façade is famous for its total lack of religious significance. The signs lead next to the Campo Francesco Morosini, named after the doge who recaptured the Morea from the Turks, but who is remembered everywhere else as the man who blew the top off the Parthenon. It's better known as **Campo Santo Stefano**, and is one of the most elegant squares in Venice, a pleasant place to sit outside at a café table—particularly at **Paolin**, Venice's best *gelateria*. At one end, built directly over a canal, the Gothic church of **Santo Stefano** has the most gravity-defying campanile of all the leaning towers in Venice (most alarmingly viewed from the adjacent Campo Sant'Angelo). The interior is worth a look for its striking wood ceiling, soaring like a ship's keel, as well as its wooden choir stalls (1488).

The Accademia

Open daily; hours vary slightly throughout the year; summer Tues–Sat 9am–10pm, Sun 9am–8pm; closed 1 May, 25 Dec and 1 Jan; adm L12,000, free for under-18s and over-60s if members of the EU. It's a good idea to get there early since a maximum of 300 visitors is allowed at a time.

Just over the Accademia bridge lies the **Galleria dell'Accademia** itself, the grand cathedral of Venetian art, ablaze with light and colour; this is the best place in the world to study both the development of the school and some of its greatest masterpieces.

The collection is arranged chronologically, beginning in the former refectory of the Scuola (**Room I**): among them, 14th-century altarpieces by Paolo and Lorenzo Veneziano, whose half-Byzantine Madonnas look like models for Venetian silks. Later altarpieces fill **Room II**, most importantly Giovanni Bellini's masterpiece the *Pala di San Giobbe*, which in its architecture repeats its original setting in the church of San Giobbe; on the left St Francis invites the viewer into a scene made timeless by the music of the angels at the Madonna's feet. Other altarpieces in the room are by Carpaccio, Basaiti, and Cima da Conegliano (the subtle *Madonna of the Orange Tree*).

The next rooms are small but, like gifts, contain the best things: Mantegna's confidently aloof *St George*, a trio of Madonnas by Giovanni Bellini, and Piero della Francesca's *St Jerome and Devotee*, a youthful study in perspective. In **Room V** you will find Giorgione's *La Vecchia*, with the warning '*Col Tempo*' ('With Time') in her hand, and the mysterious *Tempest*, two of the few paintings scholars accept as being indisputably by this artist, but how strange they are! It is said Giorgione invented easel painting for the pleasure of bored, purposeless patricians in Venice's decline, but the paintings seem somehow to reflect rather than lighten their ennui and discontent.

Highlights of the next few rooms include Lorenzo Lotto's *Gentleman in his Study*, which catches its sitter off-guard before he could clear the nervously scattered scraps of paper from his table, and Paris Bordenone's 1354 *Fisherman Presenting St Mark's Ring to the Doge*, celebrating a miracle of St Mark.

The climax of the Venetian High Renaissance comes in **Room X**, with Veronese's *Christ in the House of Levi* (1573), set in a Palladian loggia with a ghostly white imaginary background, in violent contrast to the rollicking feast of Turks, hounds, midgets, Germans and the artist himself (in the front, next to the pillar on the left). The painting was originally titled *The Last Supper*, and fell foul of the Inquisition, which took umbrage (especially at the Germans). Veronese was cross-examined, and ordered to make pious changes at his own expense; the artist, in true Venetian style, saved himself both the trouble and the money by simply giving it the title by which it has been known ever since.

Room X also contains Veronese's fine *Annunciation*, and some early masterworks by Tintoretto—*Translation of the Body of St Mark* and *St Mark Freeing a Slave*, in which the Evangelist, in true Tintorettoesque fashion, nosedives from the top of the canvas. The last great painting in the room was also the last ever by Titian, the sombre *Pietà*, which he was working on when he died, aged about 90, from the plague; he intended it for his tomb, and smeared the paint on with his fingers.

Alongside several more Tintorettos, the following few rooms mainly contain later work from the 17th and 18th centuries, but mixed in among them are a series of fascinating scenes of 15th-century Venice, by Carpaccio, Gentile Bellini and others. Compare them to Canaletto and Guardi, whose 18th-century scenes of Venice were the picture postcards of the British aristocracy on their Grand Tour, and are well represented in **Room XVII**.

The final rooms of the Accademia were formerly part of the elegantly Gothic church of Santa Maria della Carità, and house more luminous 15th-century painting by Alvise Vivarini, Giovanni and Gentile Bellini, and Crivelli, above all the fascinating series depicting the *Miracles of the True Cross* against Venetian backgrounds, originally painted for the Scuola di S. Giovanni Evangelista, in **Room XX**. **Room XXI** contains the dreamily compelling *Cycle of Saint Ursula* by Carpaccio, from the former Scuola di Sant'Orsola, and only recently restored. Finally, **Room XXIV**, the former *albergo* of the church, contains two fine paintings that were originally made for it: Titian's striking 1538 *Presentation of the Virgin* and a 1446 triptych by Antonio Vivarini and Giovanni d'Alemagna.

Dorsoduro

The Accademia lies in the *sestiere* of Dorsoduro, which can also boast the second-most-visited art gallery in Venice, the **Peggy Guggenheim Collection** (*open Easter–Oct Wed–Mon 11–6; closed Tues; adm L12,000, students L8000, © 041 520 6288*), just down the Grand Canal from the Accademia in her 18th-century Venetian palazzo. In her 30 years as a collector, until her death in 1979, Ms Guggenheim amassed an impressive quantity (if not always quality) of brand-name 20th-century art—Bacon, Brancusi, Braque, Calder, Chagall, Dali, De Chirico, Duchamp, Dubuffet, Max Ernst (her second husband), Giacometti, Gris, Kandinsky, Klee, Magritte, Miró, Moore, Mondrian, Picasso, Pollock, Rothko and Smith. Administered by the Solomon R. Guggenheim Foundation in New York, the collection can come as a welcome breath of fresh air after so much high Italian art, and also sponsors a number of temporary exhibitions, even in winter; look out for posters.

From here it's a five-minute stroll down to the serene, octagonal basilica of **Santa Maria della Salute** (*open 9–12 and 3–6*) on the pointed tip of Dorsoduro. One of five churches built in thanksgiving after the passing of plagues (Venice, a busy port isolated in its Lagoon, was particularly susceptible), La Salute (1631–81) is the masterpiece of Baldassare Longhena, its snow-white dome and marble jelly rolls dramatically set at the entrance of the Grand Canal. The interior is a relatively restrained white and grey Baroque, and the **sacristy** (*adm L2000*) contains the *Marriage at Cana* by Tintoretto and several works by Titian, including his *St Mark Enthroned Between Saints*. Almost next to the basilica, on the point, stands the distinctive profile of the **Dogana di Mare**, the Customs House (*see* 'The Grand Canal', p.124).

The **Fondamenta delle Zattere**, facing away from the city towards the freighter-filled canal and the island of Giudecca, leads from La Salute to the **Gesuati**, the only church in Venice decorated by Umbrian artists. For a more elaborate feast, take the long stroll along the Fondamenta (or take *vaporetto* Line 5 to San Basegio) to Veronese's parish church of **San Sebastiano** on Rio di San Basilio. Veronese, it is said, murdered a man in Verona and took refuge in this neighbourhood, and over the next 10 years he and his brother Benedetto Caliari embellished San Sebastiano—beginning in 1555 with the ceiling frescoes of the sacristy and ending with the magnificent ceiling, *The Story of Esther*, and illusionistic paintings in the choir. (*The church is often closed, but the custodian can usually be found there on weekday mornings or Sunday afternoons, and he will open it up for you if he has not done so already; tip him for turning on the lights.*)

From San Sebastiano you can head back towards the Grand Canal (Calle Avogaria and Calle Lunga S. Barnaba); turn left up Calle Pazienza to visit the 14th-century church of the **Carmini** with a landmark red campanile and lovely altars by Cima da Conegliano and Lorenzo Lotto. The **Scuola Grande dei Carmini** (*open Mon–Sat 9–12 and 3–6; adm L7000/5000; sometimes open for concerts*), next door, was designed by Longhena in the 1660s, and contains one of G. B. Tiepolo's best and brightest ceilings, *The Virgin in Glory*.

The Carmini is on the corner of the delightful **Campo Santa Margherita**. Traditionally the main marketplace of Dorsoduro, it's also a good spot to find relatively inexpensive pizzerias, restaurants and cafés that are not aimed primarily at tourists. It is also close to **Ca' Rezzonico** (Rio Terrà Canal down to the Fondamenta Rezzonico), home to the **Museo del Settecento Veneziano** (*open Oct–April 10–4, May–Sept 10–5; closed Fri; adm L12,000; at the time of writing only the first floor is open*), Venice's attic of 18th-century art, with bittersweet paintings by Giandomenico Tiepolo, some wild Rococo furniture, a pharmacy, genre scenes by Longhi (*The Lady and Hairdresser*), and a breathtaking view of the Grand Canal. The house was owned in the last century by Robert Browning's son Pen, and the poet died there in 1889. One of the palaces you see opposite belonged to Doge Cristoforo Moro, whom the Venetians claim Shakespeare used as his model for Othello, confusing the Doge's name with his race.

San Polo and Santa Croce

From the Ponte di Rialto, the yellow signs towards the Piazzale Roma lead past the pretty **Campo** and church of **San Polo** (*open Mon–Sat 7.10–5.30, Sun 3–5.30; adm L2000*), known for Giandomenico Tiepolo's dramatic *Stations of the Cross* in the Oratory of the Crucifix. The signs next take you before a venerable Venetian institution: the huge brick Gothic church of the **Frari** (*open Mon–Sat 9–6, Sun and hols 3–6; adm L3000*), one of the most severe medieval buildings in the city, built between 1330 and 1469.

Monteverdi, one of the founding fathers of opera and once choir director at St Mark's, is buried here, as is Titian, whose tomb follows the Italian rule—the greater the artist, the worse the tomb (*see* Michelangelo's in Florence). The strange pyramid with a half-open door was intended by Antonio Canova to be Titian's tomb, but it eventually became the sculptor's own last resting place. The Frari is celebrated for its great art, and especially for the most overrated painting in Italy, Titian's *Assumption of the Virgin* (1516–18), in the centre of the Monks' Choir. Marvel at the art, at Titian's revolutionary Mannerist use of space and movement, but its big-eyed, heaven-gazing Virgin has as much artistic vision as a Sunday school holy card.

That, however, is not true of Giovanni Bellini's lovely *Triptych of Madonna with Child and Saints* in the sacristy, or Donatello's rustic *Statue of St John the Baptist* in the choir chapel. In the north aisle Titian's less theatrical and later *Madonna di Ca' Pesaro* was modelled on his wife Celia; the painting had a greater influence on Venetian composition than the *Assumption*. Also note the beautiful Renaissance **Tomb of Doge Nicolò Tron** by Antonio Rizzo in the sanctuary (1476).

The Scuola di San Rocco

Next to the Frari, the **Scuola di San Rocco** (*open summer 9–5.30; winter mornings only; adm L8000/6000*) is one of Venice's numerous 'schools' or charitable confraternities. The school has a beautiful, lively façade by Scarpagnino, and inside it contains one of the wonders of Venice—or rather, 54 wonders—all painted by Tintoretto, who worked on the project from 1562 to 1585 without any assistance.

Tintoretto always managed to look at old, conventional subjects from a fresh point of view; while other artists of the High Renaissance often composed their subjects with the epic vision of a Cecil B. de Mille, Tintoretto had the revolutionary eye of a 16th-century Orson Welles, creating audacious, dynamic 'sets', often working out his compositions in his little box-stages, with wax figures and unusual lighting effects. In the *scuola*, especially in the upper floor, he was at the peak of his career, and created what is considered by some to be the finest painting cycle in existence. Vertigo is not an uncommon response. The greatest work in the cycle is the *Crucifixion*, where the event is the central drama of a busy human world. In the same room there are also several paintings on easels by Titian, and one of Christ that some attribute to Titian, some to Giorgione.

San Marco to Castello

Starting at the Piazzetta San Marco, the gracefully curving and ever-bustling **Riva degli Schiavoni** took its name from the Slavs of Dalmatia. A few steps beyond the Palazzo Ducale is one of the city's finest Gothic palazzi, which since 1822 has been the famous **Hotel Danieli**, its name a corruption of the Dandolo family who built it. Here on the quay stands a robust 1887 **Memorial to Vittorio Emanuele II**, where two of Venice's over 10,000 lions shelter—as often as not, with members of Venice's equally numerous if smaller feline population between their paws.

From the Riva, the Sottoportico San Zaccaria leads back to the lovely Gothic-Renaissance **San Zaccaria** (*open 10–12 and 4–6*), begun by Antonio Gambello in 1444 and completed by Mauro Codussi in 1515. Inside, look for Bellini's *Madonna and Saints* in the second chapel to the right, and the refined Florentine frescoes by Andrea del Castagno in the chapel of San Tarasio. Another church on the Riva itself, **La Pietà**, served the girls' orphanage which the red-headed priest Vivaldi made famous during his years as its concert master and composer (1704–38). The church was rebuilt shortly afterwards with a remarkable oval interior, in luscious cream and gold with G. B. Tiepolo's extravagant *Triumph of Faith* on top. It has particularly fine acoustics—due to Vivaldi's involvement in the design—and is still frequently used for concerts.

The Arsenale

From the Riva, the Fondamenta dell'Arsenale leads to the twin towers guarding the **Arsenale**. Founded in 1104, this, first of all arsenals, derived its name from the Venetian pronunciation of the Arabic *darsina'a*, or artisans' shop, and up until the 17th century these were the greatest dockyards in the world, the very foundation of the republic's wealth and power. In its heyday the Arsenale had a payroll of 16,000, and produced a ship a day to fight the Turks. Dante visited this great industrial complex twice and, as Blake would later do with his dark satanic mills, confined it to the *Inferno*.

Today the Arsenale is occupied by the Italian military and is off-limits, but you can look at the **Great Gateway** next to the towers, built in 1460 and often regarded as the earliest Venetian Renaissance building, and constructed almost entirely from marble trophies brought over from Greece. Alongside them were later placed a line of stone lions, also picked up in Greece, including one ancient beast that Doge Francesco Morosini found in Piraeus, with 11th-century runes carved in its back in the name of Harold Hardrada, a member of the Byzantine Emperor's Varangian Guard who was later crowned King of Norway. Other very innocent-looking lions, eroded into lambs, were brought from the island of Delos in 1718. The only way to get a look at the inside of the Arsenale at present is by taking the Line 5 *vaporetto*, which goes through the middle of it.

Via Garibaldi and the Fondamenta S. Anna continue to the Isola di San Pietro, site of the unmemorable **San Pietro di Castello** (*open Mon–Sat 10–5.30, Sun 3–5.30; adm L2000*), until 1807 Venice's cathedral, its lonely, distant site no small comment on the republic's attitude towards the papacy. The attractive detached campanile is by Codussi, and inside there is a marble throne incorporating a medieval Muslim tombstone inscribed with verses from the Koran, which for centuries was said to have been the Throne of St Peter in Antioch. To the south are the refreshing pines and planes of the **Public Gardens**, where the International Exhibition of Modern Art, or Biennale, takes place in even-numbered years in the artsy pavilions. This, and the **Parco delle Rimembranze** further on, were given to this sometimes claustrophobic city of stone and water by Napoleon, who knocked down four extraneous churches to plant the trees. From here you can take Line 1 or 2 back to S. Marco or the Lido.

San Marco to Santi Giovanni e Paolo

The calle that leads from the Piazzetta dei Leoncini around the back of San Marco and over the Rio di Palazzo will take you to one of Venice's newest museums, the **Museo Diocesano** (*open Mon–Sat 10.30–12.30*), in the Romanesque cloister of Sant'Apollonia. It features an exceptional collection of trappings and art salvaged from the city's churches. Through a web of alleys to the north there's more art in the 16th-century Palazzo Querini-Stampalia, home of the **Fondazione Querini-Stampalia** (*open Tues, Wed, Thurs and Sun 10–1 and 3–6, Fri and Sat 10–1 and 3–10; closed Mon; adm L10,000/5000*), which has an endearing assortment of genre paintings—the closest we have to photographs of 18th-century Venice by Pietro Longhi and the naïve Gabriel Bella, as well as works by Bellini, Palma il Vecchio and G. B. Tiepolo. Other attractions of the palazzo are its décor and furnishings, which give an idea of the look of an 18th-century Venetian patrician's residence.

Santa Maria Formosa (*open Mon–Sat 10–5.30, Sun 3–5.30; adm L2000*), in its charming campo just to the north, was rebuilt in 1492 by Codussi, who made creative use of its original Greek-cross plan. The head near the bottom of its campanile is notorious as being the most hideous thing in Venice, while inside, Palma il Vecchio's *Santa Barbara* is famed as the loveliest woman, modelled on the artist's own daughter. Another celebrated work, Bartolomeo Vivarini's *Madonna della Misericordia* (1473), is in the first chapel on the right;

the parishioners shown under the protection of the Virgin's mantle earned their exalted position by paying for the painting.

The next campo to the north is dominated by **Santi Giovanni e Paolo** (*San Zanipolo*, in Venetian dialect), after St Mark's the most important church on the right bank (*open 7–12.30 and 3–7.15*). A vast Gothic brick temple begun by the Dominicans in 1246, then almost entirely rebuilt after 1333, and finally completed in 1430, no one could accuse it of being beautiful, despite its fine front doorway. San Zanipolo contains much superb Venetian art, but is, most of all, a pantheon of the doges; all their funerals were held here after the 1300s, and some 25 of them lie in splendid Gothic and Renaissance tombs. Among them there are also monuments to other honoured servants of the Venetian state, such as Marcantonio Bragadin, the commander who in 1571 was flayed alive by the Turks after he had surrendered Famagusta, in Cyprus, after a long siege; his bust sits on an urn holding his neatly folded skin. The adjacent chapel contains Giovanni Bellini's excellent polyptych of *St Vincent Ferrer*, a fire-eating subject portrayed by the gentlest of painters; nearby is a small shrine containing the foot of St Catherine of Siena. The finest of the tombs is in the chancel, that of Doge Andrea Vendramin, by Tullio and Antonio Lombardo (1478), while the **Chapel of the Rosary** in the north transept, which was severely damaged by fire in the last century, has a fine ceiling by Veronese that was originally in the church of the Umiltà, long demolished.

Santa Maria dei Miracoli and the Ca' d'Oro

From the Campo San Zanipolo, Largo G. Gallini leads to the perfect little Renaissance church of **Santa Maria dei Miracoli** (*open Mon–Sat 10–5.30, Sun and hols 3–5.30; adm L2000*), built by Pietro Lombardo in the 1480s and often compared to an exquisite jewel box: elegant, graceful, and glowing with a soft marble sheen, inside and out. Just to the south are two enclosed courtyards, known as the **Corte Prima del Milion** and the **Corte Seconda del Milion**, which were once part of the home of Marco Polo. The latter in particular looks much as it did when the great traveller lived there; 'Million', his nickname in Venice, referred to the million tales he brought back with him from China.

Further towards the railway station up the Grand Canal, signposted off the Strada Nuova (Via 28 Aprile), stands the enchanting Gothic **Ca' d'Oro**, finished in 1440 and currently housing the **Galleria Franchetti** (*open daily 9–2; adm L6000*). In its collection are Mantegna's stern *St Sebastian*, Guardi's series of Venetian views, an excellent collection of Renaissance bronzes and medallions (some by Pisanello), a portrait of Sultan Mehmet II by Gentile Bellini, who did a stint in Istanbul, and now sadly faded fragments of the famous frescoes by Giorgione and Titian from the Fóndaco dei Tedeschi. Also present are some more minor works by Titian, including a voluptuous *Venus*, and a fine *Crucifixion* by a follower of Van Eyck. The building itself is most famous for the intricate traceries of its façade, best appreciated from the Grand Canal, and the courtyard, with a finely carved well-head by Bartolomeo Bon.

The Ghetto

Three *rii* to the south of Sant'Alvise is THE Ghetto, for, like 'arsenal', *ghetto* is a Venetian word, deriving from the word *getto* meaning 'casting in metals', and there was an iron foundry here which preceded the establishment of a special quarter to which all Jews were ordered to move in 1516. The name is poignantly, coincidentally apt, for in Hebrew ghetto comes from the root for 'cut off'. And cut off its residents were in Venice, for the Ghetto is an island, surrounded by a moat-like canal, and at night all Jews had to be within its windowless walls. Cramped for space, the houses were built tall but with very low ceilings, which, as many people have noted, eerily presages ghetto tenements of centuries to come. But the Venetians did not invent the mentality behind the Ghetto, even if they invented the name; Spanish Jews in the Middle Ages were segregated, as were the Jews of ancient Rome. Indeed, Venetian law specifically protected Jewish citizens and forbade preachers from inciting mobs against them—a common enough practice in the 16th century. Jewish refugees came to Venice from all over Europe; here they were safe, even if they had to pay for it with high taxes and rents. When Napoleon threw open the gates of the Ghetto in 1797, it is said that the impoverished residents who remained were too weak to leave.

The island of the **Ghetto Nuovo**, the oldest section, is a melancholy place, its small campo often empty and forlorn. The **Scuola Grande Tedesca** is the oldest of Venice's five synagogues, built by German Jews in 1528, and is in the same building as the small **Museo Comunità Israelitica/Ebraica**, ✆ 041 715 359 (*open 10.30–5; closed Sat and Jewish holidays; adm L12,000 for the guided tour at 30mins past the hour*). The museum organizes informative tours (in English) which take visitors around this synagogue and two others, the **Scuola Spagnola**—an opulent building by Longhena—and the **Scuola Levantina**.

San Giorgio Maggiore and the Giudecca

The little islet of San Giorgio Maggiore, crowned by Palladio's church of **San Giorgio Maggiore** (*open daily 10–12.30 and 2.30–6.30; adm, including the campanile*), dominates the view of the Lagoon from the Piazzetta San Marco (*vaporetto* Line 5). Built according to his theories on harmony, with a temple front, it seems to hang between the water and the sky, bathed by light with as many variations as Monet's series on the Cathedral of Rouen.

The austere white interior is relieved by Tintoretto's *Fall of Manna* and his celebrated *Last Supper* on the main altar, which is also notable for the fine carving on the Baroque choir stalls. A lift can whisk you to the top of the **Campanile** for a remarkable view over Venice and the Lagoon. The old monastery, partly designed by Palladio, is now the headquarters of the Giorgio Cini Foundation, dedicated to the arts and the sciences of the sea, and venue for frequent exhibitions and conferences.

La Giudecca (Line 52 or 82) actually consists of eight islands that curve gracefully like a Spanish *tilde* just south of Venice; prominent among its buildings are a string of empty mills and factories—the product of a brief 19th-century flirtation with industry—and for the most part the atmosphere is relatively quiet and homely. Like Cannaregio, it's seldom visited by the throngs, though a few people wander over to see Palladio's best church, **Il Redentore** (*open Mon–Sat 10–5.30, Sun 3–5.30; adm L2000*).

In 1576, during yet another plague that killed 46,000 Venetians, the Doge and the Senate vowed that if the catastrophe ended, they would build a church and visit it in state once a year. Palladio was duly commissioned to build the church, completed in 1592, and on the third Sunday of each July a bridge of boats was constructed to take the authorities across from the Zattere. This event, the *Festa del Redentore*, is still one of the most exciting events on the Venetian calendar. The Redentore itself provides a fitting backdrop: Palladio's temple front, with its interlocking pediments, matches it basilican interior, with curving transepts and dome. The shadowy semi circle of columns behind the altar adds a striking, mystical effect, all that survives of Palladio's desire to built a circular church, which he deemed most perfect to worship the essence of God.

The Lagoon and its Islands

Pearly and melting into the bright sky, iridescent blue or murky green, a sheet of glass yellow and pink in the dawn, or just plain grey: Venice's Lagoon is one of its wonders, a desolate, often melancholy and strange, often beautiful and seductive 'landscape' with a hundred personalities. It is 56km long and averages about 8km across, adding up to some 448 square kilometres; half of it, the *Laguna Morta* ('Dead Lagoon') consists of mud flats except in the spring, while the shallows of the *Laguna Viva* are always present, and cleansed by tides twice a day. To navigate this treacherous sea, the Venetians have developed highways of channels, marked by *bricole*—wooden posts topped by orange lamps—that keep their craft from running aground.

Once the numerous islands were densely inhabited, occupied by a town or a monastery. Now all but a few have been abandoned; many a tiny one, with its forlorn shell of a building, has been overgrown with weeds, while the whole of the Lagoon is threatened by the accumulation of algae, the curse of the post-industrial Adriatic.

The Lido and South Lagoon

The Lido, one of the long spits of land that forms the protective outer edge of the Lagoon, is by far the most glamorous of the islands, one that has given its name to countless bathing establishments, bars, amusement arcades and cinemas all over the world. On its 12 kilometres of beach the poets, potentates and plutocrats of the turn of the century spent their holidays in palatial hotels and villas, making the Lido the pinnacle of Belle Epoque fashion, so brilliantly evoked in Thomas Mann's novel *Death in Venice* and Visconti's subsequent film. The story was set and filmed in the **Grand Hotel des Bains**, just north of the renowned, Mussolini-style **Municipal Casino** and the **Palazzo del Cinema**, where Venice hosts its International Film Festival.

The Lido is still the playground of the Venetians and their visitors, with its riding clubs, tennis courts, golf courses and shooting ranges; it is also expensive, overcrowded and annoying, with its tedious hierarchy of private bathing establishments. The free beach, the **Spiaggia Comunale**, is on the north part of the island, a 15-minute walk from the *vaporetto* stop at San Nicolò (go down the Gran Viale, and turn left on the Lungomare d'Annunzio), where you can hire a changing hut and frolic in the fine sand and not-so-fine sea.

Islands in the North Lagoon

Most Venetian itineraries take in the islands of Murano, Burano and Torcello, all easily reached by inexpensive *vaporetti*, as is the cypress-studded cemetery island of **San Michele** (*vaporetto no.55 or 23*), with its simple but elegant church of **San Michele in Isola** by Mauro Codussi (1469), his first-known work and Venice's first taste of the Florentine Renaissance, albeit with a Venetian twist in the tri-lobed front. It contains the tomb of Fra Paolo Sarpi, the famous Venetian monk and philosopher who led the ideological battle against the Pope when the republic was placed under the Great Interdict of 1607, in a major duel of secular and Church authority. Venice, considering St Mark the equal of St Peter, had her priests say Mass despite the interdict and eventually won the battle of wills, thanks mainly to Sarpi, who also authored a famous Protestant-sympathizing *History of the Council of Trent*.

He also made significant discoveries in anatomy, particularly on the contraction of the iris, and shared notes on astronomy with Galileo.

The **cemetery** itself is entered through the cloister next to the church (*open daily 8.30–4*). The Protestant and Orthodox sections contain the tombs of some of the many foreigners who preferred to face eternity from Venice, among them Ezra Pound, Sergei Diaghilev, Frederick Rolfe (Baron Corvo) and Igor Stravinsky. The gate-keeper provides a basic map.

Murano

The island of Murano (*vaporetti no.52 and 23 from S. Zaccaria or no.12 and 13 from Fondamente Nuove*) is synonymous with glass, the most celebrated of Venice's industries. The Venetians were the first in the Middle Ages to rediscover the secret of making crystal glass, and especially mirrors, and it was a secret they kept a monopoly on for centuries by using the most drastic measures: if ever a glassmaker let himself be coaxed abroad, the Council of Ten sent their assassins after him in hot pursuit.

However, those who remained in Venice were treated with kid gloves. Because of the danger of fire, all the forges in Venice were relocated to Murano in 1291, and the little island became a kind of republic within a republic—minting its own coins, policing itself, even developing its own list of NHs (*nobili homini*—noblemen) in its own *Golden Book*—aristocrats of glass, who built solid palaces along Murano's own Grand Canal.

But glass-making declined like everything else in Venice, and only towards the end of the 19th century were the forges once more stoked up on Murano. Can you visit them? You betcha! In fact a trip to the glassblowers' is the single most touristy thing to do in Venice. After watching the glass being made, there's the inevitable tour of the 'museum show rooms'; these have the same atmosphere as a funeral parlour, all respect and solicitude, carpets and hush-hush—not unfitting, as some of the blooming chandeliers, befruited mirrors and poison-coloured chalices begin to make death look good. There is no admission charge, as it is hoped you might buy, though there's not too much pressure to do so. More of Murano's often grotesquely kitsch products are on sale in shops all over the island.

It wasn't always so. The **Museo Vetrario** or Glass Museum (*open 10–5; closed Wed; adm*), in the 17th-century Palazzo Giustinian on Fondamenta Cavour, has some simple pieces from Roman times, and a choice collection of 15th-century Murano glass, especially the delightful 1480 *Barovier Nuptial Cup*; later glass tends to prove that Murano's glassblowers have long had a wayward streak. A multilingual exhibit explains the history of glass-making.

Nearby stands the primary reason to visit this rather dowdy island, the Veneto-Byzantine **Santi Maria e Donato** (*open daily 8–12 and 4–7*), a contemporary of St Mark's Basilica, with a beautiful arcaded apse. Inside the floor is paved with a marvellous 12th-century mosaic, incorporating coloured pieces of ancient Murano glass, and on the wall there's a Byzantine mosaic of the Virgin. The relics of Bishop Donato of Euboea were nabbed by Venetian body-snatchers, but in this case they outdid themselves, bringing home not only San Donato's bones but those of the dragon the good bishop slew with a gob of spit; they are hanging behind the altar.

Back on the Fondamenta dei Vetrai, the 15th-century church of **San Pietro Martire** has a lovely Giovanni Bellini (*Madonna and Child with St Mark, St Augustine and Doge Barbarigo*) from 1488.

Burano

Burano (*vaporetto no.12*) is the Lego-land of the Lagoon, where everything is in brightly coloured miniature—the canals, the bridges, the leaning tower and the houses, painted with a Fauvist sensibility in the deepest of colours. Traditionally on Burano the men fish and the women make Venetian point, 'the most Italian of all lacework', beautiful, intricate and murder on the eyesight. All over Burano you can find samples on sale (of which a great deal are machine-made or imported), or you can watch it being made at the **Scuola dei Merletti** in Piazza Galuppi (*open Tues–Sat 10–4; adm*), though '*scuola*' is misleading, as no young woman in Burano wants to learn such an excruciating art. The school itself was founded in 1872, when traditional lace-making was already in decline. In the sacristy of the church of **San Martino** (with its tipsily leaning campanile) look for Giambattista Tiepolo's *Crucifixion*, which Mary McCarthy aptly described as 'a ghastly masquerade ball'.

From Burano you can hire a *sandola* (small gondola) to **San Francesco del Deserto**, some 20 minutes to the south. St Francis is said to have founded a chapel here in 1220, and the whole islet was subsequently given to his order as a site for a **monastery** (*visitors welcome daily 9–11 and 3–5.30*). In true Franciscan fashion, it's not the buildings you'll remember (though there's a fine 14th-century cloister), but the love of nature evident in the beautiful gardens. Admission is free, but donations are appreciated.

Torcello

Though fewer than 100 people remain on Torcello (*vaporetto no.12; no.14 takes twice as long*), this small island was once a serious rival to Venice herself. According to legend, its history began when God ordered the Bishop of *Altinum*, the old Roman town near Mestre, to take his flock away from the heretical Lombards into the Lagoon. From a tower the bishop saw some stars rise over Torcello, and so led the people of Altinum to this lonely island to set up their new home. The town developed quickly, and for the first few centuries seems to have been the real metropolis of the Lagoon, with 20,000 inhabitants, palaces, a mercantile fleet and five townships; but malaria decimated the population, the Sile silted up Torcello's corner of the Lagoon, and the rising star of Venice drew its citizens to the Rialto.

Torcello is now a ghost island overgrown with weeds, its palaces either sunk into the marsh or quarried for their stone, its narrow paths all that remain of once bustling thoroughfares. One of these follows a canal from the landing-stage past the picturesque Ponte del Diavolo to the grass-grown piazza in front of the magnificent Veneto-Byzantine **Cathedral of Santa Maria Assunta** with its lofty campanile, founded in 639 and rebuilt in the same Ravenna basilica-style in 1008. It is the oldest building in the Lagoon, and still one of the most impressive. The interior (*no longer functioning as a cathedral, though Mass is celebrated every Sunday during the summer; open daily 10.30–6; adm L4000*) has the finest mosaics in Venice, all done by 11th- and 12th-century Greek artists, from the wonderful floor to the spectacular, potent *Last Judgement* on the west wall and the unsettling, heart-rending *Teotoco*, the stark, gold-ground mosaic of the thin, weeping Virgin portrayed as the 'bearer of God'.

Next to the cathedral is the restored 11th-century octagonal church of **Santa Fosca**, surrounded by an attractive portico, one of the best works of late Byzantine architecture still in existence. Near here stands an ancient stone throne called the **Chair of Attila**, though the details of its connection with the Hunnish supremo are suspiciously nebulous. In the spring the basin in front of the cathedral is filled with frogs. Across the square from the cathedral the two main surviving secular buildings of Torcello, the Palazzo del Consiglio and Palazzo dell'Archivio, contain the small **Museo dell'Estuario** (*open daily 10–12.30 and 2–4; closed Mon and hols; adm L3000/1500*), with an interesting collection of archaeological finds and artefacts from Torcello's former churches.

Shopping

Venice is a fertile field for shoppers, whether you're looking for tacky bric-à-brac to brighten up the mantelpiece (just walk down the Lista di Spagna) or the latest in hand-crafted Italian design—but be warned that bargains are hard to find. Everything from fresh fish to lovely inlaid wooden boxes and huge quantities of tourist junk can be found at the **Rialto markets**. You will also come across food stalls in any number of squares and on barges along the smaller canals, but there is another large food and produce market in Castello, on **Via Garibaldi**. The main public auction house is **Franco Semezato**, Palazzo Giovanelli, Cannaregio 2292.

antiques

A flea market appears periodically in Campo San Maurizio, near Campo Santo Stefano, which is also the area with the largest concentration of antique shops. **Antonietta Santomanco della Toffola**, Frezzeria 1504, S. Marco, has Russian and English silver, prints, and antique jewellery and glass, while the establishments of the print dealer **Pietro Scarpa** at Campo S. Moisè 1464 and Calle XXII Marzo 2089, S. Marco, are as much museums as shops. Away from the San Marco area, **Salizzada**, S. Lio 5672, in Castello, has old prints of Venice, clocks, and many other curious odds and ends, and **Xanthippe**, Dorsoduro 2773, near Ca' Rezzonico, is a highly eclectic little shop specializing in the 19th century and Art Deco Venetian glass.

books

Venice has a good selection of bookshops. **Fantoni Libre Arte**, Salizzada di S. Luca 4121, S. Marco, has a monumental display of monumental art books, while **Sansovino**, Bacino Orseolo 84, S. Marco (just outside the Procuratie Vecchie), also has a large collection of art and coffee-table books combined with a huge stock of post-cards. The best stock of books in Italian about every aspect of Venice, including some rare editions, is in **Filippi**, Calle del Paradiso 5763, Castello. If you're looking for books in English, try **Sangiorgio**, Calle Larga XXII Marzo 2087, S. Marco, and **Alla Toletta**, Sacca della Toletta 1214, Dorsoduro.

fashion, fabrics and accessories

Most of Venice's high-fashion designer boutiques are located in the streets to the west of Piazza San Marco; fashion names like **Missoni**, with some of Italy's most beautiful knitwear, at Calle Vallaresso 1312, S. Marco, near Harry's Bar; **Krizia**, Mercerie del Capitello 4949, S. Marco, for more youth-oriented, colourful knits; **Laura Biagiotti**, Via XXII Marzo 2400/a, S. Marco; **Roberta di Camerino**, Lungomare Marconi 32, on the Lido, one of Venice's home-grown designers; and Giorgio Armani, at both **Giorgio Armani da Elysée**, Frezzeria 1693, S. Marco, and **Emporio Armani**, Calle dei Fabbri 989, S. Marco, with more accessible prices. For fashions by maverick Italian and French designers, try **La Coupole**, Via XXII Marzo, or its sister shop, **La Fenice**,

1674, for more everyday-wear designers. Then there's **M. Antichità**, S. Marco 1691, offering velour dresses of Renaissance richness, and jewels to match.

Most Venetians, however, buy at least some of their clothes at the **COIN** department store, Salizzada San Giovanni Crisostomo, just north of Campo San Bartolomeo, part of a national chain, and a variety of cheap clothes stalls spread along Rio Terra San Leonardo, Cannaregio. Fashionable second-hand clothes are the mainstay at **Aldo Strausse**, Campo S. Giustina, in Castello, but **Emilio Ceccato**, Sottoportico di Rialto, S. Polo, is the place to find something very typically Venetian—gondoliers' shirts, jackets and tight trousers. Meanwhile, at the **Camiceria San Marco**, at Calle Vallaresso 1340, S. Marco, they will make up men's shirts and women's dresses to order for you within 24 hours.

For sensuous and expensive lingerie, visit **Jade Martine**, S. Marco 1645. The great place to find Venetian lace, whether for lingerie or tablecloths, is on Burano, though be aware that the bargains there are probably neither handmade nor even Buranese. Back in Venice itself, **Jesurum**, Piazza S. Marco 60/61, has a vast quantity of Venetian lace and linen of all kinds on display in a 12th-century former church behind St Mark's Basilica, as well as a good selection of swimwear and summer clothes.

Not just lace but also other high-quality fabrics have figured equally among Venice's traditional specialities, using skills that in many cases have been reinvigorated in recent years. **Trois**, Campo S. Maurizio, S. Marco 2666, is an institution selling colourful pleated Fortuny silks, invented in Venice and made to traditional specifications on the Giudecca. More modern designs in silks and fabrics can be found at **Valli**, Merceria S. Zulian 783, S. Marco.

For posh shoes, **La Fenice**, Via XXII Marzo 2255, S. Marco, has a good selection by French and Italian designers. The greatest name in Venetian leather is **Vogini**, Via XXII Marzo 1300, S. Marco, which has a comprehensive selection of bags and luggage, and a complete range by Venetian designer Roberta di Camerino.

Jewellery in Venice tends to be expensive and conservative—particularly in the many shops in and around San Marco—and so may be of more interest for looking than buying. **Codognato**, S. Marco 1295, is one of the oldest jewellers in Venice, with some rare Tiffany, Cartier and Art Deco items; at **Missiaglia**, Piazza S. Marco 125, you can see some of the most elegant pieces produced by Venetian gold and silver-smiths working today.

food and drink

As well as in the markets (*see* above), other good places to pick up local specialities include **Pastificio Artigiano**, Strada Nuova 4292, Cannaregio, where Paolo Pavon has for 50 years created Venice's tastiest and most exotic pastas, among them *pasta al cacao* (chocolate pasta) and lemon, beetroot and curry varieties. Similarly, **Il Pastaio**, Calle del Varoteri 219, in the Rialto market, offers pastas in over a score of different colours. **Colussi**, Rugheta S. Apollonia 4325, near Campo Santi Filippo e Giacomo, is a *pasticceria* with an enormous range of unusual pastries.

If you do want to picnic as you make your way round Venice then **Rizzo Pane**, Calle delle Botteghe, S. Marco, just off Campo F. Morosini, is an *alimentari* where you'll find everything you need. For wines and other varieties of alcohol, **Cantinone già Schiavi**, Fondamenta S. Trovaso 992, Dorsoduro, is a fine old shop with plenty to choose from.

gifts

Anyone seeking unusual gifts will find plenty to look at in Venice, though, again, prices sometimes need to be handled with care. At **La Scialuppa**, Calle Seconda dei Saoneri 2695, S. Polo, you can buy the wares of woodworker Gilberto Penzo, who makes beautiful *forcole* (gondola oar locks, made of walnut), replicas of Venetian guild signs and many other things. **Calle Lunga 2137**, in Dorsoduro, is a workshop specializing in decorative wrought-iron, and **Fondamenta Minotto 154**, S. Croce, near S. Nicolò Tolentino and the railway station, has all sorts of gold and brass items, such as Venetian doorknockers. For children, **Signor Blum**, Calle Lunga S. Barnaba 2864, Dorsoduro, has beautiful jigsaw puzzles and brightly painted wooden toys. For an overview, the **Consorzio Artigianato Artistico Veneziano**, Calle Larga S. Marco 412, S. Marco, has a fair selection of all kinds of handmade Venetian crafts.

Burano is the centre for lace, and Murano (*see* above) is still the place to go for glassware, but in the city one of the grand names in Venetian glass is **Pauly**, at the end of Calle Larga, near Ponte Consorzi, S. Marco, with 30 rooms of traditional and contemporary designs housed in a former doge's palazzo. At a less exalted level, **Paolo Rossi**, Campo S. Zaccaria 4685, S. Marco, has attractive reproductions of ancient glassware at still-reasonable prices, and **Arte Veneto**, Campo S. Zanipolo 6335, Castello, offers glass and ceramic trinkets that escape looking tacky or ridiculous. If you can contemplate carrying them home then mosaics, one of the oldest Venetian crafts, are also available, as individual *tessere* or larger items. Try **Arte del Mosaico**, Calle Erizzo 4002, Castello, or **Angelo Orsoni**, Campiello del Battello 1045, Cannaregio. For exquisite handmade paper, blank books and photo albums try **Paulo Olbi**, Calle della Mandorla 3653 (near Campo S. Angelo), and for paper designs, silk ties and masks made by Alberto Valese fusing Persian and Italian styles, visit **Alberto Valese-Ebrû**, Campo S. Stefano 3471, S. Marco (nearly opposite the church door).

Venice ✉ *30100*   **Where to Stay**

The rule of thumb in Venice is that in whatever class of hotel you stay, expect it to cost around a third more than it would on the mainland, even before the often outrageous charge for breakfast is added to the bill. Reservations are near-essential from about April to October and for Carnival; many hotels close in the winter, though many of those that do stay open offer substantial discounts at this time. Single rooms are always very hard to find. If you arrive at any time without reservations, the tourist offices at the railway station and Piazzale Roma have a free room-finding service (a deposit is required, which is then deducted from your hotel bill), though they get very busy in season. Many hotels also have touts around the station looking for clients, who are not necessarily to be disregarded, as the prices they offer can be quite reasonable. Also, the central tourist office in Piazza San Marco will supply by post a list of agencies that rent self-catering flats in Venice and neighbouring resorts that can be reserved in advance.

★★★★★ **Cipriani**, Giudecca 10, ✆ 041 520 7744. Since 1963 this has been one of Italy's most luxurious hotels, a villa isolated in a lush garden at one end of the Giudecca that's so quiet and comfortable you could forget Venice exists, even though it's only a few minutes away by the hotel's 24-hour private launch service. An Olympic-size pool, sauna, jacuzzis in each room, tennis courts, and a superb restaurant are just some of its facilities, and no hotel anywhere could pamper you more. Room prices vary according to the view and the facilities.

★★★★★ **Danieli**, Riva degli Schiavoni 4196, ✆ 041 522 6480, ✉ 041 520 0208. The largest and most famous hotel in Venice, in what must be the most glorious location, over-looking the Lagoon and rubbing shoulders with the Palazzo Ducale. Formerly the Gothic palazzo of the Dandolo family, it has been a hotel since 1822; Dickens, Proust, George Sand and Wagner checked in here. Nearly every room has some story to tell, in a beautiful setting of silken walls, Gothic staircases, gilt mirrors and oriental rugs. The new wing, much vilified ever since it was built in the 1940s, is comfortable but lacks the charm and the stories.

★★★★★ **Gritti Palace**, S. Maria del Giglio 2467, S. Marco, ✆ 041 794 611. The 15th-century Grand Canal palace that once belonged to the dashing glutton and womanizer Doge Andrea Gritti has been preserved as a true Venetian fantasy and elegant retreat, now part of the CIGA chain. All the rooms are furnished with Venetian antiques, but for a real splurge do as Somerset Maugham did and stay in the Ducal Suite. Another of its delights is the restaurant, the **Club del Doge**, on a terrace overlooking the canal.

★★★★★ **Excelsior Palace**, Lungomare Marconi 41, Lido di Venezia, ✆ 041 526 0201, ✉ 041 526 7276. An immense confection, built in 1907 as the biggest and most luxurious resort hotel in the world and recently redesigned with as much flamboyance as ever. The outrageous exterior is part Hollywood and part Moorish neo-Gothic. Private beach, swimming pool, tennis courts, golf, nightclub and private launch service to Venice are some of its amenities. Ogling the stars at the Film Festival is another. *Closed mid-Nov–mid-Mar.*

very expensive

★★★★ **Cavalletto & Doge Orseolo**, Calle Cavalletto 1107, S. Marco, ✆ 041 520 0955. Overlooking the basin where most of the gondoliers moor their vessels, in a building that in the Middle Ages was already a hostel for pilgrims waiting to embark for the Holy Land, it has been a hotel since the 18th century. The public areas are disappoint-ingly dowdy and modern, though some of the more expensive rooms are tastefully decorated. Off-season discounts, but still over-priced.

★★★★ **Londra Palace**, Riva degli Schiavoni 4171, Castello, ✆ 041 520 0533, ✉ 041 522 5032. Tchaikovsky wrote his *Fourth Symphony* in room 108, and it was also a favourite of Stravinsky. The hotel was created by linking two palaces, and it has an elegant interior, views of the lagoon from over half the rooms, and exceptionally good service. There is also an excellent restaurant, **Les Deux Lions**.

★★★★ **Saturnia & International**, Via XXII Marzo 2398, S. Marco, ✆ 041 520 8377, ✉ 041 520 7131. A lovely hotel in a romantic quattrocento palazzo that has preserved centuries of accumulated decoration. Very near S. Marco, it has a garden court, faced by the nicest and quietest rooms. Off-season discounts.

**** **Des Bains**, Lungomare Marconi 17, Lido di Venezia, ✆ 041 526 5921, ✇ 041 526 0113. A grand old luxury hotel, now part of the Sheraton empire, that preserves much of its Belle Epoque revelries in its magnificent Liberty-style salon, private *cabanas*, and large garden designed for dalliance. Thomas Mann stayed here on several occasions, and has Aschenbach sigh his life away on the private beach. There's also a salt-water swimming pool, tennis courts, perfect service, and a launch service into Venice. *Closed Dec–mid-Mar.*

**** **Quattro Fontane**, Via delle Quattro Fontane 16, Lido di Venezia, ✆ 041 526 0227, ✇ 041 526 0726. The best of the smaller Lido hotels, it was formerly the seaside villa of a Venetian family. Its cool walled-in courtyard is inviting and tranquil, and the public and private rooms are furnished with antiques. Tennis court. Book well in advance. *Closed Nov–Mar.*

expensive

*** **Accademia 'Villa Maravege'**, Fondamenta Bollani 1058, Dorsoduro, ✆ 041 521 0188, ✇ 041 523 9152. A hotel that offers a generous dollop of slightly faded charm in a 17th-century villa with a garden, just off the Grand Canal. Its 26 rooms are furnished with a menagerie of antiques, some of which look as if they were left behind by the villa's previous occupant—the Russian Embassy.

*** **La Fenice et Des Artistes**, Campiello de la Fenice 1936, S. Marco, ✆ 041 523 2333, ✇ 041 520 3721. A favourite of opera buffs in Venice (though that's not much use until La Fenice reopens), inside there are lots of mirrors, antiques and chandeliers to make artistes feel at home. Fully air-conditioned.

*** **Do Pozzi**, Corte do Pozzi 2373, S. Marco, ✆ 041 520 7855, ✇ 041 522 9413. With a bit of the look of an Italian country inn, this hotel has 29 quiet rooms on a charming little square, only a few minutes from Piazza San Marco. It's friendly and well run. Optional air-conditioning in all rooms.

*** **Sturion**, Calle del Sturion 679, San Polo, ✆ 041 523 6243, ✇ 041 522 8378. A popular choice, as it's one of the least expensive hotels actually on the Grand Canal. It's advisable to book well ahead for one of its eight large, finely furnished rooms.

*** **Villa Parco**, Via Rodi 1, Lido di Venezia, ✆ 041 526 0015, ✇ 041 526 7620. A recently renovated villa a short way from the beach with a fine little garden for a bit of privacy. Children are welcome.

moderate

** **Falier**, Salizzada S. Pantalon 130, S. Croce, ✆ 041 710 882, ✇ 041 520 6554. A small hotel near Campo San Rocco. Elegantly furnished, it has two flower-filled terraces to lounge around on when your feet rebel; one room has its own terrace.

** **Mignon**, SS. Apostoli 4535, Cannaregio, ✆ 041 523 7388, ✇ 041 520 8658. In a fairly quiet area, not far from the Ca' d'Oro, the Mignon boasts a little garden for leisurely breakfasts, though the rooms are rather plain. Has a loyal following.

** **La Residenza**, Campo Bandiera e Moro 3608, Castello, ✆ 041 528 5315, ✇ 041 588 5042. Located in a lovely 14th-century palace in a quiet square between San

Marco and the Arsenale. The public rooms are flamboyantly decorated with 18th-century frescoes, paintings and antique furniture; the bedrooms are more simple.

cheap

The largest concentration of relatively cheap hotels in Venice is around the Lista di Spagna, running eastwards into Cannaregio from the train station, though be warned that they can be pretty tacky and noisy. A more relaxed, pleasant and attractive area in which to find less expensive accommodation is in Dorsoduro, particularly around the Campo Santa Margherita.

★ **Casa Carettoni**, Lista di Spagna 130, Cannaregio, ✆ 041 716 231. The most pleasant and comfortable cheap hotel near the station; no breakfast is a plus, as you can do as Venetians do and take it in a nearby bar.

★ **Casa Petrarca**, Calle delle Fuseri 4393, S. Marco, ✆ 041 520 0430. Petrarch didn't really sleep in one of these six friendly rooms near the Piazza, but who cares?

★ **Silva**, Fondamenta Rimedio 4423, Castello, ✆ 041 522 7643. A bit hard to find—on one of the most photographed little canals in Venice, between the S. Zaccaria *vaporetto* stop and S. Maria Formosa. The rooms are fairly basic, but quiet, and the staff are friendly.

hostels and campsites

The tourist office has a list of all inexpensive hostel accommodation in Venice; as sleeping in the streets is now discouraged, schools are often pressed into use to take in the summer overflow, charging minimal rates for a place to spread out a sleeping bag.

Ostello Venezia, Fondamenta delle Zitelle 86, Giudecca, ✆ 041 523 8211. Venice's official youth hostel enjoys one of the most striking locations of any in Italy, with views across the Giudecca Canal to San Marco. They don't take reservations over the phone, and to be assured of a place in July or August you have to write well in advance. At other times, you can chance it and book in person—the office opens at 6pm, but doors open at noon for waiting. IYHF cards required (though they're available at the hostel) and there's an 11.30pm curfew. Beds are L25,000 a head, breakfast included; meals are L14,000.

Foresteria Valdese, Calle della Madonnetta 5170, Castello, ✆ 041 528 6797. An old palazzo converted into a dormitory/*pensione* by the Waldensians. Check-in 9–1 and 6–8; beds in dorms L20,000, breakfast included, and in rooms L24,000 per person. **Domus Cavanis**, Rio Terrà Foscarini 912, Dorsoduro, ✆ 041 528 7374. A Catholic-run hostel open June–Sept only. Single (L45,000), double (L65,000) and triple (L90,000) rooms; students get about a 10% discount. Optional breakfast L7000.

Eating Out

Venetian cuisine is based on fish, shellfish, and rice, often mixed together in a succulent seafood risotto. *Risi e bisi* (rice and peas) is famous, often served with anchovy sauce, while the favourite local pasta dish is *bigoli in salsa*, thick hollow spaghetti topped with butter, onions, and anchovies or sardines. There are various types of *risotti: di mare*, with seafood, *in nero*, with cuttlefish cooked in its own ink, or *alla sbirraglia*, with vegetables, chicken and ham. For *secondo*, liver and onions (*fegato alla veneziana*) with polenta (*tecia*) shares top billing with seafood dishes like scampi, Sile eel, cuttlefish in its own ink (*seppie alla veneziana*), *fritto* (Adriatic mixed fry) and lobster (*aragosta*). Bitter red *radicchio* is a favourite side-dish, and you can top it all off with a *tiramisù*, the traditional Veneto mascarpone, coffee and chocolate dessert. Wines are of a reliably high standard in most restaurants, mainly excellent Veneto reds and whites from Friuli and Trentino-Alto Adige.

Venice, however, is famous for its bad restaurants. Not only is cooking in general well below the norm for Italy, but prices tend to be about 15% higher, and even the moderate ones can give you a nasty surprise at *conto* time with excessive service and cover charges. The cheap ones, serving up 500 tourist menus a day to the international throng, are mere providers of calories to keep you on your feet; pizza is a good standby if you're on a budget. The restaurants listed here, though, all have a history of being decent or better, so chances are they still will be when you visit.

luxury

Antico Martini, Campo S. Fantin 1983, S. Marco, ✆ 041 522 4121. This is a Venetian classic, all romance and elegance. It started out as a Turkish coffee-house in the early 18th century, but nowadays is better known for seafood, a superb wine list and the best *pennette al pomodoro* in Venice. The intimate piano bar-restaurant stays open until 2am. Its romantic flavour is temporarily swallowed up by La Fenice's rebuilding operations directly outside. *Closed Tues, Wed midday, Dec and Feb.*

Danieli Terrace, in the Danieli Hotel, Riva degli Schiavoni 4196, Castello, ✆ 041 522 6480. The Danieli's rooftop restaurant is renowned for classic cuisine (try the *spaghetti alla Danieli*, prepared at your table) and perfect service in an incomparable setting overlooking Bacino San Marco.

very expensive

La Caravella, Calle Larga XXII Marzo 2397, S. Marco, ✆ 041 520 8901, in an annexe to the Saturnia Hotel (*see* above). For sheer variety of seasonal and local dishes, prepared by a master chef, few restaurants in Italy can top this merrily corny repro of a dining hall in a 16th-century Venetian galley. Try gilt head with thyme and fennel. Despite the décor, the atmosphere is fairly formal. *Open Oct–April, closed Wed.*

Do Forni, Calle dei Specchieri 468, S. Marco, ✆ 041 523 2148. For many Italians as well as foreigners, this is *the* place to eat in Venice. There are two dining rooms, one 'Orient Express'-style, the other rustic, and both are always filled with diners partaking of its excellent seafood *antipasti*, polenta and well-prepared fish. *Closed Thurs in winter.*

Harry's Bar, Calle Vallaresso 1323, S. Marco, ✆ 041 523 6797. In a class by itself, a favourite of Hemingway and assorted other luminaries, this is as much a Venetian institution as the Doges' Palace, though food has become secondary to its celebrity atmosphere. Best to avoid the formal restaurant upstairs and just flit in for a quick hobnob while sampling a sandwich and the justly famous house cocktails (a Bellini, Tiziano or Tiepolo—delectable fruit juices mixed with Prosecco) at a table downstairs near the bar. *Closed Mon.*

Dall'Hotel Excelsior, Lungomare Marconi 40, ✆ 041 526 0201. You can still find the classic turn-of-the-century Lido experience at the hotel's restaurant which will offer you nearly everything you could desire—including a traditional Venetian meal.

expensive

Antica Besseta, Salizada da Ca'Zusto (at the end of Calle Savio), S. Croce, ✆ 041 524 0428. A family-run citadel of Venetian homecooking, where you can experience an authentic *risi e bisi*, or *bigoli in salsa*, scampi, and the family's own wine. *Closed Tues, Wed lunch, and part of July and Aug.*

Hostaria da Franz, Fondamenta San Isepo (or Giuseppe) 754, Castello, facing the side of the church, ✆ 041 522 7505. A restaurant well out of the way just north of the Giardini Pubblici, but it's well worth the trouble of getting lost *en route*. This is one of Venice's best: great oysters, *gnocchi* and seafood cooked the way it should be if all Venetians tried harder. The house wine is lovely. *Closed Tues.*

Antica Locanda Montin, Fondamenta di Borgo or Eremite 1147 (near S. Trovaso), Dorsoduro, ✆ 041 522 7151. This has long been Venice's most celebrated artists' eatery, with a vast garden, but the food can range erratically in quality from first to third division. *Closed Tues evening, Wed, and half of Aug.*

Trattoria Vini da Arturo, Calle degli Assassini 3656, S. Marco, ✆ 041 528 6974. In an infamous little street near La Fenice, this is a tiny trattoria that marches to a different drum from most Venetian restaurants, with not a speck of seafood on the menu. Instead, try the *papardelle al radicchio* or Venice's best steaks; its *tiramisù* is famous. *Closed Sun and half Aug.*

moderate

Altanella, Calle della Erbe 268, Giudecca, ✆ 041 522 7780. A delightful old seafood restaurant with an attractive setting on the Rio del Ponte Longo and a sideways glimpse of the Giudecca Canal thrown in. Any of the grilled fish will be superb, and the *risotto di pesce* and *fritto* are worth the trip in themselves. *Closed Mon evening, Tues, and half of Aug. Reserve.*

Antica Mola, Fondamenta degli Ormesini 2800, Cannaregio, near the Ghetto. All the old favourites—grilled fish, risotto and *zuppa di pesce*—as well as tables by the canal. *Closed Wed.*

Da Remigio, Salizzada dei Greci 3416, Castello, ✆ 041 523 0089. A neighbourhood favourite, with solid Venetian cooking. Very popular with the locals. *Closed Mon, and Tues eve.*

Tre Spiedi, Salizzada S. Canciano 5906, Cannaregio, ✆ 041 528 0035, near the Campiello F. Corner and the central post office. A cosy atmosphere to go with local specialities like *spaghetti alla veneziana* and *braciola Bruno* (pork chops). *Closed Mon.*

cheap

Aciughetta, Campo SS. Filippo e Giacomo, Castello, ✆ 041 522 4292. One of the best cheap restaurants and bars near the Piazza San Marco, with good pizzas and atmosphere to boot. *Closed Tues.*

Pizzeria alle Oche, Calle del Tentor 1552, S. Croce, ✆ 041 524 1161, just before Ponte del Parucheta, south of S. Giacomo dell'Orio. Cheery, young atmosphere with 85 types of pizza, and take-away. *Closed Mon in winter.*

Casa Mia, Calle dell'Oca 4430, Cannaregio, ✆ 041 528 5590, near Campo SS. Apostoli. A lively pizzeria full of locals, with six courtyard tables. *Closed Tues.*

Vino Vino, Campo S. Fantin 1983, S. Marco, ✆ 041 522 4121. A trendy offspring of the élite Antico Martini, where you can eat a well-cooked, filling dish (cooked by the same chefs!) with a glass of good wine at prices even students can afford. *Closed Tues, Wed midday, Dec and Feb.*

Entertainment and Nightlife

Sadly, in a city that's clearly made-to-order for pleasure, revelry and romance, life after dark is notoriously moribund. The Venetians take an evening stroll to their local *campo* for a chat with friends and an *aperitivo* before heading home to dinner and the TV—the hot-blooded may go on to bars and discos in Mestre, Marghera or the Lido.

Visitors are left to become even poorer at the **Municipal Casino**, out on the Lido from April to October, and at other times in the Palazzo Vendramin on the Grand Canal (hours are 3pm–2am, dress up and take your passport). You might prefer to spend less more memorably on a moonlit gondola ride, or you can do as most people do—wander about. Venice is a different city at night, when the *bricole* lights in the Lagoon are a fitting backdrop for a mer-king's birthday pageant.

Even so, there are places to go among all this peace and quiet, and against the absence of everyday nightlife should be put Venice's packed calendar of special events. For an up-to-date calendar of current events, exhibitions, shows, films, and concerts in the city, consult *Un Ospite di Venezia*, free from tourist offices.

opera, classical music and theatre

Venice's music programme is heavily oriented to the classical. Opera (from December to May only), ballet, recitals and symphonic concerts are the main fare at Venice's once stunning opera house, **La Fenice**, and its smaller chamber, Sala Apollinée, sadly closed for an indeterminate length of time following a fire in 1996 (*see* p.134). In the meantime the company is set up in a temporary pavilion at Tronchetto and tickets are sold through the Cassa di Risparmio, Campo S. Luca, ✆ 041 529 1111.

Venice's other main theatre is the **Teatro Goldoni**, Calle Goldoni 4650/b, S. Marco, ✆ 041 520 5422, which is where the Goldoni repertory holds pride of place, but there are other plays, as well as concerts; in summer performances are often moved to Campo S. Polo.

Two other concert venues that are worth visiting as much for the décor as the music are the **Palazzo Labia**, Campo S. Geremia, Cannaregio (call ahead for tickets, ✆ 041 524 2812), and Vivaldi's lovely Rococo church of **La Pietà** (information and tickets, call ✆ 041 520 8711), where prices are usually fairly high but the acoustics are well-nigh perfect.

The classic cafés of Venice face each other across Piazza San Marco: **Florian's** and its great rival **Quadri**—avoided, it is said, by all true Venetians because of its popularity with the Austrian occupiers in the last century. Prices are correspondingly exorbitant.

More fashionable with smart Venetians today, particularly on Sundays, is **Harry's Dolci**, Fondamenta S. Biagio 773 on the Giudecca, noted for its elegant teas, ice creams and cakes, as well as the Cipriani's **Cips**, which is now open for scrumptious sandwiches and cakes. **Caffè Costarica**, Rio Terrà di S. Leonardo, Cannaregio, brews Venice's most powerful *espresso* and great iced coffee (*frappé*), and also sells ground coffees and beans over the counter.

Throughout the day Venetians frequently drop into bars and wine bars (*bacaro*) for a 'shadow' (an *ombra*, a tiny glass of wine generally downed in one go) and *cichetti*, the Venetian equivalent of tapas. For the greatest variety of wines, try Venice's oldest wine bar, **Al Volta**, Calle Cavalli di S. Marco 4081, S. Marco, with over 2000 Italian and foreign labels to choose from and a sumptuous array of *cichetti*. *Open 9–2.30 and 5–9; closed Sun.* **Do Mori**, a resolutely traditional Rialto market bar, north of Ruga Vecchia San Giovanni, has delicious snacks (but no tables) to go with your *ombra*. *Open 8.30–9; closed Sun.*

Between 5pm and dinner is the time to indulge in a beer and *tramezzini*, finger sandwiches that come in a hundred varieties, and some of the best are to be found at eccentric **Bar alla Toletta**, Calle della Toletta 1191, Dorsoduro, run by a temperamental middle-aged couple with a voracious appetite for jazz.

The title of best *gelateria* in the city has by convention been accorded to **Paolin**, on the Campo Santo Stefano, S. Marco, above all for their divine pistachio. However, **Nico**, on the Zattere ai Gesuati, Dorsoduro, is also a must on anyone's ice cream tour, if the late-night queues are anything to go by.

jazz, clubs and nightspots

Venice's few late-night bars and music venues can be fun, or just posy and dull, and what you find is pretty much a matter of pot luck. **Paradiso Perduto**, Fondamenta della Misericordia 2540, Cannaregio, ✆ 041 720 581, is the city's best-known and most popular late-night bar/restaurant with inexpensive though variable food, and a relaxed, bohemian atmosphere popular with a mix of locals and English visitors. Once know for live jazz, they now often have a bit of trouble with their late-night licence, so live events are rare. *Open 6pm–midnight, sometimes later; closed Wed.*

A current favourite for young trendies is **Taverna l'Olandese Volante** ('flying Dutchman'), Campo S. Lio 5658, Castello, ✆ 041 528 9349, Venice's answer to a pub, open late with snacks and simple food. The relaxed and informal wine bar **Osteria da Codroma**, Fondamenta Briati 2540, Dorsoduro, ✆ 041 520 4161, hosts a backgammon club, art shows and occasional live jazz. *Open 7pm–2am; closed Thurs.* Another restaurant/bar with music, dancing and sometimes live rock or jazz is **Ai Canottieri**, Ponte Tre Archi 690, Cannaregio, ✆ 041 715 408. *Open 7pm–2am; closed Sun.*

There are also quite a few fairly glitzy piano bars, such as **Linea d'Ombra**, Zattere ai Saloni, near the Salute, © 041 528 5259. *Open 8pm–1am; closed Wed*. A favourite place for Venetians to make off to in Marghera is **Al Vapore**, Via Fratelli Bandiera 8, © 041 930 796, which hosts live rock and jazz. In July and August there's a disco on the Lido: **Acropolis**, Lungomare Marconi 22, © 041 526 0466. The Lido is also the place to go for a late-night game of billiards *chez* **Al Delfino**, an 'American Bar' with music and snacks at Lungomare Marconi 96, © 041 526 8309. *Open until 2am*. Or **Villa Eva**, Gran Viale 49, © 041 526 1884, with music and snacks from midnight until 4am. *Closed Thurs except in the summer*.

The main late-night drinking holes are **Harry's Bar** (*see* above, 'Eating Out'), especially if someone else is paying. **Osteria ai Assassini**, Calle degli Assassini, S. Marco, has wines, beers, and good *cichetti*. *Open till midnight; closed Sun*. For more filling victuals, try **Vino Vino** (*see* above, 'Eating Out'). *Open till 2am*. The **Creperia Poggi**, Cannaregio 2103, © 041 715 971, has music and also stays open till 2am, flipping crêpes until midnight. *Closed Sun*. The last chance for an ice cream is at 3am at the Lido's **Gelateria Bar Maleti**, Gran Viale 47. *Closed Wed*.

exhibitions and art festivals

Venice is one of Europe's top cities for exhibitions: major international shows fill the **Palazzo Grassi**, Campo S. Samuele, S. Marco, which Fiat has transformed into a lavishly equipped exhibition and cultural centre. High-calibre art and photographic exhibitions also appear frequently at the **Palazzo Querini-Stampalia**, the **Peggy Guggenheim Collection**, and **Ca' Pesaro**.

Then there's the **Biennale**, the most famous contemporary art show in the world, founded in 1895 and now held, in principle, in even-numbered years. The main exhibits of the 40 or so countries officially represented are set up in the permanent pavilions in the Giardini Pubblici, but there is also an open section for younger and less-established artists, in venues across the city.

The city's other great cultural junket is the **Venice Film Festival**, held in the Palazzo del Cinema and the Astra Cinema on the Lido every year (late August and September). As well as spotting the stars, you can sometimes get in to see films if you arrive at the cinemas really early—tickets are only sold on the same day as each showing.

traditional festivals

Venice's renowned **Carnival**, first held in the ten days preceding Lent in 1094, was revived in 1979 after several decades of dormancy. It attracts huge crowds, but battles against the inveterate Italian urge to maintain their *bella figura*—getting dressed up in elaborate costumes, wandering down to San Marco and taking each other's picture is as much as most of the revellers seem to get up to. Concerts and shows are put on all over Venice, with city and corporate sponsorship, but there's very little spontaneity or serious carousing, and certainly no trace of what Byron called the 'revel of the earth'.

Even so, a **Carnival mask** can still make a good souvenir, either in inexpensive papier mâché (*cartapesta*) or in leather. There are mask shops all over Venice, but for the real, traditionally crafted item, try **Giorgio Clanetti (Laboratorio Artigiano Maschere)**, Barbaria delle Tole 6657, Castello, near SS. Giovanni e Paolo.

In 1988 Venice revived the medieval ceremony of **La Sensa**, held on the first Sunday after Ascension Day, in which the Doge married the sea. Now the Mayor plays the groom, in a replica of the state barge or *Bucintoro*. It's as corny and pretentious as it sounds, but on the same day you can watch the gondoliers race in the **Vogalonga**, or 'long row', from San Marco to Burano and back again.

Venice's most spectacular festival, **Il Redentore**, held on the third Sunday of July, celebrates the end of the plague of 1576, when the Senate vowed that in thanksgiving they would build a church (Palladio's Il Redentore, on the Giudecca) and cross over to attend Mass there once a year on a bridge of boats—which the Venetians continue to do today. The greatest excitement happens the Saturday night before, when Venetians traditionally row out for a picnic on the water, manoeuvring for the best view of the fabulous fireworks display over the Lagoon. For landlubbers (and there are thousands of them) the prime viewing and picknicking spots are towards the eastern ends of either the Giudecca or the Zattere.

More adrenalin is expended in the **Regata Storica** (first Sunday in September), a splendid pageant of historic vessels and crews in Renaissance costumes and hotly contested races by gondoliers and a variety of other rowers down the Grand Canal. Another bridge of boats is built on 21 November, this time across the Grand Canal to the Salute, for the feast of **Santa Maria della Salute**, which also commemorates the ending of a plague, in 1631. This event provides the only opportunity to see Longhena's unique basilica as it would have been when it was built, with its doors thrown open on to the Grand Canal.

Florence

No region could be more essentially Italian. Its Renaissance culture and art became Italy's in common, and its dialect, as refined by Dante, cast a hundred others into the shadows to become the Italian language. Nevertheless, Tuscany seems to stand a bit aloof from the rest of the nation; it keeps its own counsel, never changes its ways, and faces the world with a Mona Lisa smile that has proved irresistible to northerners since the days of Shelley and Browning.

Today Britons, Dutchmen, Germans and Americans jostle each year for the privilege of paying two or three million lire for a month in a classic Tuscan farmhouse, with a view over a charmed, civilized landscape of cypresses and parasol pines, orderly rows of vines and olives, and a chapel on the hill with a quattrocento fresco. In Florence and the other cities, they stand in queues like refugees, waiting to enter the churches and museums that are the shrines of Tuscan art.

For a province that has contributed so much to Western civilization since the Middle Ages, Tuscany's career remains slightly mysterious. Some have attempted to credit its cultural prominence to an inheritance from the ancient Etruscans, but most of modern Tuscany was never more than provincial throughout Etruscan and Roman times. Out of the Dark Ages, inexplicably, new centres of learning and art appeared, first in Pisa and Florence, and then in a dozen other towns, inaugurating a cultural renaissance that really began as early as the 1100s.

As abruptly as it began, this brilliant age was extinguished in the 16th century, but it left behind a new province of Europe, finished, solid, and well-formed. Tuscany can be excused a little complacency. Though prosperous and enlightened, fully a part of modern Italy today, the region for centuries has seemed perfectly content to let the currents of culture and innovation flow elsewhere.

There's no sense in painting when anything new would have to hang next to Da Vincis and Botticellis, no incentive to build in a city full of churches and palaces by the medieval masters. After the surprising wave of bad taste that brought the Renaissance to a close, Tuscany was shamed into an introspectiveness and cultural conservatism of almost Chinese proportions.

Of course these centuries, during which Tuscany has quietly cultivated its own garden, have not been without some advantages. Its cities and their art treasures have been preserved with loving care. So has the countryside; if anything the last few hundred years have emphasized the frugal, hardworking side of the Tuscan character, the side that longs for the rural life, counts its pennies, and finds tripe with chickpeas a perfectly satisfying repast. All this at times makes a striking contrast with the motorways, the new industry around the cities, and the hordes of tourists descending on Florence, Pisa and Siena.

to Genoa

to Parma

Campo Cecina

Carrara

La Spezia

Marinella
Marina di Carrara
Marina di Massa
Cinquale Capriglia
Forte dei Marmi
Marina di Pietrasanta

Massa

Seravezza
Stazzema
Capezzano
V. Carducci
Pietrasanta
Camaiore

Lido di Camaiore

Viareggio

Torre del Lago

Massarosa

Valle Freddana

Lucca

Lago di Massaciuccoli

Pistoia

to Bologna

Prato

Florence

Gombo
San Piero a Grado
Marina di Pisa

Pisa

Certosa di Pisa

Arno

to Arezzo

Tirrenia

Livorno

Ardenza

Montenero

I. di Gorgona

Poggibonsi

Castiglioncello
Rosignano
Vada

Cecina

Volterra

Siena

Marina di Cecina

Bolgheri

TUSCANY

Castagneto-Carducci

San Vincenzo

Campiglia Marittima

Massa
Marittima

Suvereto

I. di Capraia

Porto

Golfo di Baratti
Populonia

Piombino

Follonica

Vetulonia

Braccagni

Roselle

Portoferraio

*Golfo di
Follonica*

Punta Ala

Porto Azzurro

Isola d'Elba

Castiglione
della Pescaia

Marina di Grosseto

Grosseto

Scansano

Alberese

Magliano
in Toscana

to Pitigliano

*Parco Monte
dell'Uccellina*

Talamone

Manciano

I. Pianosa

N

Porto Santo Stefano

Orbetello

Capalbio

Ansedonia

to Rome

Giglio Castello

*Monte
Argentario*

Port Ercole

Giglio Campese

Giglio Porto

I. del Giglio

Land over 200 metres

I. di Montecristo

30km

20 miles

I. di Giannutri

Venice, they say, moves one to dream a bit; Rome to contemplate the endless panorama of popes and Caesars; Naples convinces you that all is vanity. Florence (Firenze) on the other hand, a town long famed for good common sense and healthy scepticism, is different. It will not tempt you to easy conclusions; it is as romantic as a reference library. Florence, they say, moves one to *argue*.

So let's begin. Most writers have always assumed a certain point of view. You may think Florence is a museum city, they'll tell you, but you'll be wrong. Florence on the contrary is a thriving, progressive town that refuses to live in the past, insisting on earning its own way in the 20th century. Once it made Galileo's telescope, and today it still exports precision optical instruments. In the 1400s, it led Europe in fashion as well as art; today its busy seamstresses on back streets do much of the work for the designers in Milan. This argument is nice, but unfortunately untrue; despite its noise, ice cream, light industry and horrendous traffic, Florence *is* a museum city, and if you don't care to look at pictures, you'd do better just to stay on the train.

But what a museum town it is! Florence's collections easily surpass those of any other Italian city, and just from the odd bits in the back rooms its curators are able to mount a score of blockbuster special exhibitions each year. Most impressive of all is the fact that nearly all the art in them was made by the Florentines themselves, testimony to the city's position during two centuries as the great innovator of Western culture.

History

The Etruscans, who founded Florence perhaps as early as 1000 BC, were typically coy about providing any further details; the city's early history remains a puzzle. Like so many cities, however, Florence seems to begin with a bridge. Dante and many other writers commonly invoke the *marzocco*, the battered ancient icon that sat in the middle of the Ponte Vecchio and any number of bridges that preceded it until a flood swept it away in the 14th century. Often pictured as a lion (like the replacement for the original made by Donatello, now on display in the Bargello Museum), the *marzocco* may really have been a mounted cult image of the god Mars. Nothing could be more fitting, for in the centuries of its greatness Florence was a town full of trouble.

The city's apprenticeship in strife came during the endless Italian wars of the 4th–2nd centuries BC, when Rome was consolidating its hold on the peninsula. Florence seems usually to have chosen the wrong side. Sulla razed it to the ground during the Social Wars, and the town seems to have struggled back only gradually. Julius Caesar helped it along by planting a colony of veterans here in 59 BC. Roman Florence prospered, trading throughout the whole Empire. Its street plan survives in the neat rectangle of straight streets at the city's core. The town had an impressive forum right in the middle, at what is now Piazza della Repubblica.

If almost nothing remains from Roman times, it is only because Florence has been continuously occupied ever since, its centre constantly replanned and rebuilt. There were some hard times, especially during the Greek–Gothic wars of the 6th century and the Lombard occupation, but the city regained importance in the time of Charlemagne, becoming for a while the seat of the 'march' of Tuscany. Here, in what must have been one of the most fascinating eras of the city's history, once again we are left without much information. Florence, for whatever reason, was one of the first inland cities to regain its balance after the fall of the Empire. During the Dark Ages the city was already beginning to develop the free institutions of the later republic, and establishing the trading connections that were later to make it the merchant capital of Europe. About 1115, on the death of the famous Countess Matilda of Tuscany, Florence became a self-governing *comune*.

The Florentine Republic

From the beginning, circumstances forced the city into an aggressive posture against enemies within and outside its walls. Florence waged constant war against the extortionist petty nobles of the hinterlands, razing their castles and forcing them to live in the city. As an important Guelph stronghold, Florence constantly got itself into trouble with the emperors, as well as with Ghibelline Pisa, Pistoia, and Siena, towns that were to become its sworn enemies. In its darkest hour, after the crushing defeat at Montaperti in 1260, the Sienese almost succeeded in convincing their allies to bury Florence. A good sack would have been fun; Florence by the mid-13th century was possibly the richest banking and trading centre anywhere, and its gold florin had become a recognized currency across Europe.

In truth, Florence had no need of outside enemies. All through its history, the city did its level best to destroy itself. Guelph fought Ghibelline with impressive rancour, and when there were no Ghibellines left the Guelphs split into factions called the Blacks and Whites and began murdering each other. In a different dimension, the city found different causes of civil strife in the class struggles between the *popolo grosso*—the 'fat commons' or wealthy merchant class—and the members of the poorer guilds. Playing one side against the other was the newly urbanized nobility. They brought their gangster habits to town with them, turning Florence into a forest of tall brick tower-fortresses and carrying on bloody feuds in the streets that the city officials were helpless to stop. No historian has ever been able to explain how medieval Florence avoided committing suicide altogether. But despite all the troubles, this was the era of Dante (d. 1321, in political exile in Ravenna) and Giotto (d. 1337), the beginning of Florence's cultural golden age. Banking and the manufacture of wool (the leading commodity in the pre-industrial economy) were booming, and the florins kept rolling in no matter which faction was on top.

In 1282, and again in 1293, Florence tried to clean up its violent and corrupt government by a series of reforms; the *Ordinamenti della Giustizia* finally excluded the nobles from politics. It didn't work for long. Political strife continued throughout the 14th century, along with eternal wars with Lucca, Pisa and Siena, and some novel catastrophes. In 1339 Edward III of England repudiated his enormous foreign debt and Florence's two largest banks, the Bardi and Peruzzi, went bust. Plagues and famines dominated the 1340s; the plague of 1348, the Black Death, killed three-fifths of the population (and provided the frame story for Boccaccio's *Decameron*). The nobles and merchants then took advantage of the situation to establish tight boss rule. Their Guelph Party building is on Via Porta Rossa, where the spoils were divided—the original Tammany Hall. A genuine revolution in 1378 among the *ciompi*, the wool trade proletariat, might have succeeded if its leaders had been half as devious and ruthless as their opponents.

Florence's continuing good luck again saw it through, however, and prosperity gradually returned after 1400. In 1406 Pisa was finally conquered, giving Florence a seaport. Florentine armies bested the Visconti of Milan twice, and once (1410) even occupied Rome. At the dawn of the Renaissance not only Florence's artists, scholars and scientists were making innovations—the city government in the 1420s and '30s invented the progressive income tax and the national debt.

The Rise of the Medici

Although they are said to have begun as pharmacists (*medici*), by 1400 the House of Medici was the biggest merchant concern in Florence. With the resources of the Medici Bank behind him, Cosimo de' Medici installed himself as the city's political godfather, coercing or buying off the various interests and factions. In 1469 his grandson Lorenzo inherited the job, presiding over the greatest days of the Renaissance and a sustained stretch of peace and prosperity. Opposition, squashed originally by Cosimo, stayed squashed under Lorenzo. His military campaigns proved successful on the whole, and his impressive propaganda machine gave him an exaggerated reputation as a philosopher-king and patron of the arts. Lorenzo almost ruined the Medici Bank through neglect, but then made up his losses from public funds. His personal tastes in art seem to have been limited to knick-knacks, big jewels and antique bronzes, but his real hobby was nepotism. His son Giovanni, later to be made Pope Leo X at the age of 38, became a cardinal at 14.

Two years after Lorenzo's death, the wealthy classes of Florence finally succeeded in ending Medici rule when they exiled Lorenzo's weak son and successor, Piero in 1494. The republic was restored, but soon came under the influence of a remarkable Dominican demagogue, Girolamo Savonarola. Thundering out a fierce fundamentalist line, his preaching resulted in the famous 1497 'Bonfire of Vanities' on the Piazza della Signoria, when the people collected their paintings, fancy clothes, carnival masks and books and put them to the flame (a Venetian merchant offered instead to buy the whole lot from them, but the Florentines hurriedly sketched a portrait of him too, and threw it on the pyre). But Savonarola was more than a ridiculous prude. His idealistic republicanism resulted in some real democratic reforms for the new government, and his emphasis on morals provided a much needed purgative after the reigning depravity of the last 200 years. The friar reserved his strongest blasts, however, for the corruption of the Church; not a bad idea in the time of Alexander VI, the Borgia pope. When Savonarola's opponents, the *Arrabbiati* ('Infuriated'), beat his supporters, the *Piagnoni* ('snivellers'), in the 1498 elections, the way was clear for Alexander to order the friar's execution. Savonarola burned on 22 May 1498, on the same spot where the 'Bonfire of Vanities' had been held, and his ashes were thrown in the Arno.

The Medici returned in 1512, thanks to Pope Julius II and his Spanish troops. The Spaniards' exemplary sack of Prato, with remarkable atrocities, was intended as a lesson to the Florentines. It had the desired effect, and Lorenzo's nephew Giuliano de' Medici was able to re-enter the city. When Giuliano was elected Pope Clement VII in 1523 he attempted to continue running the city at a distance, but yet another Medici expulsion would take place after his humiliation in the sack of Rome in 1527, followed by the founding of the last Florentine republic.

By now Florentine politics had become a death struggle between an entire city and a single family; in the end the Medici would prove to have the stronger will. The last republic lived nervously in an atmosphere of revolutionary apocalypse; meanwhile Clement intrigued with the Spaniards for his return. An imperial army arrived in 1530 to besiege the city and, despite heroic, last-ditch resistance, Florence had to capitulate when its commander sold out to the

Pope and turned his guns on the city itself. In 1532 the Medici broke the terms of the surrender agreement by abolishing all self-government, obtaining the title of Grand Dukes of Tuscany from Emperor Charles V.

To all intents and purposes Florentine history ends here. Cosimo I Medici (d. 1574) ruled over a state that declined rapidly into a provincial backwater. When the last Medici, fat Gian Gastone, died in 1737, the powers of Europe gave the duchy to the House of Lorraine. With the rest of Tuscany, Florence was annexed to Piedmont-Sardinia in 1859, and from 1865 to 1870 it served as the capital of united Italy.

Today, despite repeated attempts to diversify the local economy through the creation of new industrial areas on the outskirts, Florence largely lives on the sheer weight of its past creativity. It suffered badly in the Second World War, when the retreating German army blew up all the bridges over the Arno except the Ponte Vecchio, and destroyed many medieval buildings along the river's edge. Still worse damage was caused by the great floods of November 1966, which left several dead and many buildings and artworks in need of restoration work that is still continuing today. The most recent damage to be inflicted on the city came in May 1993, when a bomb—planted by the Mafia—exploded near the Uffizi, killing the family of a care-taker, destroying a Renaissance library and substantially damaging parts of the Uffizi itself, particularly the Vasari corridor. The perpetrators were tried in 1998 and, as a result, 14 life sentences were given, including the conviction of Toto Riina, the 'Boss of Bosses'.

Art

Under the assault of historians and critics over the last two centuries 'Renaissance' has become such a vague and controversial word as to be nearly useless. Nevertheless, however you choose to interpret this rebirth of the arts, and whatever dates you assign it, Florence inescapably takes the credit for initiating it. This is no small claim. Combining art, science and humanist scholarship into a visual revolution that often seemed pure sorcery to their contem-poraries, a handful of Florentine geniuses taught the Western eye a new way of seeing. Perspective seems a simple enough trick to us now, but its discovery determined everything that followed, not only in art but in science and philosophy as well.

Florence in its centuries of brilliance accomplished more than any city, ever—far more than Athens in its classical age. The city's talents showed early, with the construction of the famous Baptistry, perhaps as early as 700. From the start Florence showed a remarkable adherence to the traditions of antiquity. New directions in architecture—the Romanesque after the year 1000—had little effect; what passed for Romanesque in Florence was a unique style, evolved by a self-confident city that probably believed it was accurately restoring the grand manner of the Roman world. This new architecture (*see* the Baptistry, San Miniato, Santa Maria Novella), based on elegantly simple geometry with richly inlaid marble façades and pave-ments, was utterly unlike even the creations of nearby Pisa and Siena, and began a continuity of style that would reach its climax with the work of **Brunelleschi** and **Alberti** in the 1400s.

Likewise in painting and sculpture, Florentines made an early departure from Byzantine-influ-enced forms, and avoided the International Gothic style that thrived so well in Siena. Vasari's famous *Lives of the Artists* (1547) lays down the canon of Florentine artists, the foundation of all subsequent art criticism. It begins with **Cimabue** (*c.* 1240–1302), who according to Vasari first began to draw away from Byzantine stylization towards a more 'natural' way of painting.

Cimabue found his greatest pupil **Giotto** (1266–1337) as a young shepherd boy, chalk-sketching sheep on a piece of slate. Brought to Florence, Giotto soon eclipsed his master's fame (artistic celebrity being another recent Florentine invention) and achieved the greatest advances on the road to the new painting, a plain, idiosyncratic approach that avoided Gothic prettiness while exploring new ideas in composition and expressing psychological depth in his subjects. Even more importantly Giotto, through his intuitive grasp of perspective, was able to go further than any previous artist in representing his subjects as actual figures in space. In a sense Giotto invented space; it was this, despite his often awkward and graceless draughts-manship, that so astounded his contemporaries.

Vasari, for reasons of his own, neglected the artists of the Florentine trecento, and many critics have tended to follow slavishly—a great affront to the master artist and architect **Andrea Orcagna** (d. 1368; works include the Loggia dei Lanzi and the Orsanmichele tabernacle) and others including **Taddeo and Agnolo Gaddi** (d. 1366 and 1396) whose frescoes can be compared to Giotto's at Santa Croce.

The Quattrocento

The next turn in the story, what scholars self-assuredly used to call the 'Early Renaissance', comes with the careers of two geniuses who happened to be good friends. **Donatello** (1386–1466), the greatest sculptor since the ancient Greeks, inspired a new generation of not only sculptors but painters to explore new horizons in portraiture and three-dimensional repre-sentation. **Brunelleschi** (1377–1446), neglecting his considerable talents in sculpture for architecture and science, not only built the majestic cathedral dome, but threw the Pandora's box of perspective wide open by mathematically codifying the principles of foreshortening.

The new science of painting occasioned an explosion of talent unequalled before or since, as a score of masters, most of them Florentine by birth, each followed the dictates of his own genius to create a range of themes and styles hardly believable for one single city in a few short decades of its life. To mention only the most prominent:

Lorenzo Ghiberti (d. 1455), famous for the bronze doors of the Baptistry; **Masaccio** (d. 1428), the eccentric prodigy much copied by later artists, best represented by his natural-istic frescoes in Santa Maria del Carmine and Santa Maria Novella; **Domenico Ghirlandaio** (d. 1494), Michelangelo's teacher and another master of detailed frescoes; **Fra Angelico** (d. 1455), the most spiritual, and most visionary of them all, the painter of the *Annunciation* at San Marco; **Paolo Uccello** (d. 1475), one of the most provocative of all artists, who according to Vasari drove himself bats with too-long contemplation of perspective and the newly discovered vacuum of empty space; **Benozzo Gozzoli** (d. 1497), a happier soul, best known for the springtime *Procession of the Magi* in the Medici Palace; **Luca Della Robbia** (d. 1482), greatest of a family of sculptors, famous for the *cantoria* of the Cathedral Museum and exquisite blue and white terracottas all over Tuscany; **Antonio Pollaiuolo** (d. 1498), an engraver and sculptor with a nervously perfect line; **Fra Filippo Lippi** (d. 1469), who ran off with a brown-eyed nun to produce **Filippino Lippi** (d. 1504)—both of them exceptional painters and sticklers for detail; and finally **Sandro Botticelli** (d. 1510); his progress from the secret garden of pure art, expressed in his astounding early mythological pictures, to conven-tional holy pictures, done after the artist fell under the sway of Savonarola, marks the first signs of trouble and the first failure of nerve in the Florentine imagination.

Leonardo, Michelangelo and the Cinquecento

With equal self-assurance the critics used to refer to the early 1500s as the beginning of the 'High Renaissance'. **Leonardo da Vinci**, perhaps the incarnation of Florentine achievement in both painting and scientific speculation, lived until 1519, but spent much of his time in Milan and France. **Michelangelo Buonarroti** (d. 1564) liked to identify himself with Florentine republicanism, but finally abandoned the city during the siege of 1530 (even though he was a member of the committee overseeing Florence's defence). His departure left Florence with no important artists except the surpassingly strange **Jacopo Pontormo** (d. 1556) and **Rosso Fiorentino** (d. 1540). These two, along with Michelangelo, were key figures in the bold, neurotic, avant-garde art that has come to be known as **Mannerism**. This first conscious 'movement' in Western art can be seen as a last fling amid the growing intellectual and spiritual exhaustion of 1530s Florence, conquered once and for all by the Medici. The Mannerists' calculated exoticism and exaggerated, tortured poses, together with the brooding self-absorption of Michelangelo and many others, are the prelude to Florentine art's remarkably abrupt downturn into decadence, and prophesy its final extinction.

There was another strain to Mannerism in Florence, following the cold classicism of Raphael of Urbino, less disturbed, less intense and challenging than Michelangelo or Pontormo. With artists like **Agnolo Bronzino** (d. 1572), the sculptor **Bartolomeo Ammannati** (d. 1592), **Andrea del Sarto** (d. 1531), and **Giorgio Vasari** himself (d. 1574), Florentine art loses almost all imaginative and intellectual content, becoming a virtuoso style of interior decoration perfectly adaptable to saccharine holy pictures, portraits of newly enthroned dukes, or absurd mythological fountains and ballroom ceilings. In the cinquecento, with plenty of money to spend and a long Medici tradition of patronage to uphold, this tendency soon got out of hand. Under the reign of Cosimo I, indefatigable collector of *pietra dura* tables, silver and gold gimcracks, and exotic stuffed animals, Florence gave birth to the artistic phenomenon modern critics call kitsch.

In the cinquecento, Florence taught vulgarity to the Romans, degeneracy to the Venetians, and preciosity to the French. Oddly enough the city had as great an influence in its age of decay as in its age of greatness. The cute, well-educated Florentine pranced across Europe, finding himself praised as the paragon of culture and refinement. Even in England—though that honest nation soon found him out:

> *A little Apish hatte, couched fast to the Pate, like an Oyster,*
> *French Camarick Ruffes, deepe with a witnesse, starched to the purpose,*
> *Delicate in speach, queynte in arraye: conceited in all poyntes:*
> *In Courtly guyles, a passing singular odde man...*

> *Mirror of Tuscanism*, Gabriel Harvey, 1580

It's almost disconcerting to learn that Florence gave us not only much of the best of our civilization, but even a lot of the worst. Somehow the later world of powdered wigs and chubby winged *putti* is unthinkable without 1500s Florence. Then again, so is all the last 500 years of art unthinkable without Florence, not to mention modern medicine (the careful anatomical studies of the artists did much to help set it on its way) or technology (from the endless speculations and gadgets of Leonardo) or political science (from Machiavelli). The Florentines of course found the time to invent opera too, and give music a poke into the modern world. And without that little discovery of the painters, so simple though perhaps so very hard for us in the 20th century to comprehend—the invention of space—Copernicus, Newton, Descartes and all who followed them would never have discovered anything.

But Florence soon tired of the whole business. The city withdrew into itself, made a modest living, polished its manners and its conceit, and generally avoided trouble. Not a peep has been heard out of it since 1600.

The Best of Florence

No city in Italy has such a wealth of art—perhaps only Venice comes close. If you wanted to see everything worth seeing, it would take at least two weeks, and museum admissions alone would set you back some L350,000.

For an abbreviated tour, be sure to see the **Cathedral, Baptistry**, and **Cathedral Museum**, and Florence's two great museums, the **Uffizi** and the **Bargello**, leaving time for a walk around the Ponte Vecchio and the old streets and alleys of Florence's centre, and a stop at **Orsanmichele**.

Around the edges of the old centre, the churches of **Santa Croce, Santa Maria Novella, Santa Maria del Carmine** and the monastery of **San Marco** contain some of the best of Florentine painting. Finally, try to make it up to **San Miniato**, both for the beautiful medieval church and the view over the city.

Those with more time to spend can consider the florid 16th-century art in the **Palazzo Vecchio** and **Pitti Palace**, Gozzoli's frescoes in the **Medici Palace**, the very good **Archaeology Museum** and **Museum of Science**, and Brunelleschi's **Santo Spirito**. And for devotees of the Michelangelo cult, there's the real *David* in the **Accademia**, the **Medici Chapels** at San Lorenzo, and the **Casa Buonarroti**.

Getting Around

 Florence is now one of the best Italian cities to get around; best because nearly everything you'll want to see is within easy walking distance and large areas in the centre are pedestrianized; there are no hills, and it's hard to lose your way for very long.

When you do need to get directly from A to B the city has an efficient local **bus** service. Most of the more useful routes for visitors start from the main railway station: bus no.7 goes to San Domenico and then all the way out of town to Fiesole; no.10 to the Duomo, San Marco and Settignano; no.13 to Piazzale Michelangelo and the Belvedere—especially useful if you want to avoid that long climb; no.37 goes to Galluzzo and the Certosa.

For a radio **taxi**, call ✆ 055 4798 or ✆ 055 4390. The really adventurous can **rent a bicycle** from Alinari, Via Guelfa 85r, ✆ 055 280 500, or Florence by Bike, Via della Scala 12r, ✆ 055 264 035, or a **scooter**, from Alinari, or Motorent, Via San Zanobi 9r, ✆ 055 490 113.

Just to make life difficult, Florence has two sets of address numbers on every street— red ones for business, blue for residences; your hotel might be either one.

Tourist Information

The main office is at Via Manzoni 16, ✆ 055 290 832 (*open Mon–Sat 8.30–1.30*), which is a little out of the way, near Piazza Beccaria. In the centre there is an office at Via Cavour 1r, just north of the Duomo (*open Nov–Feb Mon–Fri 8.15–1.45, Mar–Oct Mon–Sat 8.15–7.15, Sun 8.15–1.45*). There's also a very genial booth outside the station, at the end of the bus ranks, ✆ 055 212 245 (*open Mon–Sat 8.15–7.15 all year, plus Sun 8.15–2 in the summer*). There is also a new office at Borgo Santa Croce 19, ✆ 055 234 0444, ✆ 055 226 4524 (*open Mon–Sat 8.15am–9.15pm*).

Fiesole: Piazza Mino 37, ✆ 055 598 720 (*open daily 8.30–1.30*).

Police: Via Zara 2, ✆ 055 49771.

Hospital: Ospedale Santa Maria Nuova, Piazza Santa Maria Nuova, ✆ 055 27581. There is also a private **Tourist Medical Service**, Via Lorenzo il Magnifico 59, ✆ 055 475 411, which has English-speaking doctors available 24 hours.

24-hour pharmacies: Comunale della Stazione, at the main railway station, and **Molteni**, Via Calzaiuoli 7r, are both open 24 hours daily. In addition, every pharmacy has a list outside indicating those in the city on night duty each day. For information call ✆ 110.

Places that exchange money outside normal banking hours include **American Express**, Via Dante Alighieri 22r, ✆ 055 50981 (*open Mon–Fri 9–5.30, Sat 9–12.30*) and **Thomas Cook**, Piazza Stazione 5r, ✆ 055 288 456 (*open Mon–Sat 9–1 and 2–7, Sun 9.30–5*) or Lungaro Acciaiuoli 6/12, ✆ 055 289 781 (*open Mon–Sat 9–8, Sun 9.30–5*).

The **main post office** is at Via Pellicceria 8, near the Piazza della Repubblica (*open Mon–Fri 8.15–7, Sat 8.15–12*).

Lost property: Via Circondaria 17b, ✆ 055 328 3942.

Around the City

Piazza del Duomo

The Baptistry

This ancient, mysterious building, the egg from which Florence's golden age was hatched, makes as good a place to start as any. Medieval Florentines were always too busy to look back, and now and then they lost track of themselves. The men of the quattrocento believed their Baptistry to have been originally a Roman building, a Temple of Mars. After all the research that has gone into the question in the last few centuries the best guesses put the actual building in the 9th century—but maybe as far back as the 7th. The distinctive black and white marble facing, the tidily classical pattern of arches and rectangles that deceived

Piazza del Duomo　　167

Florence

Brunelleschi and Alberti, were probably added in the 10th or 11th century. The masters who built it remain unknown, but their strikingly original exercise in geometry provided the model for all Florence's great church façades. When it was new there was nothing remotely like it in Europe; to visitors from outside the city it must have seemed almost miraculous.

Every 21 March, New Year's Day on the old Florentine calendar, all the children born over the last 12 months would be brought here for a great communal baptism, a habit that helped make the Baptistry not merely a religious monument but also a civic symbol, in fact the oldest and fondest symbol of the republic, which the Florentines never finished embellishing. Under the octagonal cupola the 13th- and 14th-century gold-ground mosaics show a strong Byzantine influence, though some (*The Life of John the Baptist*) may be the work of Cimabue. To match them there is a beautiful inlaid marble floor decorated with the signs of the zodiac. Even more than the exterior, the patterned black and white marble of the interior walls is remarkable, combining influences from the ancient world and modern inspiration for something entirely new, a perfect source that the architects of the Middle Ages and Renaissance would ever strive to match. It isn't cluttered inside; only a 13th-century Pisan-style baptismal font and the tomb of anti-pope John XXIII, by Donatello and Michelozzo, stand out.

Historians used to date the coming of the 'Renaissance' as 1401, with the famous competition for the Baptistry's **bronze doors**, when Lorenzo Ghiberti defeated Brunelleschi and others for the commission. The south door had already been completed by Andrea Pisano, with scenes from the life of John the Baptist in Gothic quatrefoil frames, and in his north door Ghiberti attempted no new departures. After 1425, however, he began the great east doors (the ones with tourists piled up in front) which were to occupy much of his time for the next 27 years. These are the doors Michelangelo is said to have called the 'Gates of Paradise', and undoubtedly they made a tremendous impression on all the artists of the quattrocento, using the same advances in composition and perspective and the same wealth of detail as the painters. Unfortunately the panels currently displayed are replicas, as the originals are being restored (four are now exhibited in the **Museo dell'Opera del Duomo**, *see* below), but you can still appreciate the richness of the original design. The Old Testament scenes begin with the creation of Adam and Eve in the upper left corner, finishing with Solomon and Sheba in the Temple on the lower right-hand panel. On the frames, busts of contemporary Florentine artists peer out from tiny circles. It is a typical exhibition of Florentine pride that Ghiberti should put his friends among the prophets and sibyls that adorn the rest of the frames. Near the centre, the balding figure with arched eyebrows is Ghiberti himself.

The Duomo

For all its importance and prosperity Florence was one of the last cities to plan a great cathedral. Work began in the 1290s, with the sculptor Arnolfo di Cambio in charge, and the Florentines from the beginning attempted to make up for their delay with audacity and size. Arnolfo laid the foundations for an octagonal crossing 146ft in diameter, then died before working out a way to cover it, leaving future architects with the job of designing the biggest dome in the world. Surprisingly the Duomo shows little interest in contemporary innovations and styles; a visitor from France or England in the 1400s would certainly have found it somewhat drab and architecturally primitive. Visitors today often do not know what to think; they circle confusedly around its grimy, ponderous bulk (this is one of very few cathedrals in Italy that you can walk completely around). Instead of the striped bravura of Siena or the elegant colonnades of Pisa they behold an astonishingly eccentric pattern of marble rectangles and flowers—like Victorian wallpaper or, according to one critic, a 'cathedral wearing pyjamas'.

The west front cannot be blamed on Arnolfo; his original design, only one-quarter completed, was taken down in the late 16th century in a Medici rebuilding programme that never got off the ground. The Duomo turned a blank face to the world until 1888, when the present neo-Gothic extravaganza was added. After this façade the austerity of the interior is almost startling. There is plenty of room; contemporary writers mention 10,000 souls packed inside to hear the brimstone and hell-fire sermons of Savonarola. Even with that in mind the Duomo hardly seems a religious building—more of a *Florentine* building, with simple arches and the counterpoint of grey stone and white plaster, full of old familiar Florentine things. Near the entrance there are busts of Brunelleschi and Giotto along the right side. For building the great dome Brunelleschi was accorded a great honour—he is the only Florentine to be buried in the cathedral. On the left wall, posed inconspicuously, you will see the two most conspicuous monuments to private individuals ever commissioned by the Florentine Republic. The older one, on the right, is to Sir John Hawkwood, the famous English *condottiere* whose name the Italians mangled to Giovanni Acuto, a legendary commander who served Florence for many years. All along he had the promise of the Florentines to build him an equestrian monument after his death; it was a typical Florentine trick to cheat a dead man—but still they hired the greatest master of perspective, Paolo Uccello, to make a picture that looked like a statue. Twenty years later they pulled the same trick again, commissioning another great illusionist, Andrea del Castagno, to paint the non-existent equestrian statue of another *condottiere* named Nicolò da Tolentino. A little further down, near the entrance to Brunelleschi's dome, Florence commemorates its own secular scripture with a fresco of Dante by Michelino, a vision of the poet and his *Paradiso*. Two singular icons of Florence's fascination with science stand at opposite ends of the building: behind the west front a bizarre clock, also painted by Uccello, and in the pavement of the left apse a gnomon fixed by the astronomer Toscanelli in 1475. A beam of sunlight strikes it every year on the day of the summer solstice.

There is surprisingly little religious art. Luca della Robbia contributed terracotta lunettes above the doors to the sacristies; the scene of the Resurrection over the north sacristy is one of his earliest and best works. He also did the bronze doors beneath it, with tiny portraits on the handles of Lorenzo il Magnifico and his brother Giuliano de' Medici, targets of the Pazzi conspiracy in 1478. In this ill-fated attempt to dispose of the Medici Giuliano was stabbed during Mass, but Lorenzo managed to escape, taking refuge in this sacristy. In the middle apse there is a beautiful bronze urn by Ghiberti containing relics of the Florentine St Zenobius. The only really conventional religious decorations are the frescoes in the dome, high overhead, mostly the work of Vasari.

Brunelleschi's Dome

Open Mon–Fri 8.30–6.20, Sat 8.30–5; adm.

Losing the competition for the baptistry doors was a bitter disappointment to Brunelleschi but a piece of good luck for Florence. His reaction was typically Florentine: not content with being the second-best sculptor, he began to devote all his talents to a field where he thought no one could beat him. He launched himself into an intense study of architecture and engineering, visiting Rome and probably Ravenna to snatch secrets from the ancients. When proposals were solicited for the cathedral's dome he was ready with a brilliant *tour de force*. Not only would he build the biggest dome of that era, and the most beautiful, but he would do it without any need for expensive supports while work was in progress, making use of a cantilevered system of bricks that could support itself while it ascended. Even today architects marvel at Brunelleschi's systematic way of tackling the job. Problems with weather and air pressure were foreseen and managed; hooks were inserted to hold up scaffolding for future cleaning or repairs.

Not only had Brunelleschi recaptured the technique of the ancients, he had surpassed them, with a system simpler and better than that of the Pantheon or Hagia Sophia. To the Florentines, a people who could have invented the slogan 'form follows function' for their own tastes in building, it must have come as a revelation; the most logical way of covering the space turned out to be a work of perfect beauty. Brunelleschi, in building his dome, put a crown on the achievements of Florence, after 500 years still the city's pride and symbol. To climb it, take the door on the left aisle near the Dante fresco; the complex network of stairs and walks between the inner and outer domes provides a thorough lesson on how Brunelleschi did it, and the views from the top are priceless.

Giotto's Campanile

Open April–Oct daily 9–6.50; Nov–Mar daily 9–4.20; adm.

There's no doubt: the dome steals the show on Piazza del Duomo, putting one of Italy's most beautiful bell towers in the shade both figuratively and literally. The dome's great size—366ft to the gold ball atop the lantern—makes the campanile look small, though 280ft is not exactly tiny. Giotto was made director of the cathedral works in 1334, and his basic design was completed after his death (1337) by Andrea Pisano and Francesco Talenti. It is difficult to say whether they were entirely faithful to the plan. Giotto was an artist not an engineer; after he died his successors realized the thing was about to topple, a problem they overcame by doubling the thickness of the walls.

Besides its lovely form, the campanile's major fame rests with Pisano and Talenti's sculptural relief—a veritable encyclopaedia of the medieval world-view with prophets, saints and sibyls, allegories of the planets, virtues, and sacraments, the liberal arts and industries (the artist's craft is fittingly symbolized by a figure of Daedalus). All these are copies; the originals can be seen in the cathedral museum (*see* below). If after climbing the dome you can take another 400 steps or so, the terrace on top offers a slightly different view of Florence. Some lesser-known monuments line the southern edge of the Piazza del Duomo.

The **Loggia del Bigallo**, headquarters of one of Florence's still-operating charitable confraternities, was the place where mothers dropped off children they couldn't support. Inside there is a small museum of works commissioned by the confraternity in the 1400s (open by request, © 055 215 440). A little way to the east, **Dante's Seat** is the ancient stone bench where, according to local legend, the poet would take the air, observing his fellow citizens and the building of the Duomo.

Museo dell'Opera del Duomo

Open April–Oct Mon–Sat 9–6.50, Sun 9–2; Nov–Mar Mon–Sat 9–6.20, Sun 10–1; adm exp.

Relatively few tourists find their way to the cathedral museum, hidden away in an inconspicuous building behind the central apse, but it contains some of the finest works of art in Florence, along with fascinating relics of the Duomo's past: brick moulds, tools, and a block and tackle from the original construction; models of the dome, and even Brunelleschi's death mask. Arnolfo di Cambio's sculpture from the original façade is here, along with drawings that show how it would have looked. There are a dozen big models of proposed reconstructions from the 1580s in various hack-Mannerist styles—the façade could have been much, much worse. Florentines were never enthusiastic about the worship of relics, and long ago they shipped San Girolamo's jawbone, John the Baptist's index finger and St Philip's arm across the street to this museum.

In the 1430s Donatello and Luca della Robbia were commissioned to create a matching pair of *cantorie*, marble choir balconies, with exquisite low reliefs. Both works rank among the Renaissance's greatest productions: Donatello's features dancing *putti* in a setting of quattrocento decorative motifs, and della Robbia's a delightful horde of children dancing, singing, and playing instruments, a truly angelic choir; one imagines the artist enjoying himself thoroughly making them, dragging in all the children of the neighbourhood for models. From the campanile, besides the reliefs of Pisano, there are some fine Old Testament figures by Donatello, as well as his gruesome wood statue of Mary Magdalen, something the Florentines no longer wished to see in their Baptistry.

In the 1980s Michelangelo's last *Pietà* also joined the company, a strange, unfinished work that so exasperated the artist that he finally took a hammer to it, breaking Christ's left arm and leg. The tall, hooded figure supporting Christ, Nicodemus, dominates the composition; according to Vasari its face is that of Michelangelo himself. The finished, polished sections of the work, Mary Magdalen and part of the body of Jesus, are not Michelangelo's work at all, but that of a student, who also did his best to patch the arm. The most recent additions to the museum are some of Ghiberti's original bronze panels from the 'Gates of Paradise' of the Baptistry, newly restored.

Orsanmichele

Florence likes things neat and in their place. To balance Piazza del Duomo, the religious centre, there is Piazza della Signoria, the civic centre, with an equally formidable array of architecture and art, directly to the south at the other end of Via dei Calzaiuoli, long the city's main artery. On your way there, through the crowds navigating past the *via*'s fashionable jewellery shops and street knick-knack sellers, you pass the very unusual church of **Orsanmichele**. This stately square building, built up to the street, is easy to miss; it doesn't look anything like a church, and in fact began its life as a grain market, with an open loggia at street level and emergency storehouses above where grain was kept against a siege. In 1304 when the market was relocated, the building was left to the city's powerful guilds, the *Arti*, as a trade and meeting hall. In 1380 Simone Talenti was hired to close in the arches of the loggia and make the 'Oratory of St Michael' (as the building was familiarly known because of the ancient chapel that had preceded it) into a church, although throughout the following century it continued to be closely associated with the guilds, the leaders of each of which strove to outdo the other by commissioning sculptures from the finest artists of the day.

All around the exterior the guilds erected statues of their patron saints: a remarkable collection, including Donatello's famed *St George* (now a copy; the original is in the Bargello) and *St Mark*, a work much admired by Michelangelo. *Saints Stephen* and *Matthew* are by Ghiberti. *Doubting Thomas* is by Verrocchio. The dim interior, full of stained glass and painted vaults, is ornate and cosy, with more of the air of a guildhall than a church. It makes a picture-book medieval setting for the wonderful **Tabernacle**, a free-standing chapel with fine reliefs and sculpted angels by Andrea Orcagna (1350), precious stones and metalwork (every guild contributed something if it could), and a *Madonna* by Bernardo Daddi.

Piazza della Signoria

Now that the city has finally chased the cars out of this big medieval piazza it serves as a great corral for tourists, endlessly snapping pictures of the Palazzo Vecchio or strutting in circles like pigeons. In the old days it would be full of Florentines, the stage set for the tempestuous life of their republic. The public assemblies met here, and at times of danger the bells would ring and the piazza fill with citizen militias, assembling under the banners of their quarters and guilds. Savonarola held his Bonfire of Vanities here, and only a few years later the disenchanted Florentines ignited their Bonfire of Savonarola on the same spot. (You can see a painting of the event at San Marco.) Today the piazza is still the favoured spot for political rallies.

The three graceful arches of the **Loggia dei Lanzi**, next to the Palazzo Vecchio, were the reviewing stand for city officials during assemblies and celebrations. Florentines often call it the *Loggia dell'Orcagna*, after the architect who designed it in the 1370s. In its simple classicism the Loggia anticipates the architecture of Brunelleschi and all those who came after him. The city has made it an outdoor sculpture gallery, with some of the best-known works in Florence: Cellini's triumphant *Perseus* (currently being restored) and Giambologna's *Rape of the Sabines*, other works by Giambologna, and a chorus of Roman-era Vestal Virgins along the back wall. Cosimo himself stands imperiously at the centre of the piazza, a bronze equestrian statue also by Giambologna.

All the statues in the piazza are dear to the Florentines for one reason or another. Some are fine works of art; others have only historical associations. Michelangelo's *David*, a copy of which stands in front of the palazzo near the spot the artist intended for it, was meant as a symbol of republican virtue and Florentine excellence. At the opposite extreme, Florentines are taught almost from birth to ridicule the **Neptune Fountain**, a pompous monstrosity with a giant marble figure of the god. The sculptor, Ammannati, thought he would upstage Michelangelo, though the result is derisively known to all Florence as *Il Biancone* ('Big Whitey'). Bandinelli's statue of *Hercules and Cacus* is almost as big and just as awful; according to Cellini, it looks like a 'sack of melons'.

Palazzo Vecchio

Open Mon–Wed, Fri and Sat 9–7, Sun 8–1; closed Thurs and Sun; adm exp.

Florence's republican government was never perfect. In the better times chronic factionalism was barely kept in check, usually by the utter destruction or exile of one side or the other. Typically, however, the Florentines managed to give their aspirations a perfect symbol. The proud republic would accept nothing less than the most imposing 'Palazzo del Popolo' (as it was originally called) and Arnolfo di Cambio was able to give it to them. Even though the 94m tower was for a long time Florence's tallest, Arnolfo avoided the sort of theatrical façade he was planning for the Duomo. The **Palazzo Vecchio** is part council hall, part fortress and part prison, and looks to fit all three roles well. Its rugged façade, copied in so many Florentine palaces, is not quite as frank and plain as it looks; all its proportions are based on the Golden Section of the ancient Greeks, rediscovered by medieval mathematicians. You may also accuse it of politically playing both sides—with square Guelph crenellations on the cornice and the swallowtail Ghibelline style on the tower.

The palace is often called the Palazzo della Signoria, the name it had under the rule of the Medici. After the final consolidation of their new government, the Duchy of Tuscany, the Medici turned the Palazzo Vecchio upside down. The house where Guelphs and Ghibellines once brawled in the council hall, and where lions were kept in the basement as a totem animal for the state, now became a florid Mannerist bower fit for a duke. Cosimo de' Medici's pet architect, Giorgio Vasari, oversaw the work in the 1550s and 1560s. Though the Medici did not reside there for long, the palazzo was always used for state functions.

Today the palazzo has somewhat recovered its old purpose. It serves as Florence's city hall, and the Council holds its meetings in the **Salone dei Cinquecento**, built by the republic in 1495. At that time Leonardo da Vinci and Michelangelo were commissioned to fresco the two longer sides, a contest of talents that everyone in Florence looked forward to. For a number of reasons it never came off; only a small part of Leonardo's fresco was ever completed, and Vasari painted it over sixty years later. Even the designs for both men's concepts have been lost. However, Michelangelo's statue of *Victory*, originally intended for the tomb of Pope Julius II in San Pietro in Vincoli in Rome, stands in this room, installed here by Vasari in the 1560s.

Despite the palazzo's functional role as a base for the city administration, nearly all of the more historic rooms are open to the public. Without even buying a ticket you can look round the ferociously over-decorated **Cortile**, or courtyard, redone by Vasari. Inside, upstairs on the first floor, there is the fascinating **Studiolo di Francesco I**, a little retreat created for Duke Cosimo's son, who liked to dabble in poisons, where Vasari and his assistants created a vast allegory of mythology, science and alchemy; more Vasari in the Chambers of Leo X and Clement VII (including a famous scene of the 1527 siege); and even more Vasari in the 'Quartiere degli Elementi'. Vasari's workshop was perhaps the fastest and most reliable fresco machine in history—he never turned down a request from the dukes. Rooms with frescoes glorifying the Medici go on and on, but try not to miss the rooms of Eleanor of Toledo (Cosimo I's consort) done by Bronzino, or the **Sala del Giglio**, with a fine ceiling by the da Maiano brothers and the recently restored *Judith and Holofernes* by Donatello.

Bargello

Open daily 8.30–1.50; closed alternate Sun and Mon; adm.

For hundreds of years this medieval fortress-palace on the Via del Proconsolo, behind the Palazzo Vecchio, served as Florence's prison; today the inmates are men of marble—Italy's finest collection of sculpture, a fitting complement to the paintings in the Uffizi. When it was begun, about 1250, the Bargello was the *palazzo del popolo*, though by 1271 it was home to the foreign *podestà* installed by Charles of Anjou. When the republic was reconstructed under the *Ordinamenti*, the decision was made to erect a bigger and grander seat of government—the Palazzo Vecchio. Just as that structure served as the model for so many Florentine palaces, so the Bargello was the model for the palazzo, a rugged, austere work with a solid air of civic virtue about it. The Medici made a jail of it, but a thorough—and perhaps somewhat imaginative—restoration of the interior in the 19th century got it ready for its current job of housing the **Museo Nazionale**.

After the plain façade the delightful arcaded courtyard comes as a surprise, full of interesting architectural fragments, plaques and coats of arms in a wild vocabulary of symbols. In the first-floor galleries there are some early works of Michelangelo, including the *Bacchus*, and also Giambologna's *Mercury*—a work so popular it has entered everyone's consciousness as the way Mercury should look. There are also a number of works by Cellini, including his preliminary model for *Perseus* and his bust of *Cosimo I*.

Upstairs, passing through the **Loggia**, now converted into an 'aviary' for Giambologna's charming bronze birds, you come to the **Salone del Consiglio**. This 14th-century hall contains many of the greatest works of Donatello: the fascinatingly androgynous *David*, the *St George* from Orsanmichele and the enigmatic Cupid or *Amor Atys*. These three alone make a powerful case for considering Donatello the greatest of Renaissance sculptors. The alert watchfulness of *St George* created new possibilities in expressing movement, emotion and depth of character in stone, a revolution in art that was obvious even to Donatello's contemporaries. The *David*, obviously from a different planet from Michelangelo's, explores depths of the Florentine psyche the Florentines probably didn't know they had. The same could be said of the dangerous-looking little-boy *Cupid*. No one knows for whom Donatello made it, or who it is really meant to represent. With its poppies, serpents and winged sandals, it could easily be the ancient idol people in the 18th century mistook it for. Like Botticelli's mythological paintings it reflects the artistic and intellectual undercurrents of the quattrocento, full of pagan philosophy and eroticism, a possibility rooted out in the terror of the Counter-Reformation and quite forgotten soon after.

Among the other artists represented in the hall are Luca della Robbia, Verrocchio, Bernini, Michelozzo and di Duccio. The two bronze panels made by Brunelleschi and Ghiberti for the Baptistry doors competition are preserved here; judge for yourself which is the better. Above, on the second floor, the collection continues with works mainly by Antonio Pollaiuolo and Verrocchio. The Bargello also houses an important collection of the decorative arts—rooms full of pretty bric-à-brac such as combs, mirrors, jewel caskets, reliquaries, Turkish helmets, vases and silks, wax anatomical figures and majolica from Urbino. Some of the most beautiful pieces are in a collection of medieval French ivory—intricately carved scenes like the 'Assault on the Castle of Love' and other medieval fancies. The Bargello's **Chapel** has frescoes by an unknown follower of Giotto.

Dante's Florence

Dante would contemplate his Beatrice, the story goes, at Mass in the **Badia Fiorentina**, a Benedictine church on Via del Proconsolo across from the Bargello, with a lovely Gothic spire to grace this corner of the Florentine skyline. The church has undergone many rebuildings since Willa, widow of a Margrave of Tuscany, began it in around 990, but there is still a monument to Ugo, the 'Good Margrave' mentioned in Dante, and a painting of the *Madonna Appearing to St Bernard* by Filippino Lippi.

Between the Badia and Via dei Calzaiuoli, a little corner of medieval Florence has survived the changes of centuries. In these quiet, narrow streets you can visit the **Casa di Dante** (*open Mon, Tues, Thurs–Sat 9.30–12.30 and 3.30–6.30, Sun 9.30–12.30; closed Wed*), which was actually built in 1911 over the ruins of an amputated tower house, although scholars all agree that the Alighieri lived somewhere in the vicinity.

Nearby, the stoutly medieval **Torre del Castagna** is the last extant part of the original Palazzo del Popolo, predecessor to the Bargello and Palazzo Vecchio. After giving up on Beatrice, Dante married his second choice, Gemma Donati, in the **Santa Margherita** church on the same block. Another church nearby, **San Martino del Vescovo**, has a fine set of frescoes from the workshop of Ghirlandaio—worth a look inside if it's open.

The Uffizi Gallery

Open Tues–Sat 8.30am–10pm; Sun and hols 8.30–8, closed Mon; adm exp.

Poor Giorgio Vasari. His roosterish boastfulness and conviction that his was the best of all possible artistic worlds, set next to his very modest talents, have made him almost a comic figure in some art criticism. Even the Florentines don't like him. On one of the rare occasions when he tried his hand at being an architect, though, he at last gave Florence something to be proud of.

The Uffizi ('offices') were meant as Cosimo's secretariat, incorporating the old mint and archive buildings, with plenty of room for the bureaucrats needed to run the efficient, modern state Cosimo was building. Vasari's plan, a matched pair of arcaded buildings with restrained, elegant façades, conceals a revolutionary but little-known innovation. Iron reinforcements inside the façades make the huge amount of window area possible, and keep the building stable on the soft ground below; it was a trick that would almost be forgotten until the building of the Crystal Palace and the first American skyscrapers.

The architects of the Renaissance in Florence were astoundingly indifferent to matters of urban design. They thought like painters, and gave as little attention to streets and squares as a painter would to the design of a museum gallery. The Uffizi is the noble exception, an intelligent conception that unites the Piazza della Signoria with the Arno. Almost from the start the Medici began to store their huge art collections in parts of the Uffizi. The last of the Medici, Duchess Anna Maria Lodovica, willed the entire hoard to the people of Florence in 1737. Give yourself a day or two to spend on the most important picture gallery in Italy, and come early in the day, especially in summer, when queues sometimes stretch around the arcades and beyond by 11am.

The size of the collection in the Uffizi is not overwhelming, but every work is choice. All the Florentine masters are represented, and the Medici even deigned to purchase a few foreigners. Here is a brief list of the works most worth seeing: near the entrance, amid halls of Medici clutter, the series of *Illustrious Men* (which includes the Cumean sibyl!) in the dry precise style of **Andrea del Castagno**, then some fine trecento works by **Duccio di Boninsegna** and **Cimabue**. If you can't make it to Siena this trip, be sure to see the works of that city's school, especially **the Lorenzetti brothers** and **Simone Martini**. From the early quattrocento Florentine painters there is **Uccello**'s *Battle of San Romano*; even with only one-third of the original present this is one of the most provocative of all paintings, a surreal vision of war with pink, white and blue toy horses. **Piero della Francesca** contributes a *Portrait of Federico di*

Montefeltro with his famous nose; among the works by **Filippo** and **Filippino Lippi** there is a powerful grey *St Jerome*. **Botticelli** gets one big room to himself, in which are displayed his uncanny, erotic masterpieces including *The Birth of Venus*, *Primavera* and *Pallas and the Centaur* (another subtle allegory of the Medici triumph—the rings on Athena's gown were a family symbol), as well as some of his religious paintings and the disturbing *Calumny*, an introduction to the dark side of the quattrocento psyche.

Be sure to visit Room 15 and **Leonardo**'s *Annunciation*, an intellectual rather than divine revelation that is one of the foremost achievements of Florentine art. Nearby are works by **Verrocchio** (Leonardo's teacher) and **Luca Signorelli**, and a formidable sea monster in **Piero di Cosimo**'s *Perseus and Andromeda*. In the Tribuna, a gaudy chamber designed by Bernardo Buontalenti, the Medici kept a valuable collection of Hellenistic and Roman sculpture, as well as portraits of *Cosimo* and *Eleanor of Toledo* by **Bronzino**.

There's a surprising amount of German and Flemish painting, including **Dürer**'s *Adoration of the Magi* and *Adam and Eve*, both looking as much like Italian painting as he could make them—and for a still bigger surprise, **Cranach**'s *Portraits of Luther and Melanchthon*, spying on the Catholics. Venetians aren't as well represented, but there is the *Judgement of Solomon* by **Giorgione** and a *Sacred Allegory* by **Giovanni Bellini**.

Michelangelo always maintained that sculpture and fresco were the only arts fit for a man; oil painting he disdained, and just coincidentally he wasn't very good at it. The *Sacra Famiglia* here is the only canvas he ever finished. Next come some portraits by **Raphael**, **Rosso Fiorentino** and **Pontormo**. Those of **Andrea del Sarto** have been been singled out for restoration—they will light up the room when the bright original colours are revealed. **Titian**'s overdressed Spaniards and well-upholstered girls get a room to themselves.

The collections continue through painters of the 17th and 18th centuries—works of **Rembrandt** (two self-portraits), **Rubens**, **Van Dyck**, even **Goya**; the one exceptional picture here is the *Boy Playing at Cards* by **Chardin**.

In May 1993 the gallery became a victim of Italy's ongoing political drama, when a mysterious bomb exploded in one of the streets outside. The blast affected various parts of the structure, and—although the restoration of the Uffizi is being carried out with much more alacrity than the routine 'restoration' work in most Italian museums—for the next few years you will find more rooms than usual closed for restoration, and some pictures withdrawn from show. Thankfully, no major works of art were lost, and the most important paintings and sculpture from the rooms that are closed have in the meantime all been relocated to undamaged areas of the gallery.

However, the one section of the Uffizi that was seriously damaged was the fascinating *Corridoio Vasariano*, or Vasari Corridor (*now reopened*). Vasari built it at the request of Cosimo I, who wanted to pass from the Palazzo Vecchio and the Uffizi to his new home across the river in the Pitti Palace without rubbing elbows with his subjects—from the bottom end of the Uffizi, facing the Arno, a covered passageway up above street level leads along the river, then over the top of the Ponte Vecchio, through the rooftops on the other side and into the Pitti. The corridor contains a unique collection of artists' self-portraits, by Vasari himself, Velázquez, Rubens, Hogarth and many French artists, most of which are still unharmed. (*Admission with ticket for the Uffizi; opening hours vary so check with the tourist office.*)

Ponte Vecchio and Ponte S. Trinità

The 'Old Bridge' is to Florence what London Bridge is to London. No one knows how long the Arno has been spanned at this point. The present bridge, built in 1345, replaced a wooden construction from the 970s, which in turn was the successor to a span that may have gone back to the Romans. Like medieval bridges in London and many other European cities, the new 14th-century bridge had shops and houses built all along it. By the 1500s it had become the street of the butchers; after Vasari built Cosimo's secret passage over the top the duke evicted the butchers (he didn't like the pong) and gave their places to the goldsmiths. They have kept their spot ever since, and hordes of shoppers from around the world descend on it each year to scrutinize the Florentine talent for jewellery. This is the most prestigious shopping location in Florence, and the jewellers are happy to stay—they could not be deterred even by the 1966 flood, when a fortune in gold was washed down the Arno.

In the summer of 1944 the river briefly became a German defensive line during the slow painful retreat across central Italy. Before they left Florence the Germans took it upon themselves to blow up every one of the city's bridges, saving only the Ponte Vecchio. Somehow the city managed to talk them out of it, and instead buildings on both sides were destroyed and the rubble piled up to block the approaches.

Florence's most beautiful span, the **Ponte Santa Trinità**, had to go, however. The Florentines like their city just as it is, and immediately after the war they set about replacing the bridges exactly as they were. In the case of Santa Trinità it was quite a task. Old quarries had to be reopened to duplicate the stone, and old methods used to cut it (modern power saws would have done it too cleanly). The graceful curve of the three arches was a problem; they cannot be constructed geometrically and considerable speculation went on over how the architect (Ammannati, in 1567) had done it. Finally, remembering that Michelangelo had advised Ammannati on the project, someone discovered that the same form of arch could be seen on the decoration of Michelangelo's Medici Chapels, constructed most likely not by mathematics and common engineering, but by pure artistic imagination. Fortune lent a hand in the reconstruction; of the original statues of the 'Four Seasons', almost all the pieces were fished out of the Arno and reconstructed. *Spring*'s head was missing, however, and controversy raged for a decade over whether to replace it or leave it as it was, until some divers found it, completely by accident, in 1961.

Around Piazza della Repubblica

On the map it is easy to pick out the small rectangle of narrow, straight streets at the heart of Florence; these remain unchanged from the little *castrum* of Roman days. At its centre the old forum deteriorated through the Dark Ages into a shabby market square, surrounded by the Jewish ghetto. So it remained until Florence, in a fit of post-Risorgimento ambition, decided to make it a symbol of the city's reawakening. The square was given a new design and a thorough facelift, and a grand arch was built, with a big inscription: THE ANCIENT CITY CENTRE RESTORED TO NEW LIFE FROM THE SQUALOR OF CENTURIES. Unfortunately the results were the same as in the new façade for the Duomo; Piazza della Repubblica is one of the ghastliest squares in Italy. Just the same, it is a popular place with tourists and natives alike, full of cafés with outside tables, and something of an oasis among the severe, unwelcoming streets of old Florence.

Those streets are worth walking. Dreary as they look at first sight, they are part of the soul of Florence. Also they are full of surprises; walk down Calimala, an important shopping street south of the piazza, and you will encounter the **Arte della Lana**, behind Orsanmichele and connected to it by an overhead passageway. The 'Wool Corporation', richest of the guilds save that of the bankers, was really a sort of manufacturers' co-operative; its headquarters, built in 1308, was restored in 1905 in a delightful William Morris style of medieval picturesque. Nearby, further towards the river, is one of Florence's oldest marketplaces, covered by a beautiful loggia built in the 1500s. The **Mercato Nuovo**, where vendors hawk purses, toys and every sort of trinket, was in medieval times a merchants' exchange; it was also the place where the *carroccio*, the decorated wagon that served as a rallying point for the citizen armies during battles, was kept in time of peace. Florentines often call this the *Loggia del Porcellino*, after the drooling bronze boar put up as a decoration in 1612, a copy of a Greek sculpture in the Uffizi.

Between Via delle Terme and Via Porta Rossa the 14th-century **Palazzo Davanzati** recreates the atmosphere of a wealthy merchant's house of the 1400s as the **Museo della Casa Fiorentina Antica** (*closed for restoration; exhibition on ground floor open 8.30–1.50; closed alternate Sun and Mon*). Though some of the furnishings are from a century or two later, the late medieval atmosphere is certainly present and, if historically accurate, a tribute to the taste of the honest burghers of the time. Two fine rooms, called the 'Room of the Parrot' and the 'Room of the Peacocks', have murals, tapestries, furniture (especially wedding chests) and ceramics, and even 14th-century high-heeled shoes are part of the furnishings; the dumbwaiter and bathrooms were luxurious at the time. Some of Florence's oldest and most typical town houses lie between here and the river. Off Via Pellicceria, behind the Mercato Nuovo, is the 14th-century Guelph Party building, often the real seat of power in the city, built with money confiscated from exiled Ghibellines.

Conspicuous Consumption *alla Fiorentina*

The streets west of Piazza della Repubblica have always been the choicest district of Florence. Via Tornabuoni, the fanciest shopping street, is as well-known in fashion as Via Montenapoleone in Milan or Via dei Condotti in Rome. In the 15th century this was the area most of the new merchant élite chose for their palaces. Today's bankers build great skyscrapers for the firm and settle for modest mansions themselves; in medieval Florence, things were reversed. The bankers and wool tycoons really owned their businesses, and in absolute terms probably had more money than anyone had ever had before. While their places of business were usually quite simple, for themselves they constructed imposing city palaces, all in the same conservative style, and competing with each other in size like some Millionaire's Row of Victorian-era America.

The style, derived from the Palazzo Vecchio, began at the **Rucellai Palace** on Via della Vigna Nuova (*closed for lengthy restoration*), a building designed by Alberti in 1446 for a prominent manufacturer and patron of learning. Much has been made of this building as a turning point in architecture; its only real innovation, though, is a consistent and skilful use of the classical 'orders', the system of proportion learned from Vitruvius. Of the other palaces in the neighbourhood north of Piazza S. Trinità, two stand out—the 1465 **Palazzo Antinori** at the northern end of Tornabuoni, and the **Palazzo Strozzi**, two streets south. The Strozzi is the daddy of them all, the accustomed design blown up to heroic proportions; though three storeys like the rest, here each floor is as tall as three or four normal ones. Filippo Strozzi, head of a family of bankers who often felt strong enough to challenge the leadership of the Medici, built it in 1489 at the height of the clan's fortunes. Fifty years later his grandchildren were all exiles, bankers and advisers to the King of France. Both the Antinori and Strozzi palaces were the work of Benedetto da Maiano; for their use of classical proportions, the Florentines counted them among their highest achievements, surpassing the architecture of the ancients. The Strozzi houses a large library, and often hosts art exhibitions.

Santa Maria Novella

The broad piazza in front of this church bears two fat obelisks set on bronze turtles and placed like the monuments in a Roman circus. They served the same purpose; in the 1600s the wealthy families of the neighbourhood would hold an annual carriage race around them. But Santa Maria Novella, begun by the Dominicans in 1246, was always associated with the great families. Between them they bestowed so much money to embellish it that by the 1500s the church had become a museum in itself, with important works of many late medieval and Renaissance artists.

The brilliant black and white patterned façade, badly in need of a cleaning but still the finest in Florence, shows the continuity of the city's style from medieval times. The lower half is part of the original work, finished before 1360, but the rest had to wait for one of the Rucellai family to commission Alberti to finish the job. It's his best work in Florence, a synthesis of classical architecture and medieval Florentine tradition, with volutes and arabesques that seem already to prefigure the Baroque. An odd touch is the image of the sun at the apex, the only image or symbol of any kind in Alberti's plan. Lower down, Cosimo I added the two unusual sundials over the left- and right-hand arches.

Inside, above the portal, there is a recently restored *Nativity* by Botticelli. From there, proceeding clockwise around the church: a pulpit with reliefs by Brunelleschi, and Masaccio's *Trinità* fresco, perhaps one of the earliest works with the temerity to depict God the Father, and then a *Resurrection* by Vasari. In the left transept, the Gondi Chapel has Brunelleschi's only wood sculpture, a crucifix—Vasari tells the story of how he made it to show Donatello a Christ with proper dignity, after complaining that his friend's crucifix (now in Santa Croce) made the Redeemer 'look like a peasant'. A great series of frescoes of the *Lives of St John and*

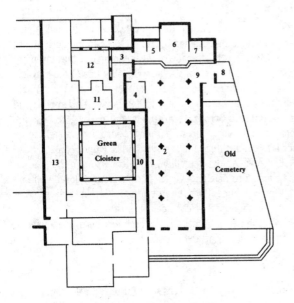

1 Masaccio's *Trinity*
2 Brunelleschi's Pulpit
3 Cappèlla Strozzi
4 Sacristy
5 Cappella Gondi
6 Sanctuary
7 Filippo Strozzi Chapel
8 Rucellai Chapel
9 Gothic Tombs
10 *Universal Deluge*
11 Spanish Chapel
12 Chiostrino dei Morti
13 Refectory

the Virgin by Ghirlandaio surrounds the main altar. All his students helped him complete it—little Michelangelo included. Some equally fine frescoes by Filippino Lippi adorn the Filippo Strozzi Chapel in the right transept, where Strozzi is buried; the architect who designed his palace, da Maiano, also carved his tomb. Another tomb nearby belongs to a Patriarch of Constantinople who accompanied the Byzantine Emperor to Italy in 1440 seeking last-minute aid against the Turks.

There's little of interest in the right-hand chapels, but just outside the left transept are some of the best parts of this surprisingly large monastic complex. Another Strozzi Chapel, this one from the 1360s, has a fine early fresco series of the *Last Judgement* by Nardo di Cione, brother of Orcagna. The Spanish Chapel, commissioned by Cosimo I's Spanish wife Eleanor of Toledo, offers a chilling touch of Counter-Reformation with a series of frescoes detailing the history of the Dominicans: the *domini canes* ('dogs of the Lord') sit at the Pope's feet, symbolizing the order that ran the Inquisition and sniffed out heretics and freethinkers. In the background an interesting view of the Duomo as a fairly pink confection may in fact represent the original plans of Arnolfo di Cambio.

Best of all, however, is the famous **Green Cloister** (*open Mon–Thurs, Sat 9–2, Sun 8–1; adm*), decorated with the most important frescoes by Paolo Uccello, a mysterious interpretation of the story of Noah that has stoked controversy for centuries. Unfortunately the frescoes are much deteriorated, but the best preserved one, the *Universal Deluge*, is uncanny enough to haunt your imagination for years.

San Lorenzo

Around the railway station beats the true heart of tourist Florence, dozens of streets around the Via Nazionale packed with hotels, restaurants and bars. There's an almost Neapolitan air about the boisterous street market that surrounds the **Mercato Centrale**, built in the 1890s to replace the old market evicted from the Piazza della Repubblica, and known locally as 'Shanghai'. The market *bancarelle* extend all the way to **San Lorenzo**, a church always associated with the Medici, and a shrine to the art of Brunelleschi and Michelangelo. Brunelleschi built it in the 1420s; Michelangelo designed a façade that was never realized, leaving the odd-shaped church as charming as a huge dreadnought docked in the piazza. The interior, however, is essential Brunelleschi, a contemplative repetition of arches and columns in grey and white, while nothing else in Florence prepares you for the two pulpits in the nave, the last violent, near-impressionistic works of Donatello. Off the left transept the **Old Sacristy** is a beautiful vaulted chamber with calmer sculptural decoration by Donatello.

The real interest is outside the church; a separate entrance on Piazza Madonna degli Aldobrandini leads to the famous **Medici Chapels** (*open Mon–Sat 8.30–5; Sun 8.30–1.50; closed alternate Sun and Mon; adm exp*) and their celebrated sculptures by Michelangelo. First, however, you will have to pass through the Prince's Chapel, under a huge eight-sided dome that dwarfs the rest of San Lorenzo, begun in 1604 following a design by a dilettante architect member of the Medici family.

Several of the Medici dukes are buried in this dreary, trashy rotunda, the true monument of the ducal period and a sobering demonstration of just how soon Florence's great age of art declined into provincialism and preciosity. It certainly cost enough—the entire lower walls and floor are done in *pietra dura* with rich marbles from around the world, a job not completed until this century.

From here a corridor to the left leads to the **New Sacristy**, designed by Michelangelo in a severe style to match the Old Sacristy on the other side. The two tombs, of Giuliano, Duke of Nemours, and Lorenzo, Duke of Urbino, the ruler to whom Machiavelli dedicated *The Prince*, are decorated with an allegorical sculptural scheme that has caused much discussion over the centuries. Giuliano is portrayed as a soldier representing the Active Life, with figures representing Day and Night reclining on his sarcophagus below. Lorenzo, as the Contemplative Life, sits and contemplates, overlooking figures of Dawn and Dusk (true to life in one respect; the passive Lorenzo was a disappointment to Machiavelli and everyone else). The male figures, at least, are among Michelangelo's triumphs. The women, Dawn and Night, come off less well. Michelangelo never had much use for the ladies—he wouldn't even use female models—and whatever role they played in his personal mythology he portrays them here as imperfect men, male forms with flabbier musculature and breasts stuck on like superfluous appendages.

In front of San Lorenzo a separate entrance leads to the **Biblioteca Laurenziana** (*currently closed for restoration*), designed for the Medici by Michelangelo and built by Ammannati, an important landmark in architecture: it was Michelangelo's first commission (along with the Medici Chapels), and one of the first steps on the slippery slope to Mannerism.

Palazzo Medici Riccardi

San Lorenzo became the Medici's church because it stood just round the corner from the family palace—a huge, stately building on Via Cavour constructed by Alberti and Michelozzo about the same time as the Rucellai Palace. The family's coat-of-arms, which you've probably already noticed everywhere in Florence, is prominently displayed in the corners. The seven, sometimes six, red boluses probably come from the family's origin as pharmacists (*medici*), and opponents called them 'the pills'. Medici supporters, however, made them their battle cry in street battles: 'Balls! Balls!'.

The main reason for visiting is one of Florence's hidden delights: the **Chapel** (*open Mon, Tues, Thurs–Sat 9–1 and 3–6, Sun 9–1 Sun; closed Wed; adm*) with extravagantly colourful frescoes by Benozzo Gozzoli. The *Procession of the Magi* is hardly a religious painting, a merry scene full of portraits of the Medici and others among the crowd following the Three Kings. The artist included himself, with his name on his hat. In the foreground of one of the panels note the black man carrying a bow. Blacks (also Turks, Circassians, Tartars and other non-Europeans) were common enough in Renaissance Florence. Though originally brought as slaves, by the 1400s not all were still servants. Contemporary writers mention them as artisans, fencing masters, soldiers and, in one famous case, as an archery instructor, who may be the man pictured here. For an extraordinary contrast pop into the **gallery** (up the second set of stairs) with its 17th-century ceiling by Neopolitan Luca Giordano, showing the last, unspeakable Medici floating around in marshmallow clouds.

Fra Angelico's San Marco

Open daily 8.30–1.50; closed alternate Sun and Mon; adm.

Despite all the others who contributed to this Dominican monastery and church, it has always been best known for the work of its most famous resident. Fra Angelico lived here from 1436 until his death in 1455, spending the time turning Michelozzo's simple **cloister** into a complete exposition of his own deep faith, expressed in bright playroom colours and angelic pastels. Fra Angelico painted the frescoes in the corners of the cloister, and on the first floor there is a small museum of his work, collected from various Florentine churches, as well as a number of early 15th-century portraits by Fra Bartolomeo, capturing some of the most sincere spirituality of that age. The *Last Supper* in the refectory is by Ghirlandaio. Other Fra Angelico works include the series of the *Life of Christ*, telling the story sweetly and succinctly, and a serenely confident *Last Judgement* in which all the saved are well-dressed Italians holding hands. They get to keep their clothes in heaven, while the bad (mostly princes and prelates) are stripped to receive their interesting tortures.

Right at the top of the stairs to the monks' dormitory, your eyes meet the Angelic Friar's masterpiece, a miraculous *Annunciation* that offers an intriguing comparison to Leonardo's *Annunciation* in the Uffizi. The subject was a favourite with Florentine artists, not only because it was a severe test—expressing a divine revelation with a composition of strict economy—but because the Annunciation, falling near the spring equinox, was New Year's

Day for Florence until the Medici adopted the Pope's calendar in the 17th century. In each of the monks' cells, Fra Angelico and students painted the Crucifixion, all the same but for some slight differences in pose; glancing in the cells down the corridor in turn gives the impression of a cartoon. One of the cells belonged to Savonarola, who was the prior here during his period of dominance in Florence; it has simple furniture of the period and a portrait of Savonarola by Fra Bartolomeo. In a nearby corridor, you can see an anonymous painting of the monk and two of his followers being led to the stake on Piazza della Signoria. Michelozzo's Library, off the main corridor (*currently closed for restoration*), is as light and airy as the cloisters below; in it is displayed a collection of choir books, one illuminated by Fra Angelico.

Piazza Santissima Annunziata

This square, really the only Renaissance attempt at a unified ensemble in Florence, is surrounded by arcades on three sides. The earliest of its buildings, one of Brunelleschi's most famous works, is also a monument to Renaissance Italy's long, hard and ultimately unsuccessful struggle towards some kind of social consciousness. Even in the best times Florence's poor were treated like dirt; if any enlightened soul had been so bold as to propose even a modern conservative 'trickle down' theory to the Medici and the banking élite, their first thought would have been how to stop the leaks. Babies, at least, had it a little better. The **Spedale degli Innocenti** (*open Thurs–Tues 8.30–2; adm*), built in the 1440s, was Italy's first foundling hospital (in most Italian cities unwanted children were commonly abandoned in alleyways), and still functions as an orphanage today. Brunelleschi's beautiful arcade, decorated with the famous *tondi* of infants in swaddling clothes by Luca della Robbia, was one of the early classicizing experiments in architecture. There's a small picture gallery containing Ghirlandaio's *Adoration of the Magi* and several other works.

To complement Brunelleschi's arches, the old church of **Santissima Annunziata** was rebuilt and given a broad arcaded portico by Michelozzo facing the street. Behind the portico the architect added the *Chiostrino dei Voti*, a porch decorated with a collection of early 16th-century frescoes, including two by Andrea del Sarto. The best of these, faded as it is, is a finely detailed *Nativity* by Alessio Baldovinetti, one of the quattrocento's underappreciated masters. The church itself is the gaudiest in Florence; its freshly gilded elliptical dome, its unusual polygonal tribune around the sanctuary and megatons of *pietra dura* have helped it become the city's high-society parish, where even funerals are major social events. The huge candlelit chapel in the rear is the Tempietta, also by Michelozzo, sheltering a miraculous painting of *The Annunciation*.

The Accademia

Open Tues–Sat 8.30am–10pm; Sun 8.30–8; adm exp.

It may not be Florence's most interesting museum, but in summer the queues at the Accademia, just off the Piazza Santissima Annunziata, are often as long as those at the Uffizi. What they are most anxious to get a look at is of course Michelangelo's *David*. Just over a hundred years ago Florence decided to take this precocious symbol of republican liberty in out of the rain. The artist completed it for the city in 1501, when he was 26, and it was this work that established the overwhelming reputation he had in his own time. Looking entirely contented with his own perfection, he stands in a classical exedra built just for him (behind protective glass). As the political symbol the republic commissioned he may be excessive—the irony of a David the size of Goliath is disconcerting—but as a symbol of the artistic and intellectual aspirations of the Renaissance he is unsurpassed. Other works by Michelangelo include the famous *non finiti*: the *Prisoners* and *St Matthew*, tortured forms still waiting for Michelangelo to come back and finish liberating them from the stone; also one of his three versions of the *Pietà*.

There is plenty of indifferent painting in the Accademia, but persevere for such works as the *Deposition from the Cross* by Perugino, the sweet and small *Madonna del Mare* by Botticelli, and Uccello's very dirty *Thebaid*. Some of the best works are in a room of lesser-known masters of the quattrocento, especially Mariotto di Cristoforo and the 'Maestro del Casione Adimare', the latter known only for the painted chest here, a delightful scene of a marriage in Florence in the 1450s that has been reproduced in half the books ever written about the Renaissance. There is also a collection of musical instruments.

Santa Croce

Santa Maria Novella was the Dominicans' church, and so naturally the Franciscans had to have one just as big and grand. The original church, said to have been founded by St Francis himself, went by the board in Florence's colossal building programme of the 1290s. Arnolfo di Cambio planned its successor, largely completed by the 1450s, but a job of 'restoration' by Vasari in the 1560s ruined much of the original interior. The façade, in the accustomed Florentine black and white marble, nevertheless has something of the Victorian Gothic about it—just as it should, since it was only added in the 1850s, a gift from Sir Francis Sloane. Of all the modern façades on Italy's churches, built to atone finally for the chronic Renaissance inability ever to finish anything, this one may be the best.

Like Santa Maria Novella the interior is a museum in itself. Starting clockwise from the left side: near the door is the **tomb of Galileo**, whose remains were moved here only after the Church grudgingly consented to allow him a Christian burial in 1737. For a while it was the custom to bury great Italians here, as a sort of Tuscan Westminster Abbey, and you'll see plenty of tombs along both sides, mostly of thoroughly forgotten men of the 19th century. Two chapels down, the *Monument to Carlo Marsuppini* is a mine of good quattrocento sculpture, mostly by Verrocchio and Desiderio da Settignano. Look in the Bardi Chapel in the left transept for the *Crucifix* by Donatello (the one Brunelleschi said looked like a peasant). Many of the small vaulted chapels that flank the high altar contain important late (1330s) works by Giotto, his assistants and his followers. In the second **Bardi Chapel** is a series of frescoes on the *Life of St Francis* that can be compared with the more famous ones at Assisi.

The **Peruzzi Chapel** frescoes detail the *Lives of St John the Evangelist and St John the Baptist*. These works had a tremendous influence on all the later Florentine artists, but by the 18th century they were considered eyesores and whitewashed for 150 years—hence their fragmentary state.

Two of Giotto's immediate artistic heirs, the Gaddi, also contributed much to Santa Croce. Agnolo Gaddi did the stained glass around the high altar, as well as the fascinating series of frescoes on the *Legend of the Cross*—how Seth received a branch from St Michael and planted it over Adam's grave, how the tree that grew from it was shaped into a beam for a

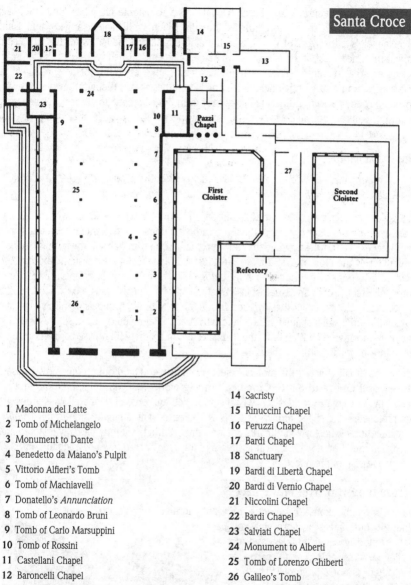

bridge, then buried by Solomon when his guest the Queen of Sheba prophesied that it would someday bring about the end of the Jews. The beam was dug up and shaped into Christ's cross, later found by St Helena, Constantine's mother, and then stolen by a Persian king and eventually recovered by the Emperor Heraclius. In the **Sacristy**, off to the right, there are more fine frescoes by Agnolo Gaddi's father Taddeo, and yet more Gaddis in the Castellani Chapel (Agnolo) and Baroncelli Chapel (Taddeo).

Back down the right side of the church, Donatello's **Tabernacle** has a beautiful relief of the *Annunciation.* Then some more **tombs**: Rossini, Machiavelli, Michelangelo, and Dante. Michelangelo's is the work of Vasari, who thought himself just the fellow for the job. Vasari's vandalism ruined most of the chapels on this side, once embellished with frescoes by Orcagna and other great trecento painters. His replacements, like his tomb for Michelangelo, are misfortunes. Dante isn't buried here at all. The Florentines always thought they would eventually get his body back from Ravenna; once they even bribed a pope to order the Ravennese to give it up, whereupon the body mysteriously disappeared for a decade or two until the affair was forgotten.

The Pazzi Chapel

Open April–Sept daily 10–12.30 and 2–6.30; Oct–Mar daily 10–12.30 and 3–5; closed Wed; adm; one charge for both Pazzi Chapel and museum.

One of Santa Croce's chapels carries an entrance fee, but it's well worth it. Brunelleschi, who could excel on the monumental scale of the cathedral dome, saved some of his best work for small places. Without knowing the architect, and something about the austere religious tendencies of the Florentines, the Pazzi Chapel is inexplicable, a Protestant reformation in architecture, unlike anything ever built before. The 'vocabulary' is essential Brunelleschi: simple pilasters, arches and rosettes in grey stone and white plaster. The only decoration is a set of modest terracotta apostles by Luca della Robbia, coloured roundels of the Evangelists by Donatello, and a small stained-glass window by Alessio Baldovinetti. Even so, this is enough. The contemplative repetition of elements makes for an aesthetic that posed a direct challenge to the international Gothic of the time.

Across the broad cloister, the monks' refectory and several adjoining rooms now house the **Museo dell'Opera di Santa Croce**, with more works by della Robbia, bits from a large fresco by Orcagna wrecked by Vasari's remodelling, one of Donatello's statues from Orsanmichele—the gilded bronze *St Louis of Toulouse*—and a famous, mournful *Crucifix* by Cimabue, one of the early landmarks of Florentine painting, but only partially restored after damage in the 1966 flood. Yet another fresco of the *Tree of the Cross*, by Taddeo Gaddi, adorns one wall of the refectory.

Across the Arno: The Pitti Palace

Once across the Ponte Vecchio, a different Florence reveals itself—not too different, but at least a more pleasant place to walk around: greener, quieter, and less burdened with traffic. The **Oltrarno**, as it is called, is not a large district. A chain of hills squeezes it against the river, and their summits afford the best views over the city. Across the bridge, the Medici's catwalk passes almost over the top of **Santa Felicità** church, best known as a monument to the quirky Mannerist painter Jacopo Pontormo. This artist, a recluse who lived atop a tower he built for himself, often pulling up the ladder to keep his friends at bay, frequently got himself into trouble with his neighbours for keeping the place full of dead animals and even human bodies, from which he studied form and anatomy. His work in Santa Felicità includes his masterpiece, the *Deposition*, with its luminous, distorted figures and exaggerated expressions, as well as frescoes of the Annunciation and the Evangelists.

As the Medici consolidated their power in Florence they made a point of buying up all the important properties of their former rivals, especially their family palaces. The most spectacular example of this ducal eminent domain was the acquisition by Cosimo I of the **Pitti Palace**, built in 1457 by a powerful banker named Luca Pitti who seems to have had vague ambitions of toppling the Medici and becoming the big boss himself. The palace and its extensive grounds, now the **Boboli Gardens**, were purchased by Cosimo in the 1540s; he and his wife Eleanor of Toledo liked it much better than the medieval Palazzo Vecchio, and soon moved in for good, and the palace remained the residence of the Medici, and later the House of Lorraine, until 1868. The original building, said to have been designed by Brunelleschi, was only as wide as the seven central windows of the façade. Succeeding generations of Medici and Lorraines found it too small for their burgeoning collections of bric-à-brac, and made several stages of symmetrical additions, resulting in a long bulky profile, resembling some sort of Stalinist ministry on its bleak asphalt piazza. The grand dukes kept it better landscaped. Piazza Pitti was a prized address in the old days—the greatest of all Florence fans, the Brownings, kept house across from the palace, and so for a time did Dostoevsky.

Boboli Gardens

Open daily 9–one hour before sunset; adm.

It is the loveliest park in the centre of Florence, the only park in the centre of Florence, and if you're visiting in the summer, the sooner you become acquainted with it the better. The Boboli is the only escape from the sun, humidity and crowds of July and August. Cosimo I began the planning and landscaping in the 1550s. The tone for what was to be the first Mannerist park was set early on by the incredible **Grotta del Buontalenti**, near the entrance behind the Pitti Palace. The Florentines do not seem to like this artificial cavern. In Rome or Venice, cities where decadence is properly valued and honoured, it would be one of the biggest tourist attractions; here in Florence it is forgotten and allowed to deteriorate. The grotto is sheer madness, Gaudiesque dripping stone with peculiar creatures seeming to grow out of it. Inside are fantastic painted landscapes, surrounded by leopards, bears, satyrs, and others harder to define.

The groves and walks of the Boboli are haunted by platoons of statuary, some Roman and some absurd Mannerist work, like the fat baby Bacchus riding a turtle. There's a genuine obelisk, in the centre of a miniature Roman circus, and a fountain from the Baths of Caracalla. Some of the best parts of the gardens are the furthest away: shady paths and flower beds towards the south, near Florence's southern gate, the Porta Romana.

Santo Spirito

The centre of the Oltrarno district, Piazza Santo Spirito usually has a small market going under the plane trees, as well as restaurants and a quiet café or two. The church, **Santo Spirito**, shows a severe 18th-century façade that conceals one of Brunelleschi's triumphs, a characteristic, contemplative interior of grey and white surrounded by ranks of semi-circular chapels.

Even though later architects tinkered grievously with the plan after Brunelleschi's death, many consider this to be one of his best churches. Among the paintings in the chapels are works by Filippino Lippi (south transept, a *Madonna and Child*) and Orcagna (a fresco of the *Crucifixion*, in the refectory of the adjacent monastery).

Santa Maria del Carmine

With its walls of rough stone—the projected façade was never completed—**Santa Maria del Carmine** looks more like a country farmhouse than a church. Most of it was destroyed in a fire and reconstructed in the 1700s, but the **Brancacci Chapel** (*open Mon and Wed–Sat 10–5, Sun 1–5; adm*), another of the landmarks of Florentine art, somehow survived, and has recently been restored. Three artists worked on the chapel frescoes: Masolino, beginning in 1424, his pupil Masaccio, working alone from 1428, and Filippino Lippi, who completed the work in the 1480s. Scholars never tire of disputing the attributions of the various scenes, especially those that could be either Masolino's or Masaccio's. It doesn't matter; 'Little Tom' and 'Shabby Tom' both contributed greatly to the visual revolution of quattrocento painting. Both were revolutionary in their understanding of light and space, though art historians these days make more of a fuss over the precocious, eccentric Shabby Tom, who died at the age of 27 shortly after his work here. Some of the scenes—the *Expulsion of Adam and Eve*, the *Tribute Money* and scenes from the life of St Peter—are among Masaccio's masterpieces. Almost every artist of the later 1400s and 1500s came here to do sketches and study how Shabby Tom did it; some of Michelangelo's sketches after Masaccio still survive.

San Miniato

Despite the fact that the lovely Romanesque façade of this church can be glimpsed from almost anywhere in Florence, few visitors are ever moved to see it up close. As a result, you may have one of Florence's best churches all to yourself. Built in 1015 over an earlier church, on the spot where the head of obscure St Minias bounced after the Romans decapitated him, the exterior echoes the black and white geometric style of the Baptistry. The playful patterns are continued inside, framing a richly coloured 13th-century mosaic of Christ Pantocrator in the apse. Despite its distance from the city centre, this has always been a church dear to the hearts of the Florentines. At the top of the façade you'll notice the gold eagle symbol of the Calimala, the medieval cloth merchants' guild. These rich businessmen had the church in their care, and over the centuries they bestowed on it many lovely things. Inside, be sure to see the wonderful inlaid marble floor, with signs of the zodiac and fantastical animals; also the **Cappella del Crocifisso**, a joint effort by Michelozzo and Luca della Robbia. The fine pulpit and choir screen date from the early 1200s, and the Chapel of the Cardinal of Portugal contains work by Baldovinetti (who also restored the apse mosaic), della Robbia, Pollaiuolo, and Rossellino.

Fiesole

No ordinary suburb, **Fiesole** can claim to be the mother city of Florence itself. In fact the town is of Etruscan origin, the northernmost member of the federation of city-states called the Dodecapolis. *Faesulum* dwindled in the heyday of Roman-era Florence, but in the Dark Ages its secure hilltop site ensured its survival. When times became a little bit safer its families began moving back down to the Arno to rebuild Florence. For centuries now Fiesole has played the role of Florence's aristocratic suburb; its cool breezes and belvedere views make it the perfect retreat from the torrid Florentine summers. The no.7 city bus from the Piazza della Stazione will have you there in less than half an hour.

Mino da Fiesole is a favourite son, a quattrocento sculptor whose best work can be seen in the early 11th-century **Duomo** on the piazza. Behind the cathedral on Via Dupré is the **Bandini Museum** (*open winter 9.30–5, summer 9.30–7, closed Tues; adm*), a must for anybody who loves the iridescent della Robbia terracottas on Tuscany's churches and would like a chance to see some up close. Not much is left of Etruscan or Roman Fiesole, but you can visit the small **Roman Theatre**, excavated in 1911 and often used for plays and concerts in the summer. Perhaps the best sights Fiesole has to offer, though, are the perfect views over Florence and the surrounding area from old streets like Via Francesco on the edge of town.

Shopping

Although central Florence sometimes seems like one solid boutique, the city is no longer the queen of Italian fashion—the long lack of a central airport, more than anything else, sent most of the big designers to Milan. Nevertheless, the big **fashion** names of the 1960s and '70s, and the international chain stores of the 1980s, are well represented in smart Via Tornabuoni, Via Calzaiuoli and in the streets around the Duomo, and if you come to Florence itching to spend some cash, there are still plenty of opportunities: **jewellery**, surprisingly, heads the list. The shops that line the Ponte Vecchio are forced by the nature of their location into competition, and good prices for Florentine brushed gold, cameos and antique jewellery (much of it actually made in Arezzo these days) are more common than you might think. They do not set up shop here just to exploit tourists—they've been on the bridge for over 300 years. Near the Oltrarno end there's also one shop that specializes in fascinating antique telescopes and other instruments.

Leather goods are also still something Florence is known for; you can have a look in a number of choice shops around Via della Vigna Nuova and Via del Parione, and less expensively at an unusual institution called the **Leather School** that occupies part of Santa Croce's cloister and has a showroom on the square in front.

For bargains and surprises, try Florence's famous and boisterous **street markets**, usually open every day. The big San Lorenzo market, which has spread all over the neighbourhood around San Lorenzo Church, is where ordinary Florentines probably buy most of their clothes. In this little bit of Naples transplanted to Tuscany, the range of choice is equal to three department stores; you'll see plenty of fake designer labels, and even some real ones. Further west in Santa Croce, in the Piazza dei Ciompi, the *mercato delle pulci* (flea market) carries on daily, with a wide array of desirable junk, beneath Vasari's Fish Loggia; the shopkeepers, being Florentines, are a little smug and not inclined to bargain. At both locations there are also lavishly stocked **food markets** where you should find what you're looking for, whether you want to stock up for a train journey or find local specialities, like *stracchino* cheese, to take home. More serious **antique** shops, and Florence has plenty of them, tend to cluster in the streets between Via Tornabuoni and the Ognissanti Church, and on Via Maggio. The **Mercato Nuovo**, or *Mercato del Porcellino*, right in the centre of town, still performs its age-old function of selling Florentine straw goods—hats and bags—though tourist trinkets have taken over most of the stalls. There is also a small market in Piazza Santo Spirito in the Oltrarno (mornings) and a larger one in the Cascine Park (Tuesday mornings). Some of the real finds are in the towns around Florence: **glassware** in the shops of Empoli, and **ceramics** (including the inevitable della Robbia reproductions) in Impruneta, and especially in Montelupo.

Florence ✉ *50100*   **Where to Stay**

An alternative to staying in the centre of Florence is to look for a hotel in Fiesole, which is cooler, and quieter at night, when you can appreciate the wonderful views over the city far below, twinkling like a mass of fairy lights.

luxury

★★★★★ **Helvetia & Bristol**, Via dei Pescioni 2, ✆ 055 287 814, 🖷 055 288 353. Just 52 luxurious bedrooms, each one different, and each exquisitely furnished with antiques and rich fabrics; service is discreet and the atmosphere understated. Stravinsky, Bertrand Russell and Pirandello have stayed here. There is also a superb restaurant.

★★★★ **J & J**, Via di Mezzo 20, ✆ 055 234 5005, 🖷 055 240 282. Occupying an unassuming ex-convent, in a quiet residential street near Sant'Ambrogio. The interiors are fresh and new, combining original 16th-century features and antique furniture with chic contemporary design. Each room is totally different. The suites are enormous, with sitting areas and luxurious bathrooms.

★★★★★ **Villa San Michele**, Via Doccia 4, ✆ 055 59451, 🖷 055 598 734, is in a breathtaking location just below Fiesole. This 14th-century monastery has a façade and loggia reputedly designed by Michelangelo. Carefully reconstructed after bomb damage in the Second World War, it has become one of the most beautiful hotels in Italy, set in a lovely Tuscan garden, complete with a pool. The prices are seriously astronomical, but the food is wonderful. *Closed mid-Nov–mid-Mar.*

very expensive

★★★★ **Monna Lisa**, Borgo Pinti 27, ✆ 055 247 9751, 🖷 055 247 9755, is one of the most charming, well-situated small hotels in Florence, a well-preserved Renaissance palace owned by the descendants of sculptor Giovanni Dupre. The furnishings and works of art are family heirlooms. Try to reserve one of the tranquil rooms overlooking the garden. There is private parking.

★★★★ **Kraft**, Via Solferino 2, ✆ 055 284 273, ✉ 055 239 8267. Just two minutes' walk from the Teatro Comunale. Bedrooms are light and sunny, comfortably furnished with cheerful fabrics. The suites on the top floor have great views and there is a small rooftop pool, and a restaurant.

★★★★ **Lungarno**, Borgo San Jacopo 14, ✆ 055 264 211, ✉ 055 268 437. A discreet, fairly modern building near the Ponte Vecchio which incorporates a medieval tower. Recently refurbished, the smallish bedrooms are decorated in smart blue and cream, and the best have balconies with 'The View'. Book ahead if you want one of these. There is also a lovely view from the ground-floor sitting/breakfast room and bar.

expensive

★★★ **Loggiato dei Serviti**, Piazza SS. Annunziata 3, ✆ 055 289 592. Designed for the Servite Fathers by Antonio da Sangallo the Elder, who added a loggia to match Brunelleschi's Spedale degli Innocenti across the square. Redone with the best of Florentine taste and refinement, with Italian and English antiques; all rooms have air-conditioning, parking is possible in a nearby garage, and there is a lovely garden.

★★★ **Hermitage**, Vicolo Marzio 1, ✆ 055 287 216, very near the Ponte Vecchio, is one of the best places to stay in the very heart of Florence; reserve well in advance to get one of its 14 cosy old rooms, and even further in advance to get one overlooking the Arno.

★★★ **Morandi all Crocetta**, Via Laura 50, ✆ 055 234 4747, ✉ 055 248 0954, is a popular, 10-room hotel in the university area northeast of Piazza San Marco. Run by an Irish family, the building was a convent in the 16th century, and some of the comfortable rooms still have the odd fresco. Two have private terraces.

moderate

★★ **Pensione Alessandra**, Borgo SS. Apostoli 17, ✆ 055 283 438, ✉ 055 210 619. A 1507 palazzo designed by Baccio d'Agnolo, near the Ponte Vecchio. There are 25 rooms, the best with waxed parquet floors and antique furniture.

★★★ **Casci**, Via Cavour 13, ✆ 055 211 686, ✉ 055 239 6461. This 15th-century palazzo (once home to Rossini) is now a family-run hotel. The atmosphere is relaxed and cheerful, the breakfast room has a frescoed ceiling, and the recently refurbished bedrooms are bright and modern. Some look on to a garden at the back. Good value.

★★★ **Classic Hotel**, Viale Machiavelli 25, ✆ 055 229 351, ✉ 055 229 353. Just above Porta Romana on the way to Piazzale Michelangelo, this pink-washed villa stands in a shady garden. Rooms are furnished with a mixture of old and new; walls are white, parquet floors are polished. There is even the odd fresco. Excellent value for money.

cheap

Most of Florence's budget (or at least budget-ish) hotels are grouped together around the railway station. Most of them send touts to the station to pick up wandering bed-less backpackers, and if you're getting stuck it's worth at least checking the prices they are offering. Except in very high season it's usually possible to bargain.

★ **Firenze**, Piazza dei Donati, ✆ 055 214 203. Near the Duomo, this is the classiest inexpensive hotel in Florence. Book in advance, and ask for one of the newer rooms.

★ **Scoti**, Via Tornabuoni 7, © 055 292 128. A simple and cheap *pensione* run by new, friendly owners (Doreen is Australian). Large rooms have up to four beds and there's bags of atmosphere—and floor-to-ceiling frescoes in the sitting room.

Besides hotels, a number of **institutions and private homes** let rooms—there's a list in the back of the annual provincial hotel book (*Elenco degli Alberghi*), available from tourist offices. There are two main **youth hostels** in Florence: the **Ostello Europa Villa Camerata**, Viale A. Righi 2/4, © 055 601 451 (bus 17b from the station), and the **Ostello Santa Monaca**, Via S. Monaca 6, © 055 268 338, in Oltrarno.

Eating Out

For better or worse, the real Florentine specialities rarely turn up on many restaurant menus, and you'll probably finish your stay without ever learning what a Florentine cook can do with cocks' combs, calves' feet and tripe. Florence in its loftier moods likes to call itself the 'birthplace of international *haute cuisine*', but in fact the city's contribution to the Italian kitchen is minimal; everyone knows its only really popular dish, *bistecca alla Fiorentina*—thick grilled steaks seasoned with salt and pepper. Nevertheless, like any sophisticated city with lots of visitors, Florence has plenty of fine restaurants; even in the cheaper places, standards are high, and if you don't care for anything fancier there will be lots of good red Chianti to wash it down.

very expensive

Florence is blessed with one of the finest gourmet restaurants in Italy, the **Enoteca Pinchiorri**, Via Ghibellina 87, © 055 242 777, near the Casa Buonarroti. The owners inherited the building, a wine shop, some 10 years ago, and have converted it into a beautifully appointed restaurant, with meals served in a garden court in the summer; they've also accumulated an astonishing collection of some 80,000 bottles of the best Italian and French wine. The cooking, a mixture of *nouvelle cuisine* and traditional Tuscan recipes, wins prizes every year. Be warned that you can leave behind as much as L200,000 per person here. *Closed Sun, Mon midday, and Aug.*

Relais le Jardin, the restaurant in the Regency hotel in Piazza d'Azeglio, is rapidly establishing itself as one of Florence's best; the setting is lovely and refined, the dishes sublime: delicate crêpes filled with courgette blossoms, artichoke hearts, or asparagus, and medallions of veal with rhubarb. *Closed Sun.*

Cibreo, Via dei Macci 118r, © 055 234 1100, overlooking Sant'Ambrogio's market, has simple décor—food is the main concern: tripe *antipasto*, pumpkin soup, *prosciutto* from the Casentino, leg of lamb stuffed with artichokes, a delicious lemon *crostata*. There's an excellent selection of Italian or French wines, and Armagnac. *Open for lunch and dinner; closed Sun and Mon, Easter, and mid-July–mid-Sep.*

expensive

If *cucina nuova fiorentina* sounds intriguing, try the fare at **Caffè Concerto**, Lungarno C. Colombo 7, © 055 677 377, served on a veranda overlooking the Arno. It remains open late, for light midnight suppers. *Closed Sun.*

Coco Lezzone, Via del Parioncino 26r, off Lungarno Corsini, © 055 287 178. In old Florentine dialect, the name means big, smelly cook, but the food here—Tuscan classics using ingredients of the highest quality—is excellent, the ambience informal.

Pane e Vino, Via San Niccolò 70r (in the Oltrarno, just in from Ponte alla Grazie), © 055 247 6956. This informal restaurant started life as an *enoteca* and still has a superb wine list. The *menu degustazione* changes daily, has seven small courses and is very good value. With any luck, the porcini mushroom flan will be available—it is superb. *Open for lunch and dinner; closed Sun.*

moderate

Ila Vecchia Bettola, west of the Carmine in Viale Ariosto 32–4r, © 055 224 158, is a noisy trattoria with marble-topped tables and wooden benches. The menu changes daily, but you can nearly always find their classic *tagliolini con funghi porcini*; the grilled meats are tasty and succulent. *Open for lunch and dinner; closed Sun.*

Ristoro di Cambi, Via Sant'Onofrio 1r, © 055 217 134, in the Oltrarno, is popular with the Florentine intelligentsia. The food is genuinely Florentine, the décor rustic. The soups—classic *ribollita* and *pappa al pomodoro*—are tasty and warming, and the *bistecca alla fiorentina* the real McCoy. *Open for lunch and dinner; closed Sun.*

cheap

Central Florence, by popular demand, is full of *tavole calde*, pizzerias, cafeterias and snack bars, where you can grab a sandwich or a salad instead of a full sit-down meal (one of the best pizza-by-the-slice places is just across from the Medici Chapels).

Trattoria Cibreo, Via de' Macci 118r, is an annexe at the back of the smart Cibreo (see above), and a real find. The food is more or less the same, just served on less expensive porcelain. Open for lunch and dinner; closed Sun and Mon.

Le Belle Donne, Via delle Belle Donne 16r, © 055 238 2609, is easy to miss, just off Via Tornabuoni. There is an emphasis on vegetable dishes, although it's not exclusively vegetarian. It's always crowded, so book. *Open Mon–Fri for lunch and dinner.*

Il Pizzaiuolo, Via dei Macci 113r, near S. Ambrogio, © 055 241 171, is a relatively new pizzeria, but one of the best. The *pizzaiuolo* is Neapolitan, and his creations are puffy and light. There's lots more to choose from as well if you can get past the queues. *Open for lunch and dinner; closed Tues and Aug.*

The cheapest meal in Florence, though, will almost certainly be found at the lunch counter, the **Tavola Calda**, in the Sant'Ambrogio market, where once you've fought your way through the crowds of market traders you can get a full three courses for around L20,000, served with a complete absence of the usual restaurant courtesies.

Entertainment and Nightlife

opera, classical music, theatre

Florence is not renowned for its nightlife, but it does have plenty of theatre and music. The main **opera** season runs only from September to December, but the city's main cultural festival, the **Maggio Musicale**, combining opera and classical concerts, runs from April to

June, with events at a variety of venues. For festival information inquire at tourist offices or call ✆ 055 211 158. There is also a festival in Fiesole each summer, the **Estate Fiesolana**, featuring concerts, dance, film screenings and theatre. In addition, at almost any time of the year there is a busy concert calendar in Florence including many of the world's best-known musicians.

The city also takes **theatre** seriously, and at any given time you are likely to find the likes of Pirandello, Shakespeare, Brecht—even Niccolò Machiavelli—playing alongside contemporary works. *Firenze Spettacolo* and the English language *Events*, available from the city tourist office, have full listings of upcoming events. **Goldoni**, Via de' Serragli 109, ✆ 055 222 437, and **Odeon**, Via Sassetti 1, ✆ 055 214 068, show recent original-language (usually English) films (*Mon and occasionally Tues*); the **Cinema Astro**, on Piazza San Simone near Santa Croce, has older movies in English (*every night except Mon and July*).

cafés and bars

Florence has plenty of stylish and pretty expensive bars, most of all around the main shopping and tourist streets such as the Via Tornabuoni. A more relaxed atmosphere—and lower prices—will more likely be found around San Marco, the main student area, or in Oltrarno.

The city's most classic and elegant *gran caffè* is **Rivoire**, on the Piazza Signoria, a fine place to watch the milling throng once you've got over the prices. Also elegant and a traditionally fashionable venue for fine-quality snacks is **Procacci**, Via Tornabuoni 64, bizarrely an Italian bar that doesn't serve coffee.

For a livelier, younger clientèle, the long-established main meeting-point in San Marco is the **Gran Caffè San Marco**, on the piazza of the same name. Nearby, **La Mescita**, Via degli Alfani 70, is a good-value snacks and wine bar. For ice cream, Florence's most lavish range of varieties is on offer at **Festival del Gelato**, Via del Corso 75r, but the most famous is **Vivoli**, Via Isola delle Stinche 7r (between the Bargello and S. Croce). *Closed Mon.*

clubs and discos

Although Florence after dark isn't exactly humming, in the last few years a number of new clubs, discos and late-night music bars have opened up. The best way to find out about what's going on is to buy *Firenze Spettacolo* (available from news-stands), look out for posters, particularly in the San Marco area, or inquire at one of the many English pubs.

A funky time can also usually be had at **Stonehenge**, Via dell'Amorino 16, near S. Lorenzo, which serves rock and cocktails from 10pm until after 1am. **Central Park**, Parco delle Cascine, is a summer club with live music, three dance floors, shows and snacks. Possibly the trendiest place in Florence. The **Jazz Café**, Via Nuova de' Caccini 3, has a pleasant but smoky atmosphere, with live jazz on Friday and Saturday nights, and a free jam session on Tuesdays. *Closed Sun and Mon.* There are two gay clubs in Florence: **Satanassa**, Via Pandolfini 26r, has a disco and cocktail bar, *closed Mon*; **Tabasco**, Piazza Santa Cecilia 3r, was Italy's first gay bar.

The fathers of modern Italian were Dante, Manzoni and television. Each had a part in creating a national language from an infinity of regional and local dialects; the Florentine Dante, the first to write in the vernacular, did much to put the Tuscan dialect in the foreground of Italian literature. Manzoni's revolutionary novel, *I Promessi Sposi*, heightened national consciousness by using an everyday language all could understand in the 19th century.

Television in the last few decades is performing an even more spectacular linguistic unification; although the majority of Italians still speak a dialect at home, school and work, their TV idols insist on proper Italian.

Perhaps because they are so busy learning their own beautiful but grammatically complex language, Italians are not especially apt at learning others. English lessons, however, have been the rage for years, and at most hotels and restaurants there will be someone who speaks some English. In small towns and out-of-the-way places, finding an Anglophone may prove more difficult. The words and phrases below should help you out in most situations, but the ideal way to come to Italy is with some Italian under your belt; your visit will be richer, and you're much more likely to make some Italian friends.

Italian words are pronounced phonetically. Every vowel and consonant is sounded. Consonants are the same as in English, except the 'c' which, when followed by an 'e' or 'i', is pronounced like the English 'ch' (*cinque* thus becomes cheenquay). Italian 'g' is also soft before 'i' or 'e' as in *gira*, or jee-ra. 'H' is never sounded; 'z' is pronounced like 'ts'.

The consonants 'sc' before the vowels 'i' or 'e' becomes like the English 'sh' as in 'sci', pronounced shee; 'ch' is pronouced like a 'k' as in Chianti, kee-an-tee; 'gn' as 'ny' in English (*bagno*, pronounced ban-yo); while 'gli' is pronounced like the middle of the word million (Castiglione, pronounced Ca-stee-lyon-ay).

Vowel pronunciation is: 'a' as in English father; 'e' when unstressed is pronounced like 'a' in fate as in *mele*, when stressed can be the same or like the 'e' in pet (*bello*); 'i' is like the 'i' in

Language

machine; 'o', like 'e', has two sounds, 'o' as in hope when unstressed (*tacchino*), and usually 'o' as in rock when stressed (*morte*); 'u' is pronounced like the 'u' in June.

The accent usually (but not always!) falls on the penultimate syllable. Also note that in the big northern cities, the informal way of addressing someone as you, *tu*, is widely used; the more formal *lei* or *voi* is commonly used in provincial districts.

Useful Words and Phrases

yes/no/maybe	*sì/no/forse*	Good night	*Buona notte*
I don't know	*Non lo so*	Goodbye	*Arrivederla* (formal), *arrivederci, ciao* (informal)
I don't understand (Italian)	*Non capisco (italiano)*		
Does someone here speak English?	*C'è qualcuno qui che parla inglese?*	What?/Who?/Where?	*Che?/Chi?/Dove?*
		When?/Why?	*Quando?/Perché?*
Speak slowly	*Parla lentamente*	How?	*Come?*
Could you assist me?	*Potrebbe aiutarmi?*	How much?	*Quanto?*
Help!	*Aiuto!*	I am lost	*Mi sono smarrito*
Please	*Per favore*	I am hungry	*Ho fame*
Thank you (very much)	*(Molte) grazie*	I am thirsty	*Ho sete*
You're welcome	*Prego*	I am sleepy	*Ho sonno*
What do you call this in Italian?	*Come si chiama questo in italiano?*	I am sorry	*Mi dispiace*
		I am tired	*Sono stanco*
It doesn't matter	*Non importa*	I am ill	*Mi sento male*
All right	*Va bene*	Leave me alone	*Lasciami in pace*
Excuse me	*Mi scusi*	good	*buono/bravo*
Be careful!	*Attenzione!*	bad	*male/cattivo*
Nothing	*Niente*	It's all the same	*Fa lo stesso*
It is urgent!	*È urgente!*	fast	*rapido*
How are you?	*Come sta?*	slow	*lento*
Well, and you?	*Bene, e lei?*	big	*grande*
What is your name?	*Come si chiama?*	small	*piccolo*
Hello	*Salve* or *ciao* (both informal)	hot	*caldo*
		cold	*freddo*
Good morning	*Buongiorno* (formal hello)	up	*su*
		down	*giù*
Good afternoon, evening	*Buonasera* (also formal hello)	here	*qui*
		there	*lì*

Shopping, Service, Sightseeing

I would like...	*Vorrei...*	money	*soldi*
Where is/are...	*Dov'è/Dove sono...*	newspaper (foreign)	*giornale (straniero)*
How much is it?	*Quanto viene questo?*	pharmacy	*farmacia*
open	*aperto*	police station	*commissariato*
closed	*chiuso*	policeman	*poliziotto*
cheap/expensive	*a buon prezzo/caro*	post office	*ufficio postale*
bank	*banca*	sea	*mare*
beach	*spiaggia*	shop	*negozio*
bed	*letto*	room	*camera*
church	*chiesa*	tobacco shop	*tabaccaio*
entrance	*entrata*	WC	*toilette/bagno*
exit	*uscita*	men	*Signori/Uomini*
hospital	*ospedale*	women	*Signore/Donne*

Time

What time is it?	*Che ore sono?*	today	*oggi*
month	*mese*	yesterday	*ieri*
week	*settimana*	tomorrow	*domani*
day	*giorno*	soon	*fra poco*
morning	*mattina*	later	*dopo/più tardi*
afternoon	*pomeriggio*	It is too early	*È troppo presto*
evening	*sera*	It is too late	*È troppo tardi*

Days

Monday	*lunedì*	Friday	*venerdì*
Tuesday	*martedì*	Saturday	*sabato*
Wednesday	*mercoledì*	Sunday	*domenica*
Thursday	*giovedì*		

Numbers

one	*uno/una*	twenty	*venti*
two	*due*	twenty-one	*ventuno*
three	*tre*	twenty-two	*ventidue*
four	*quattro*	thirty	*trenta*
five	*cinque*	thirty-one	*trentuno*
six	*sei*	forty	*quaranta*
seven	*sette*	fifty	*cinquanta*
eight	*otto*	sixty	*sessanta*
nine	*nove*	seventy	*settanta*
ten	*dieci*	eighty	*ottanta*
eleven	*undici*	ninety	*novanta*
twelve	*dodici*	hundred	*cento*
thirteen	*tredici*	one hundred & one	*centouno*
fourteen	*quattordici*	two hundred	*duecento*
fifteen	*quindici*	one thousand	*mille*
sixteen	*sedici*	two thousand	*duemila*
seventeen	*diciassette*	million	*milione*
eighteen	*diciotto*	a thousand million	*miliardo*
nineteen	*diciannove*		

Transport

airport	*aeroporto*	port station	*stazione marittima*
automobile	*macchina*	railway station	*stazione ferroviaria*
bus/coach	*autobus/pullman*	seat (reserved)	*posto (prenotato)*
bus stop	*fermata*	ship	*nave*
customs	*dogana*	taxi	*tassì*
platform	*binario*	ticket	*biglietto*
port	*porto*	train	*treno*

Travel Directions

I want to go to...	*Desidero andare a...*	Have a good trip	*Buon viaggio!*
How can I get to...?	*Come posso andare a...?*	near	*vicino*
Do you stop at...?	*Ferma a...?*	far	*lontano*
Where is...?	*Dov'è...?*	left	*sinistra*
How far is it to...?	*Quanto siamo lontani da...?*	right	*destra*
		straight ahead	*sempre diritto*
When does the ... leave?	*A che ora parte ... ?*	forward	*avanti*
What is the name of this station?	*Come si chiama questa stazione?*	backwards	*indietro*
		north	*nord*
When does the next ... leave?	*Quando parte il prossimo...?*	south	*sud*
		east	*est/oriente*
From where does it leave?	*Da dove parte?*	west	*ovest/occidente*
		round the corner	*dietro l'angolo*
How long does the trip take...?	*Quanto tempo dura il viaggio?*	crossroads	*bivio*
		street/road	*strada*
How much is the fare?	*Quant'è il biglietto?*	square	*piazza*

Driving

bicycle	*bicicletta*	motorbike/scooter	*motocicletta/Vespa*
breakdown	*guasto* or *panne*	narrow	*stretto*
bridge	*ponte*	no parking	*sosta vietata*
car hire	*noleggio macchina*	parking	*parcheggio*
danger	*pericolo*	petrol/diesel	*benzina/gasolio*
driver	*guidatore*	slow down	*rallentare*speed
driving licence	*patente di guida*	*velocità*	
garage	*garage*	This doesn't work	*Questo non funziona*
map/town plan	*carta/pianta*	toll	*pedaggio*
mechanic	*meccanico*	Where is the road to...?	*Dov'è la strada per...?*

Italian Menu Vocabulary

Antipasti

These before-meal treats can include almost anything; among the most common are:

antipasto misto	mixed antipasto
bruschetta	garlic toast (sometimes with tomatoes)
carciofi (sott'olio)	artichokes (in oil)
frutti di mare	seafood
funghi (trifolati)	mushrooms (with anchovies, garlic, and lemon)
gamberi ai fagioli	prawns (shrimps) with white beans
mozzarella (in carrozza)	cow or buffalo cheese (fried with bread in batter)
olive	olives
prosciutto (con melone)	raw ham (with melon)
salsicce	sausages

Minestre (Soups) and Pasta

These dishes are the principal typical first courses (*primi*) served throughout Italy.

agnolotti	ravioli with meat
cacciucco	spiced fish soup
cannelloni	meat and cheese rolled in pasta tubes
cappelletti	small ravioli, often in broth
crespelle	crêpes
fettuccine	long strips of pasta
frittata	omelette
gnocchi	potato dumplings
lasagne	pasta sheets baked with meat and cheese sauce
minestra di verdura	thick vegetable soup
minestrone	soup with meat, vegetables, and pasta
orecchiette	ear-shaped pasta, served with turnip greens
panzerotti	ravioli filled with mozzarella, anchovies, egg
pappardelle alla lepre	pasta with hare sauce
pasta e fagioli	soup with beans, bacon, and tomatoes
pastina in brodo	tiny pasta in broth
penne all'arrabbiata	quill-shaped pasta with tomatoes, hot peppers
polenta	cake or pudding of corn semolina
risotto (alla milanese)	Italian rice (with stock, saffron and wine)
spaghetti all'amatriciana	with spicy sauce (salt pork, tomato, onion, chilli)
spaghetti alla bolognese	with ground meat, ham, mushrooms,etc
spaghetti alla carbonara	with bacon, eggs, and black pepper
spaghetti al pomodoro	with tomato sauce
spaghetti al sugo/ragù	with meat sauce
spaghetti alle vongole	with clam sauce
stracciatella	broth with eggs and cheese
sagliatelle	flat egg noodles
tortellini al pomodoro	pasta caps filled with meat and cheese
vermicelli	very thin spaghetti

Carne (Meat)

abbacchio	milk-fed lamb	*bresaola*	dried raw meat
agnello	lamb	*capretto*	kid
anatra	duck	*capriolo*	roebuck
animelle	sweetbreads	*carne di castrato*	mutton
arista	pork loin	*carne di suino*	pork
arrosto misto	mixed roast meats	*carpaccio*	thin slices of raw beef
bistecca alla fiorentina	Florentine beef steak	*cassoeula*	winter stew with pork and cabbage
bocconcini	veal mixed with ham and cheese and fried	*cervello (al burro nero)*	brains (in black butter)
bollito misto	stew of boiled meats	*cervo*	venison
braciola	chop	*cinghiale*	boar
brasato di manzo	braised beef with vegetables	*coniglio*	rabbit

cotoletta	veal cutlet	alla diavola	grilled
fagiano	pheasant	alla Marengo	fried with tomatoes, garlic and wine
faraona	guinea fowl		
fegato alla veneziana	liver (usually of veal) with filling	polpette	meatballs
		quaglie	quails
lepre (in salmi)	hare (marinated in wine)	rane	frogs
		rognoni	kidneys
lombo di maiale	pork loin	saltimbocca	veal scallop with prosciutto and sage, cooked in wine and butter
lumache	snails		
maiale (al latte)	pork (cooked in milk)		
manzo	beef		
ossobuco	braised veal knuckle with herbs	scaloppine	thin slices of veal sautéed in butter
pancetta	rolled pork	spezzatino	pieces of beef or veal, usually stewed
pernice	partridge		
petto di pollo	boned chicken breast	spiedino	meat on a skewer or stick
piccione	pigeon		
pizzaiola	beef steak with tomato and oregano sauce	stufato	beef braised in white wine with vegetables
pollo	chicken	tacchino	turkey
alla cacciatora	with tomatoes and mushrooms in wine	trippa	tripe
		uccelletti	small birds on a skewer
		vitello	veal

Pesce (Fish)

acciughe or alici	anchovies	merluzzo	cod
anguilla	eel	nasello	hake
aragosta	lobster	orata	bream
aringa	herring	ostriche	oysters
baccalà	dried salt cod	pescespada	swordfish
bonito	small tuna	polipi/ polpi	octopus
branzino	sea bass	pesce azzurro	various types of small fish
calamari	squid		
cappe sante	scallops	pesce di San Pietro	John Dory
cefalo	grey mullet	rombo	turbot
coda di rospo	angler fish	sarde	sardines
cozze	mussels	seppie	cuttlefish
datteri di mare	razor (or date) mussels	sgombro	mackerel
dentice	dentex (perch-like fish)	sogliola	sole
dorato	gilt head	squadro	monkfish
fritto misto	mixed fried delicacies, usually fish	tonno	tuna
		triglia	red mullet (rouget)
gamberetto	shrimp	trota	trout
gamberi (di fiume)	prawns (crayfish)	atrota salmonata	salmon trout
granchio	crab	vongole	small clams
insalata di mare	seafood salad	zuppa di pesce	mixed fish in sauce or stew
lampreda	lamprey		

Contorni (Side Dishes, Vegetables)

asparagi	asparagus	lenticchie	lentils
broccoli	broccoli	melanzane (al forno)	aubergine/eggplant
calabrese	green		(filled and baked)
romana	spiral	patate (fritte)	potatoes (fried)
carciofi (alla giudia)	artichokes (deep fried)	peperoni	sweet peppers
cardi	cardoons, thistles	peperonata	stewed peppers, onions,
carote	carrots		etc., similar to
cavolfiore	cauliflower		ratatouille
cavolo	cabbage	piselli (al prosciutto)	peas (with ham)
ceci	chickpeas	pomodoro (i)	tomato(es)
cetriolo	cucumber	porri	leeks
cipolla	onion	radicchio	red chicory
fagioli	white beans	radice	radish
fagiolini	French (green) beans	rapa	turnip
fave	broad beans	sedano	celery
finocchio	fennel	spinaci	spinach
funghi (porcini)	mushrooms (boletus)	verdure	greens
insalata (mista, verde)	salad (mixed, green)	zucca	pumpkin
lattuga	lettuce	zucchini	courgettes

Dolci (Desserts)

amaretti	macaroons
cannoli	crisp pastry tubes filled with ricotta, cream, chocolate or fruit
coppa gelato	assorted ice cream
crema caramella	caramel-topped custard
crostata	fruit flan
gelato (produzione propria)	ice-cream (homemade)
granita	flavoured ice, usually lemon or coffee
Monte Bianco	chestnut pudding with whipped cream
panettone	sponge cake with candied fruit and raisins
panforte	dense cake of almonds and preserved fruit
Saint-Honoré	meringue cake
semifreddo	refrigerated cake
sorbetto	sorbet/sherbet
spumone	a soft ice cream
tiramisù	sponge fingers, mascarpone, coffee, chocolate
torrone	nougat
torta	cake, tart
torta millefoglie	layered pastry with custard cream
zabaglione	whipped eggs, sugar and Marsala, served hot
zuppa inglese	trifle

Formaggio (Cheese)

bel paese	a soft white cow's cheese
cacio/caciocavallo	pale yellow, often sharp cheese
fontina	rich cow's milk cheese
groviera	mild cheese (gruyère)
gorgonzola	soft blue cheese
parmigiano	Parmesan cheese
pecorino	sharp sheep's cheese
provolone	sharp, tangy cheese; *dolce* is less strong
stracchino	soft white cheese

Frutta (Fruit, Nuts)

albicocche	apricots	mandorle	almonds
ananas	pineapple	melagrana	pomegranate
arance	oranges	mele	apples
banane	bananas	melone	melon
cachi	persimmon	mirtilli	bilberries
ciliege	cherries	more	blackberries
cocomero	watermelon	nespola	medlar fruit
composta di frutta	stewed fruit	nocciole	hazelnuts
datteri	dates	noci	walnuts
fichi	figs	pera	pear
fragole (con panna)	strawberries (with cream)	pesca	peach
		pesca noce	nectarine
frutta di stagione	fruit in season	pinoli	pine nuts
lamponi	raspberries	pompelmo	grapefruit
macedonia di frutta	fruit salad	prugna/susina	prune/plum
mandarino	tangerine	uva	grapes

Bevande (Beverages)

acqua minerale con/senza gas	mineral water with/without fizz
aranciata	orange soda
birra (alla spina)	beer (draught)
caffè (freddo)	coffee (iced)
cioccolata (con panna)	chocolate (with cream)
gassosa	lemon-flavoured soda
latte	milk
limonata	lemon soda
succo di frutta	fruit juice
tè	tea
vino (rosso, bianco, rosato)	wine (red, white, rosé)

Cooking Terms, Miscellaneous

aceto (balsamico)	vinegar (balsamic)	*mostarda*	candied mustard sauce
affumicato	smoked	*olio*	oil
aglio	garlic	*pane (tostato)*	bread (toasted)
alla brace	on embers	*panini*	sandwiches
bicchiere	glass	*panna*	cream
burro	butter	*pepe*	pepper
cacciagione	game	*peperoncini*	hot chilli peppers
conto	bill	*piatto*	plate
costoletta/cotoletta	chop	*prezzemolo*	parsley
coltello	knife	*ripieno*	stuffed
cucchiaio	spoon	*rosmarino*	rosemary
filetto	fillet	*sale*	salt
forchetta	fork	*salmi*	wine marinade
forno	oven	*salsa*	sauce
fritto	fried	*salvia*	sage
ghiaccio	ice	*senape*	mustard
griglia	grill	*sartufi*	truffles
in bianco	without tomato	*tazza*	cup
limone	lemon	*tavola*	table
magro	lean meat/or pasta without meat	*tovagliolo*	napkin
		tramezzini	finger sandwiches
marmellata	jam	*umido*	cooked in sauce
menta	mint	*uovo*	egg
miele	honey	*zucchero*	sugar

General and Travel

Barzini, Luigi, *The Italians* (Hamish Hamilton, 1964). A perhaps too clever account of the Italians by an Italian journalist living in London, but one of the classics.

Goethe, J. W., *Italian Journey* (Penguin Classics, 1982). An excellent example of a genius turned to mush by Italy; brilliant insights and big, big mistakes.

Haycraft, John, *Italian Labyrinth* (Penguin, 1987). One of the latest attempts to unravel the Italian mess.

Hutton, Edward, *Florence, Assisi and Umbria Revisited, Venice and Venetia* and *Rome* (Hollis & Carter).

McCarthy, Mary, *The Stones of Florence and Venice Observed* (Penguin, 1986). Brilliant evocations of Italy's two great art cities, with an understanding that makes many other works on the subject seem sluggish and pedantic; don't visit them without it.

Morris, James, *Venice* (Faber & Faber, 1960). Another classic account of 'the world's most beautiful city'.

Morton, H. V., *A Traveller in Rome* and *A Traveller in Southern Italy* (Methuen, 1957, 1969). Among the most readable and delightful accounts of the region in print. Morton is a sincere scholar, and a true gentleman. Also a good friend to cats.

Nichols, Peter, *Italia, Italia* (Macmillan, 1973). Account of modern Italy by an old Italy hand.

History

Burckhardt, Jacob, *The Civilization of the Renaissance in Italy* (Harper & Row, 1975). The classic on the subject (first published 1860), the mark against which scholars still level their poison arrows of revisionism.

Carcopino, Jérome, *Daily Life in Ancient Rome* (Penguin, 1981). A thorough and lively account of Rome at the height of Empire—guaranteed to evoke empathy from modern city dwellers.

Ginsborg, Paul, A *History of Contemporary Italy: Society and Politics 1943–1988* (Penguin, 1990). A good modern account of events up to the fall of Rome.

Hale, J. R. (ed.), *A Concise Encyclopaedia of the Italian Renaissance* (Thames and Hudson, 1981). An excellent reference guide, with many concise, well-written essays.

Hibbert, Christopher, *Benito Mussolini, Rise and Fall of the House of Medici* and *Rome* (Penguin, 1965, 1979, 1985).

Joll, James, *Gramsci* (Fontana, 1977). A look at the father of modern Italian communism, someone we all should get to know better.

Morris, Jan, *The Venetian Empire* (Faber & Faber, 1980). A fascinating account of the Serenissima's glory days.

Procacci, Giuliano, *History of the Italian People* (Penguin, 1973). An in-depth view from the year 1000 to the present—also an introduction to the wit and subtlety of the best Italian scholarship.

Rand, Edward Kennard, *Founders of the Middle Ages* (Dover reprint, New York), a little-known but incandescently brilliant work that can explain Jerome, Augustine, Boethius and other intellectual currents of the decaying classical world.

Art and Literature

Boccaccio, Giovanni, *The Decameron* (Penguin, 1972). The ever-young classic by one of the fathers of Italian literature. Its irreverent worldliness still provides a salutary antidote to whatever dubious ideas persist in your mental baggage.

Calvino, Italo, *Invisible Cities*, *If Upon a Winter's Night a Traveller* (Picador). Provocative fantasies that could only have been written by an Italian. Something even better is his compilation of *Italian Folktales*, a little bit Brothers Grimm and a little bit Fellini.

Cellini, *Autobiography of Benvenuto Cellini* (Penguin, trans. by George Bull). Fun reading by a swashbuckling braggart and world-class liar.

Clark, Kenneth, *Leonardo da Vinci* (Penguin).

Dante Alighieri, *The Divine Comedy* (plenty of good translations). Few poems have ever had such a mythical significance for a nation. Anyone serious about understanding Italy and the Italian world-view will need more than a passing acquaintance with Dante.

Gadda, Carlo Emilio, *That Awful Mess on Via Merulana* (Quartet Books, 1980). Italy during the Fascist era.

Gilbert/Linscott (ed.), *Complete Poems and Selected Letters of Michelangelo* (Princeton Press, 1984).

Henig, Martin (ed.), *A Handbook of Roman Art* (Phaidon, 1983). Essays on all aspects of ancient Roman art.

Levi, Carlo, *Christ Stopped at Eboli* (Penguin, 1982). Disturbing post-War realism.

Levy, Michael, *Early Renaissance* and *High Renaissance* (both Penguin, 1975). Old-fashioned accounts of the period, with a breathless reverence for the 1500s—but still full of intriguing interpretations.

Murray, Linda, *The High Renaissance* and *The Late Renaissance and Mannerism* (Thames and Hudson, both 1977). Excellent introduction to the period; also Peter and Linda Murray, *The Art of the Renaissance* (Thames and Hudson, 1963).

Petrarch, Francesco, *Canzoniere and Other Works* (Oxford, 1985). The most famous poems by the 'First Modern Man'.

Further Reading

Vasari, Giorgio, *Lives of the Artists* (Penguin, 1985). Readable, anecdotal accounts of the Renaissance greats by the father of art history, also the first professional philistine.

Wittkower, Rudolf, *Art and Architecture in Italy 1600–1750* (Pelican, 1986). The bible on Baroque, erudite and full of wit.

Index

Also Available from CADOGAN Guides...

Country Guides

Antarctica
Belize
Central Asia
China: The Silk Routes
Egypt
France: Southwest France;
    Dordogne, Lot & Bordeaux
France: Southwest France;
    Gascony & the Pyrenees
France: Brittany
France: The South of France
France: The Loire

Germany: Bavaria

India
India: South India
India: Goa

Ireland
Ireland: Southwest Ireland
Ireland: Northern Ireland

Italy
Italy: The Bay of Naples and
    Southern Italy

Italy: Lombardy, Milan and the
    Italian Lakes
Italy: Tuscany and Umbria
Italy: Venetia and the Dolomites

Japan
Morocco

Portugal
Portugal: The Algarve

Scotland
Scotland's Highlands and Islands

South Africa

Spain
Spain: Southern Spain
Spain: Northern Spain

Syria & Lebanon
Tunisia
Turkey
Yucatán and Southern Mexico
Zimbabwe, Botswana and
    Namibia

City Guides

Amsterdam
Brussels, Bruges, Ghent & Antwerp
Florence, Siena, Pisa & Lucca
London
Manhattan
Moscow & St Petersburg
Paris

Prague
Rome
Venice
Italy: Three Cities—Rome, Venice
    and Florence

Island Guides

Plus...

Available from good bookshops or via, in the UK, **Grantham Book Services**, Isaac Newton Way, Alma Park Industrial Estate, Grantham NG31 9SD, ✆ (01476) 541 080, ℻ (01476) 541 061; and in North America from **The Globe Pequot Press**, 6 Business Park Road, Old Saybrook, Connecticut 06475-0833, ✆ (800) 243 0495, ℻ (800) 820 2329.

By the same authors

Rome

1-86011-028-2   £12.99

CADOGAN's city guide to Rome explores the little-known nooks as well as the sights you know you want to see. From Roman ruins to Baroque glories, catacombs to the Coppedé quarter, the twelve walks pace the streets with clarity, knowledge and wit, and the eleven day trips whisk you out of the hustle and into the countryside.

Venice

1-86011-054-1   £10.99

CADOGAN's cliché-busting guide to Venice re-enchants the most beautiful city in the world, revealing the secrets and unique civilization behind the waterlogged myths. Six walks—each one a treasure hunt—lead you through the labyrinths of lagoon-land, and a new colour section helps you pick out the palaces along the Grand Canal while lazing back in your gondola.

Florence, Siena, Pisa & Lucca

1-86011-034-7   £10.99

The **CADOGAN** guide to Florence, Siena, Pisa & Lucca captures the outstanding wealth of history and culture in four of Italy's most illustrious cities, with illuminating insights into Tuscan city life and style, and fourteen detailed city walks through the ancient streets, chock-a-block with monuments and museums.